Marketing DeMystified

A Self-Teaching Guide

Donna Anselmo

New York   Chicago   San Francisco   Lisbon   London
Madrid   Mexico City   Milan   New Delhi   San Juan
Seoul   Singapore   Sydney   Toronto

The **McGraw·Hill** Companies

Copyright © 2010 by The McGraw-Hill Companies, Inc. All rights reserved. Printed in the United States of America. Except as permitted under the United States Copyright Act of 1976, no part of this publication may be reproduced or distributed in any form or by any means, or stored in a database or retrieval system, without the prior written permission of the publisher.

1 2 3 4 5 6 7 8 9 10 WFR/WFR 1 9 8 7 6 5 4 3 2 1 0

ISBN 978-0-07-171391-7
MHID   0-07-171391-3

This publication is designed to provide accurate and authoritative information in regard to the subject matter covered. It is sold with the understanding that neither the author nor the publisher is not engaged in rendering legal, accounting, securities trading, or other professional services. If legal advice or other expert assistance is required, the services of a competent professional person should be sought.
    —*From a Declaration of Principles Jointly Adopted by a Committee of the American Bar Association and a Committee of Publishers and Associations*

Trademarks: McGraw-Hill, the McGraw-Hill Publishing logo, DeMystified, and related trade dress are trademarks or registered trademarks of The McGraw-Hill Companies and/or its affiliates in the United States and other countries and may not be used without written permission. All other trademarks are the property of their respective owners. The McGraw-Hill Companies is not associated with any product or vendor mentioned in this book.

Product or brand names used in this book may be trade names or trademarks. Where we believe that there may be proprietary claims to such trade names or trademarks, the name has been used with an initial capital or it has been capitalized in the style used by the name claimant. Regardless of the capitalization used, all such names have been used in an editorial manner without any intent to convey endorsement of or other affiliation with the name claimant. Neither the author nor the publisher intends to express any judgment as to the validity or legal status of any such proprietary claims.

McGraw-Hill books are available at special quantity discounts to use as premiums and sales promotions, or for use in corporate training programs. To contact a representative, please e-mail us at bulksales@mcgraw-hill.com.

This book is printed on acid-free paper.

CONTENTS

Contents

Contents

Contents

ACKNOWLEDGMENTS

Writing this book is a privilege and a blessing. I am humbled by the opportunity to serve the very many people who also have so much to teach *me*. I wish all readers of *Marketing DeMystified* many opportunities to build extraordinary outcomes in business and life through bold action and by following the lessons inside. To your success!

I extend my deepest gratitude to literary agent Grace Freedson for advocating this book; editors Brian Foster and Maureen Dennehy for your exceptional insight and support; and the team at McGraw-Hill for your commitment to publishing this book in a tight economy. Your leadership makes it possible for others to succeed by putting this information to good use. I salute you.

Many thanks to Stephanie Leibowitz, colleague and friend, for your unflagging support. You are my magic bullet, and I am grateful for your research and editorial contributions.

Thanks also to Dr. Diane Kramer, mentor, friend, and spiritual visionary, for your contributions to this book, creating the Extraordinary Self development programs, and teaching me how to let go of patterns that kept me from writing this book sooner. I am enjoying extraordinary results now because of you.

Ms. Andrea Kantor, of Bond Street Coaching, one day spoke two little words that resounded in my soul. My heart rhythm now goes, "be-bold, be-bold, be-bold, be-bold," which keeps my life and work flowing. Thanks for your inspiration.

Thanks, too, to Ellen Cooperperson's Corporate Performance Consultants, Inc. for your leadership vision, resourceful and cooperative spirit, and contribution to this book; Ellen Barohn, publicist, for sharing perspectives on public relations; Carol Heuser, virtual assistant, for help with final logistics; and John Harper and Vern Harper of AM1300 WMEL, home of BOLD*TALK* Business Radio, for insights on promotion; thanks also to Zion Michtavy, Estelle Cooper, Ceil Cleveland, Ellen Cleary, Judy Martin, Dr. Carolyn Fausnaugh, Dr. Elaine Christine, and my many clients, colleagues, and friends, for your unbounded support, insight, and inspiration; special thanks to Dr. Ivan Misner, founder and chairman of BNI and the Referral Institute, for sharing information on how to master networking and referral marketing.

Special thanks to Gerri and Joe Dundie; Eli Pacino; Susan, Bill, Michael, and Samantha Glamore; Jonathan Jones; Addy and Bill Yushuk; Nicki, John, Jenna, and John Laronga; and Rosalie Perrino, whose spirit of encouragement, enthusiasm, presence, insight, feedback, and deep support enrich my life and work.

Finally, I am deeply grateful to my husband, Peter H. Anselmo, daughters Suzanne and Elizabeth, and son, Peter Nicholas. Your love and support for my choices and my work are more deeply appreciated than you know. Thanks to my parents, who always told me to write a book, and to Chloe, the best dog in the world, for waiting patiently by my side, morning till night, until I could make time to play. You are the best!

All good thoughts!

INTRODUCTION:
The New Marketing Paradigm

If you are living, breathing, and conscious at all, you already know that life can change in an instant. So can business. Half the world woke up in the fall of 2008 to acknowledge a serious unraveling of the U.S. national economy. It wasn't long before the entire world took note. Yes, change can seemingly happen overnight, and we need to be prepared.

Likewise, the speed at which business communication evolves makes it necessary to write this book in a different way than I would have written it even a year ago. *Marketing DeMystified* brings several *powerful new marketing realities* into sharp focus. It guides you in considering what aspects of your marketing strategy must adapt to changes in our quickly transforming *marketsphere*. And, it shows you how to do that—through information, strategies, tips, and tools. This book is not intended to be an academic treatise. While it provides insight on marketing philosophy and principles, it serves as a practical, process-oriented guide for the hands-on marketer. It is designed to be fast and factual, supported by real-life marketing experiences. It acknowledges, in detail, the very best of the traditional marketing disciplines. It also will help you adjust your thinking to fit demands of shifting markets, new communication platforms, and the enduring power of perception.

Without a doubt, the Internet is today's dominant marketing force and the most highly capable, cost-effective, timesaving marketing medium available. But make no mistake: this is *not* just a handbook for Internet marketing. It is a journey inside a world shaped by marketing concepts and strategies.

Written with small business owners, entrepreneurs, and marketing students in mind, this book will help you gain the insight, focus, and tools you need to be successful in marketing endeavors. Marketing success unfolds with understanding of the environments in which we operate; the desires, perceptions, and basic needs of those we serve; and the courage to step out of our own comfort zones to confront and overcome inevitable challenges.

The Power of Transformational Thinking

In a large way, this book is about transformation: how you can shift your thinking, your strategies, your marketing efforts, and your business operations for greater success. To do that, you'll need to become highly aware of your own personal assumptions, beliefs, and thoughts about the marketing process and how your products and services bring value to consumers. You'll also need to become intimately aware of the needs, assumptions, and perceptions of those consumers.

The Marketing Challenge

Let's begin with one obvious note: we no longer dwell in the same small business world in which we grew up. Unlike our prototypical business forebears, we operate in a global business environment, driven more strongly by the Internet every day. Regardless of which service or commodity you sell, be assured that it is very likely to be available for purchase, for less money, elsewhere online. Many domestic buyers choose products based on price and send payment not only to a different town or city but also into the banks of offshore operators, distinctly apart from our domestic economy. That leaves less money in community pocketbooks to shop in your store or office. Therein lies your marketing challenge: *Position. Differentiate. Market. Promote. Or, go home.*

Shifting the Odds

That's the end of the tough news. From here forward, you will gain the confidence you need to succeed against the odds by learning everything necessary to maximize your marketing effort. So, fold up your old road map of preconceptions, and get ready to draw a new route with a thick, colorful marker that reflects your newfound marketing wisdom. Along the way you may find yourself guided by lessons learned through the eyes, ears, and finger clicks of a teenager, college student, or computer geek—consider them your tutors.

Without any conscious agenda, the playful, innovative communication behavior of a younger generation of Internet adopters has influenced the business landscape. Harnessing the mega-power of Internet connectivity, young techno-geeks inspired the world's largest companies and industries to transform their own marketing operations or face the consequence of inaction. Now, businesses large and small, as well as government hopefuls and officials, nonprofit organizations, celebrities, families, and bloggers from across the world are communicating through Facebook and tweeting on Twitter. There's no longer a question about how the Internet will create business.

By honoring one of the greatest social doctrines in history—the need for people to connect and belong to society—the luminary purveyors of MySpace, Facebook, LinkedIn, Plaxo, and YouTube, to name a few, have created the fastest and most dynamic linking strategies in our universe. And those links have relevance for the marketing community.

Connecting with Consumer Communities

Since Tom Anderson launched MySpace in 2003, social networking sites have exploded. Following the lead of cutting-edge social marketers, companies in a broad spectrum of industries have launched their own membership sites. Businesses now allow customers to create profiles; chat in forums, bulletin boards, and e-mails; upload images and photos; and share ideas, product ratings, and even less pertinent information on company blogs and shopping sites. Don't be fooled; it's not just for fun. Membership sites enable businesses to collect critical data about customers and their buying behavior, while affording visitors the opportunity to connect with one another. Simultaneously, the business builds brand and cultivates customer loyalty. It happens in offices, living rooms, and Internet cafés across the globe. No holds barred, 24/7.

Interactive media should no longer be an afterthought—its impact is exponential. According to an article in *Radio Ink* magazine, interactive media has become to the industry as a whole what programming and sales departments have traditionally been to a radio station. In essence, interactive media can be the product, positioning, messaging, and sales platform all rolled into one.

So, while this book presents best practices of traditional positioning, branding, and marketing, the discussion inside also prompts readers toward a new, more relevant marketing vanguard. It is propelled by the power of interactive media and lessons from what has become the *Brave New World* that Aldous Huxley once predicted.

Set Your Marketing Intention

Let's face it—marketing is about dreams. And dreamers—from devotees of *The Secret* to would-be entrepreneurs, and masters of business and spirituality—have one thing in common: the need to be clear on their intention before they can reach their goals.

So, what is your intention? What impact do you need? Are you seeking to gain insight to the principles of marketing? Learn how to capture market demographics, competitor information, and media attention? Build a brand image? Or embark on Internet marketing? Whatever your goal, take a moment now to set your intention for marketing success. Decide what you are looking for, prepare your mind for the journey, and read with purpose.

Understanding the Consumer's Perceptual Map

With the emergence of new digital imaging equipment, scientists now can peek inside an active brain and see the stuff of thoughts. Today's neurophysicists and quantum physicists are defining thoughts not as amorphous inspiration but as chemical processes that have

carved specific neural pathways in our brain. The more often we think a particular thought, the faster that series of microimpulses jumps the nerve synapse and creates the impetus for what we perceive as beliefs, sensations, emotions, and their resultant behaviors.

For more than a century, classical and operational theorists have documented the power of repetition and learning to reinforce and strengthen behavior. In the 1890s and early 1900s, Russian physiologist Ivan Pavlov noticed that dogs salivated even before they had food in their mouths. Pavlov's study, of what he termed "psychic secretion," led to experiments in which he altered external stimuli, then observed the dogs' reactions, and eventually defined what he called "conditioned responses." The classic story told in Psychology 101 classes is that Pavlov's dogs learned to salivate whenever Pavlov rang a bell, even before food was presented. Pavlov demonstrated that behavior could be influenced by seemingly unrelated stimuli. The science of classical conditioning was born.

In the 1950s, Harvard University's Burrhus Frederic Skinner made famous the theory of operant conditioning while studying rats in what now is called a "Skinner Box." The point is that Skinner's theory held that every organism operates within the framework of its environment. When it encounters a stimulus with the power to strengthen a behavior (positive reinforcement), or weaken a behavior (negative reinforcement), learning occurs and behavior adapts. Such is also the stuff of marketing.

Influencing Beliefs, Perceptions and Behavior

In recent years, experts recognized that language could be scientifically engineered to impact behavior, too. Every communication is a two-way operation. There is a sender and a receiver. What receivers hear and process, and how they respond, depends on the power of their perceptions, sensory filters, and their own neural systems for processing language. For example, researchers found that when visual learners are cued visually, they learn better. Some people are more stimulated by auditory cues than visual ones; others learn more from physical sensation and performing a task.

The rule holds that when people are stimulated in the way that best matches their neural wiring, learning happens faster and the "subjects" learn more. So, when communicators can figure out (based on responses, behaviors, and language cues) how a receiver is most likely to process information, they can adjust communication accordingly.

It didn't take long for marketers and sales gurus to take hold of that knowledge and transform what they learned into competitive advantage. Either communicate in the preferred modality of your prospective customer or pepper your communication with all learning modalities so that you don't miss customers who, if tuned in, would pay attention.

After you tackle "Principles of Integrated Marketing" (Chapter 1), Chapter 2 will provide exercises to help you uncover the beliefs and learning strategies of prospective customers.

By the time you have finished Chapter 3, you'll have the structure for a marketing plan, and in Chapter 4, you will learn how to formulate a plan based on the information you gain about customer beliefs, perceptions, and behavior through marketing research. As you read on, you'll address the Seven Ps of Marketing; learn helpful tips for Web communication and online advertising, and how to embark on an integrated marketing campaign. Before you've finished, you'll consider how to connect with, nurture, and retain the customers your marketing efforts attract. And before you're done, you'll consider ethics, social responsibility, expectations, budgeting, and marketing management.

This book forges several important keys to marketing success. Use it, along with the exercises, project worksheets, and evaluation tools that are supplied, and you will leapfrog your way to ongoing marketing success.

PART ONE

Understanding Marketing Principles

CHAPTER 1

Principles of Integrated Marketing

Whether you've just entered the market with spanking new products and services, plan to stretch a growing brand across new geographic terrain, or extend a successful brand into different product lines, chances are that your business concept began with a heartfelt "*a-ha!*" That exclamation probably left you giddy with the belief that you had just hit upon something that the world was missing. No doubt you were tempted to bring that unique idea to buyers who would clamor for your concept, if only they knew about it. At that point, you may have launched your new business venture with devil-take-all bravado. Then, you set your sights on a killer plan that would jump-start your success.

It's the same with a marketing plan. Once you transform inspiration into a viable concept, its time to uncover the right marketing strategies to catapult you to victory. It may be that you didn't come up with the concept at all. Perhaps you don't own the business but are responsible for marketing a set of ideas, products, or services. Whichever scenario describes your current situation, this book will help.

A marketing manager working to build excellent outcomes is a lot like an architect in the process of design. The architect begins with a vision for a compelling structure as well as a concept of how the building will relate to the environment. The architect lines up planning tools: grids, tracing paper, compass, charcoal, sharpeners, erasers, and maybe even renderings of beautiful buildings, cities, columns, and artistic treatments for inspiration.

He then pencils in painstakingly scaled lines. Next, he lays over tracing paper, and begins a second layer of planning. Or, he enters thoughtful keystrokes into a computer-aided drafting (CAD) program. As the form begins to emerge, he thinks about aesthetics, client wishes, construction materials, practical budget concerns, and code requirements, not to mention the presentation he must make to teammates, partners, clients, and planning boards. Throughout the process, the architect blends his artistic talents with insight from team members, engineers, product experts, and even zoning regulators and code enforcers. The process is at once mathematical (with calculations that shift as perceptions change) and musical (as the work is fine-tuned).

To set the stage for sales, marketing managers build their platforms in much the same way. They consider their products, study the competitive landscape, uncover opportunities in target markets, and then weave together various elements of the marketing mix to create a harmonious message that will be tested, sensed, perceived, tried, and appreciated by the right audiences.

To create a truly powerful marketing enterprise, the manager must stretch beyond traditional activities associated with marketing disciplines. She also must find a way to integrate the goals, tactics, and cultures of the sales, operations, training, human resource, customer service, finance, and executive teams into a consistent, synergistic brand message across the organization. Then, she must channel that message *beyond* the organization. Marketing begins at home.

Extraordinary marketing managers spread their marketing vision inside and beyond the company. They make it a priority to ensure that all company teams speak a common brand language and understand their roles in the marketing process. You can develop the skill set of an extraordinary marketing manager by incorporating strategic, integrated marketing principles and sound teamwork. As you do, you will reach breakthrough outcomes that other managers only hope for. You will know how to brand your organization in a consistent way and reach the markets you seek.

Developing a Strategic, Integrated Approach

Integrated marketing is a strategic, *process-driven* approach to marketing management. It incorporates traditional marketing disciplines with the still-emerging discipline of Internet marketing. But it doesn't end there. The integrated process aligns the interest of mission-critical business teams, such as sales, operations, finance, and customer service, with marketing goals so that the marketing enterprise does not churn in a vacuum.

It's sad but true that many marketing managers are called to the table well after products have been developed, names chosen, and the initial sales process is underway. That is backward marketing. It puts the cart before your marketing workhorse and then expects that horse to leap straight over the cart to promotion. Can that work? Sure. Should you operate like that on purpose? Absolutely not. While marketing horses can certainly accommodate unruly processes and demands, it makes more sense to take advantage of marketing wisdom at the beginning of the product cycle. Leaders and planners need to bring in the marketing team early on, involving them in information gathering and marketing research that will prove either the wisdom of business decisions or the need for a critical shift in direction.

When marketing is approached as an add-on, marketers enter the game in landmine territory. After some effort and resources have been expended, chief executive officers (CEOs) may be reluctant to change course, even when change is needed. The best-case marketing scenario then becomes founded on hope rather than the process of success. The risks are often costly in both time and money.

> ### CAUTION
>
> To prepare for success, first choose the right team members; then involve them in early strategic discussions and evaluate options before committing to a course. Even a very small company can make sure that marketing issues are addressed alongside planning and product development.

MAKE FEEDBACK A PRIORITY

Whether starting at ground zero or jumping in to an existing project, you'll need a process to gather and integrate feedback from multiple business units into your marketing plan and promotions. Every segment of a business should operate in connection to the marketing enterprise and purpose. The earlier you involve your marketing team in gathering internal and customer feedback, the more information you will have for decision making. Better information translates to better outcomes.

THE LINK BETWEEN MARKETING AND BRANDING

Marketing and branding go hand in glove. Marketing is the umbrella under which branding resides. It is a multifaceted process used to develop and connect your brand presence and message with target customers. Marketing requires an understanding of consumer needs, products, planning, pricing, promotion, placement, and positioning, as well as the importance of people involved in the process. Together, these elements make up the marketing mix.

Branding is one aspect of promotional marketing, and it represents way more than your outer mark. It becomes your image, inside and out, reflecting the impression you make on people's minds. Brand image conveys the kinds of experiences that people—prospects, customers, employees, investors, and other stakeholders—can expect from your products, services, and company. This expectation is translated as your brand promise. It communicates how you connect and engage with prospects and customers. It colors the business of every department in every company. Likewise, every department colors the brand in some way.

> **CAUTION**
>
> Guide your branding by the rule that people will forget what you say and do, but they will never forget how you make them feel.

Branding is more about consumers' actual experience with your products, services, and people than with what you tell them about your brand. The feeling people take away from engaging with your products, services, or company is what drives your brand. Engage people from inside and outside your organization. Work to positively influence their sense of connection with your company and products, and you will build a marketing success story.

Branding may begin when research indicates a viable business concept. But brands grow based on missions and beliefs. They are promoted through marketing messages, taglines, expertise, and experiences. They are marketed in print, in person, and on the Web. They are built through internal relationships with employees and external relationships with customers, the community, and the media. Then, they are validated by consumer experience. When consumers experience predictable positive outcomes—and when they are regularly exposed to a brand via marketing services—brand awareness, presence, and value grow.

THE MARKETER'S ROLE IN BRANDING

As a marketer, your job is to position and differentiate your brand(s) in the minds of consumers. That takes strategy. Learning to employ the full spectrum of the marketing mix, in a strategic way, will help you shape and reinforce your brand image. As you speed up brand recognition, you will provide critical support that tees up and reinforces the sales effort and paves the road to profit.

Defining the Marketing Mix: The Seven Ps of Marketing

Many marketing handbooks reveal the various "Ps" of marketing. Many sources cite the four most popular Ps: *product, place, price,* and *promotion.* Others add *positioning* to the mix. To cover all the bases well, I've included *people.* And to leave no stone unturned, I present the seventh P (arguably the most important of all), *planning,* as a critical measure to ensure stable, predictable results.

The right data can validate your premise, help you decide how well your strategy will work, determine whether your reasoning is sound, and indicate whether or not it is the right time to go forward. While gung-ho enthusiasts might tell you to "go big or go home," it's my job to help you learn to decide how big is too big and when it's better to play at home than risk your booty in a market that may just swallow up your investment.

Consider marketing research to be your marketing safety net. If you gather enough evidence about what need there is for your products or services, where they are likely to sell best, what the perceived value and price points are to be, how they are to be positioned, and who can help you get your products to market, you will be gunning for success. Then with a plan in hand, you can move forward with confidence.

SIMPLIFYING THE SEVEN P PREMISE

Learning the Seven P Premise will deepen your understanding of the marketing mix and help you develop a framework for thinking through issues that will impact your marketing plan. As you answer the questions that follow, you will increase your chance of enjoying solid return on your marketing investment. As you gain awareness of the many factors influencing marketing success, you will gain the confidence to manage your marketing effort effectively. That confidence will emerge as you enjoy even small successes along the way.

Product

The first step in your marketing mix is to identify and develop a *product* or service to sell. The process of developing products and services is called research and development (R&D). But choosing the right products or services requires more than an idea and a manufacturer. It takes marketing research to get it right. Here are several questions that will help you round out your approach to product analysis:

- What need or needs will our product(s) or service(s) fill?
- What product(s) will we offer to meet that need or those needs?
- For whom will we design the products and services?
- Where are those people? How old are they?
- What do they buy now? How will our product be different from others they might buy?
- How will we reach them?
- Who will build our products and develop our service processes?
- What will it cost to build those products?
- Can we afford to build these products or services now?
- How long will it take?
- Who will oversee product development? What special skills do they need?
- How will we know that our products or services have value to prospective customers?
- What quality management systems must be in place to ensure product quality?
- What user guide will be needed for our products?
- What is needed to shift from planning to execution?

- What special knowledge will we need to sell those products?
- How many do we have to sell, at what price, to cover production costs?
- What is our product development budget?
- How will we turn our product decisions into profit?

Positioning

Positioning is the process of choosing where your brand of products and services will stand in the minds of your target audience when compared to those of your competitors'. Positioning is designed to stimulate the senses and tease out inner responses that make people want to buy. The game board is as much in the consumer's mind as it is laid out in your marketing plan. After you've decided where to position your products or brand, you'll need to create a plan and then take action to fill that mental space.

For example, look at face cream. Thoughts of face cream can elicit dreams of extended youth and beauty. To entice the minds of luxury buyers, a face cream can be positioned as a high-end product with fancy packaging, point-of-sale displays, boutique placements, ad campaigns, and a high price tag. Or, the exact same cream can be positioned as a cost-effective alternative to luxury creams. It can be packaged to appeal to the practical buyer's cost-saving instinct and marketed to less fussy buyers. This lower-level positioning can open access to a much broader market; profit can then be made up in volume sales.

Product and brand position is tightly linked to the sensory and emotional connections discussed in the introduction to this book. In *Positioning: A Battle for Your Mind*, authors Al Reis and Jack Trout recognized that buying behavior is ruled by emotions as well as practical needs and have brought positioning theory to the forefront of marketing strategy.

Positioning decisions will influence your product's cachet. The position you choose to create in the minds of consumers will depend on the level of distinction your company wants for your products, services, or branding. Positioning is an important brand management tool. It starts with a decision to influence perception in some way, and it takes root as you create preference. You can influence positioning through advertising. You can employ word-of-mouth power as a viral strategy to create consumer buzz. As a marketing manager, your day-to-day actions both influence and are influenced by your company's positioning decisions. Consider these questions when thinking about your firm's market position:

- What fantasy comes to mind when I think of our product? What do I see changing in my life as a result?
- Who are our target customers? What do they want most?
- How can our product fulfill that fantasy?
- Will our products or services represent a premier, luxury, or economy model?
- Will they convey fun, spirit, and a wild ride? Or will they conjure a sense of safety and stability? Or something else? What is that?

- Where do we want customers to come from?
- Where do our customers come from now? What can they afford?
- What are those customers like? Create a consumer profile of the perfect consumer.
- What do we want customers to say, feel, and believe about us?
- How do we think prospective customers will view our brand?
- How important are our products or services to the customers we want to reach?
- Why is that?
- Where do we stand now in the minds of potential customers? Do we have any market presence now?
- How do intended products fit with our current products?
- How will our products compare with our competitors' in customers' minds?
- Where do we stand now in terms of our competition?
- What do we want our customers to think, say, and feel about our brand?
- What can our products or services do for our customers?
- What will it take for them to see our brand as valuable to them?
- What can we do about that?
- What will it take for us to perform well in our chosen industry tier?
- How will we turn that positioning into profit?

Marketing research and statistical analysis can help you answer those questions and determine the scope of work you need to do to influence customer perceptions. We'll discuss this in more detail in Chapter 4.

Price

More than a number on a tag, pricing is a marketing strategy in itself. You can price right when you align it with your overall business strategy, choose target markets that need and can afford your products, engage the right sales channels, and budget accordingly to extract a reasonable profit. This approach seems obvious, but believe it or not, entrepreneurs sometimes neglect to reason this out. Their mistakes usually come from lack of experience and/or reliable research. (So, do your homework.)

Be sure to work up all of your costs when pricing a product, from research and product development, through ongoing overhead and incremental expenditures. We discuss this topic more fully in Chapter 7. For now, remember to calculate all costs, before settling on the markup you need to stay solvent. When pricing your products, be sure to include all R&D costs (including a projected budget in the event product changes are needed), general and administrative costs, tax burden, anticipated discount promotions, delivery costs, the cost of money (interest owed and the cost of waiting for payments, if you plan to extend credit), and how much you will need to stay afloat while in product development or early marketing stages. Consider everything that can impact your profit *before* you set your price. If you don't know what you don't know, ask advice from friends in other businesses, an accountant, business consultant, and/or financial experts.

> **CAUTION**
>
> Profit is the reason you are in business. Without profit, you have a hobby—and a potentially costly hobby at that.

Some experts say that manufacturers must charge a minimum of five times their unit cost to run a profit. To assess your business tolerance, research your product options and market opportunities, buyer behavior, and profit-or-loss tolerance before moving forward. Here are some pricing questions to consider:

- What will (or does) it cost us to develop this product?
- What are our labor costs per product or service?
- How much overhead must we add to the cost to cover our R&D outlay?
- How will costs change based on added volume?
- What will be the impact of discounts or coupons to get people to try our product? What will those discounts cost us in profit?
- Will we need additional labor or facilities to cover growth? How soon will we need it?
- How much will those marginal growth expenses add to our business costs? At what point will they be added?
- What is the current pricing for similar products in our market?
- What external factors influence our pricing?
- Have we based our pricing strategy on marketing research?
- What beliefs, thoughts, feelings, or conditions will influence customers to pay our price?
- Have we prepared a cost-benefit analysis, based on different pricing models?
- What does our cost-benefit analysis tell us about our pricing strategy?
- What will we do with the profits we make?
- What is our tolerance for risk? What is the impact of a pricing mistake?
- How will we sustain our business if our pricing strategy returns less than anticipated?
- What controls will we have in place to monitor and manage costs?
- Where can we go for pricing advice?

Place

Placement is an issue of product distribution. Decide where and how you will be most effective in distributing your products and services. Placement can be as simple as creating an online catalog and offering products through a self-managed e-commerce shop on your own Web site. It can be more complex, taking your product to market through multiple Internet portals, bricks-and-mortar stores, and various channel partners. A *marketing channel* is a conduit for getting products from the factory into buyers' hands. Channel partners may include wholesalers and manufacturers' representatives, distributors, packaging companies, shipping and fulfillment houses, franchisees, licensees, and product affiliates.

When planning your product placement, think of the many ways and locales through which you can sell your product. While you're at it, consider how those placements will tie in with your marketing promotion. For example, will your products sell better if they are located near the cash register? Will you need a point-of- purchase (POP) display? Perhaps you represent insurance or financial products. If so, you may place your products by creating strategic affiliations with insurance brokers, financial consultants, accountants, and related providers who can introduce your products directly to your targeted customers while on sales calls at their homes or offices.

Think of the marketing channel as a supply chain with multiple stop points. Some channels are composed of long chains with various middlemen who help to promote you in exchange for compensation. To decide on the best channel partners for you, consult a finance expert who can help you conduct a cost-benefit analysis. Or, if you are good at finance, conduct your own analysis.

To get the most out of your placement effort, go back to your marketing plan and reflect on your product positioning, pricing, people relationships, and promotional strategies. We'll discuss placement in more detail in Chapter 6. In the meantime, think of your supply chain as part of your marketing mix. Create a plan that will enable you to identify, manage, satisfy, protect, and take advantage of every participating partner in your supply channel, for mutual benefit. Remember that, as with every other aspect of marketing, your *relationship* with channel partners will turn the key to success. Here are some placement questions to consider:

- What quality of business will we do in a designated region?
- What distribution channels have we considered and evaluated?
- Which distributors, wholesalers, resellers, agents, and retailers offer the best pricing points for channeling our product to buyers at the required profit margins?
- Which distributors, wholesalers, resellers, agents, and retailers offer the easiest and fastest payment terms and quickest return on investment?
- Where can we gain quick transactional sales?
- Where will we need to make adjustments for longer sales cycles?
- Are there gatekeepers to consider?

- Where can we find the right vendor management systems (VMS) to ensure smooth, cost-effective product placement?
- What business volume can we do in a specific market or via a special distribution channel, such as a reseller or affiliate marketing program?
- What special information might we require to get our products in a particular market?
- What resources will we need to get our products to those markets?
- How will we gain entry to the market(s)?
- Do we need partners or affiliates to help us reach our clients or to facilitate our delivery?
- How will we handle logistical issues?
- What does our operations team say about our placement plan?
- What size market do we intend to cover? How long will our resources cover us there?
- Who else is already doing business there?
- Who can help us enter a new market?
- What will it cost to place our product in a single market or multiple markets?
- Have we considered all placement options? Geographic? Industry? Niche? Internet? Reseller? Joint venture? Affiliate?
- To whom can we turn for advice?
- What is our placement budget?
- How will we evaluate profit based on placement costs?

Promotion

Promotion is the process of reaching, communicating with, and influencing targeted customers. The chance to plan promotions is what lures most managers and creative spirits to the marketing table. The promotion game is where creative juices flow and warm, fuzzy thinking begins. It's the part everybody loves.

But promotion takes real work, requiring you to step outside the playroom and into the war room. Your marketing team—whether a team of one or a multifaceted, cross-functional group—must ask and answer hard business questions that will decide the utility or *value* of every marketing promotion and expense.

Promotions can range from coupons to major sales events, ads to print materials, parties to trade shows, and promotional gifts to e-blasts. When planning your promotion, start with the "Why question." For example, why are we choosing to attend this trade show in this particular geographic region or market? What will it do for us? Are we doing a trade show just to expose our brand image? If we attend that trade show, how will we collect leads? Who will follow up on those leads? How many sales must we close before we will see a return on our trade show investment?

Trade Shows as a Promotional Vehicle

There are only three reasons for doing a trade show:

1. To foster brand image.

2. To make sales on site.

3. To collect leads.

Once you've gathered those leads, you have to follow up to justify the expense. Trade shows are costly to attend. They can range from as little as $50 for a booth to $50,000 and more for the whole enchilada. There are costs to register your place, secure electric outlets, create attractive display booths, purchase promotional giveaways, print product literature (most of which gets tossed by attendees after the show), host parties, and conduct seminars. In addition, you should factor in the cost of time and other opportunities lost because you invested in a show. What would you have been doing to secure business if you weren't at the show? Alternatively, what is the avoidance cost? What is the cost of *not* going to the show? What opportunities will you miss?

If you haven't figured it out yet, marketing is as much about asking questions as answering them. You now may be asking, how do I know *which* promotions to launch? If you are very new to marketing, you may be asking, what exactly *is* a marketing promotion? Promotions include print advertisements, brochures, bookmarks, and premium gifts such as pencils, pens, and assorted paraphernalia with your name printed boldly on top. They also include banner ads on Web sites, pay-per-click advertising campaigns, live in-person events, and online Webcasts. They can be radio ads, public service announcements, television commercials, and just about any public relations method you choose for getting the word out.

Some promotions, such as tying your name to a social cause, can be subtle. Johnson & Johnson serves as a founding sponsor of the SAFE KIDS USA, connecting its name with a cause, and a fragrance manufacturer targeting women may donate products to a breast cancer charity event or causes of interest to women, without even a listing on the event program. Other promotions are way more obvious. Skywriting planes, blimps, banners at sports stadiums, signs on buses and subways, and light boxes at concert halls all make messages pop. Less flashy promotions, such as greeting cards to celebrate client birthdays or employee anniversaries with your company, work too. Every time you make a concerted effort to make your product or service visible in the community that you call a target market, you are in the act of promotion. Here are some promotion questions to consider:

- Where do we need and want to promote products and services?

- How big is that market? How much of a share do we need to capture to break even or profit from a promotion in that area? What will help us do that?

- Why do we want to go there?

- What do we want people to experience when they consume our products, services, or company?

- What do we want people to believe about us? Which promotion will communicate that?
- What do we want to say about our products, services, or company?
- How do people in this market get their product information now?
- Who else influences consumers in this market?
- What level of literacy do these consumers typically have?
- What language(s) do they speak?
- What age or special interests does this demographic represent?
- What kind of promotions will work best for us with which audience(s)?
- How much will it cost us to do that?
- Do we have the resources to cover that?
- What is our priority?
- What is our time frame?
- What are the risks involved if we place our money on one promotion instead of another?
- What are the benefits if we place our money on one promotion instead of another?
- In what order should we launch our promotions?
- What is our promotions budget?
- How will we evaluate if this promotion was profitable?

People

While planning your promotions, you decided *what* you intend to tell the world about your products, services, and company. Now it's time to shift your focus to another critical segment of your marketing mix—the people who promote it and the people who buy it. People are the tellers of your story, and the most effective purveyors of your brand. They will share your story in many places and in many ways. Understanding the power of people, and taking proactive steps to maximize their own satisfaction with your company, services, and products will pay dividends as they influence prospects and customers. In Chapter 8, we will explore the impact of people and culture on marketing. In the meantime, consider the questions below:

- If my company were a person, what would (s)he be like?
- What would that person do best?
- How do we want our customer service and sales teams to relate with our customers?
- How do our people interact with one another?
- How should our people present themselves? How should they dress and speak?

- Who will train them to dress that way?
- Who would benefit from a consultation with a personal image consultant?
- How can a personal image consultant enhance our brand impact?
- How will we keep our people knowledgeable about product changes and market launches?
- What will our inside customer service and outside client service teams (sales teams and account managers) believe about our products and services?
- How will we keep our people happy, interested, and engaged as part of an integrated customer contact and feedback loop?
- How will we ensure that our people provide high-quality service and positive regard for our products and services?
- How often should we conduct trainings?
- What is our strategy for sustainable development of our human assets?
- How can we involve people in policy making and branding decisions, so they will feel engaged and part of our team?
- What incentives and reward systems will ensure that we hold on to valuable people resources?
- Have there been events in our history that affected the perceptions our people have about our company brand?
- What is the average longevity of our employees? Why is that? Should we do something to change it?
- What future do our people have with us? How do they feel about that?
- How do we communicate with our people?
- Have we effectively communicated our organizational values to our people?
- Are we timely and consistent in addressing violations of ethical values if and when they occur?
- Can our people predict our response to day-to-day actions?
- Do our people know what the organizational managers and leaders expect from them?
- Do our people know what to expect from organizational managers and leaders?
- Do our people share the values of organizational leaders?
- Do we have a system and resources for cultivating new leaders with the power to positively impact our brand well into the future?

Answers to those questions will provide many insights into the impact that your company's people have on your customers now and will have into the future.

Planning

Planning is the space and time in which the other six Ps converge. Plans do not need to be complicated to add value to the mix. Even a simple plan can move you forward without wasted effort and resources. You will develop an excellent marketing plan by following a few simple rules. Think about the outcome you want. Then lay out steps that will get you there. Decide who belongs at the table with you when you are planning. Whenever possible, pull together a cross-functional team to uncover needs, concerns, goals, and dreams. Then, set the ground rules for your planning process and create an environment that fosters communication, teamwork, and accountability for results. Make it a point to brainstorm all ideas without passing judgment; then prioritize what is needed, and match ideas accordingly. By gathering people from different levels and functions in your organization, you will round out your perspective and develop a plan that meets needs across the organization. Plans developed with input from a group have the best chance of success. These questions will help prime your planning pump:

- What are we planning for? What is our goal?
- How will planning and promoting specific products and services help us achieve our goal?
- How do our marketing goal(s) fit in with our company mission?
- What problem(s) are we trying to solve?
- What resources do we need in place to make planning worthwhile?
- What is our specific challenge? What gets in our way now?
- What steps do we need to take to reach our goal?
- In what order?
- If we get off track, how will we get back on track?
- What will it cost us to market this product or service effectively and see an acceptable return on investment?
- How long will it take us to reach profitability?
- Do we have the money in our budget? If not, can we get it? Where?
- How well does our specific marketing plan align with the overall objectives of the organization?
- From whom do we need input or approval?
- Who else should we be speaking with about this?
- Is our plan research founded and driven by reliable data?
- How will we implement it?
- Who will help?
- What special communications will we need?

- How will we evaluate our plan and success?
- How will we know when it is time to change it?
- Who else can help us?

Engage the right people in your planning process—goal-oriented people—and you will reap rewards. By engaging people from the beginning, you will find the support you need to move forward. More often than not, your colleagues will be pleased that you asked for their input. When they are happy about their involvement, they will be more likely to take responsibility for helping to achieve the group's desired outcomes.

The Value of an Integrated Marketing Approach

Through a strategic, integrated approach to the seven Ps of marketing, you can increase the likelihood of achieving not only a creative marketing campaign but also a successful and profitable investment. Paying special attention to the role of people in your organization—as well as planning, products, positioning, price, placement, and promotion—will help advance your brand image in the market.

An integrated marketing framework is the keystone of a well-rounded, cohesive marketing strategy. (See Figure 1.1.) An integrated approach fosters communication among business functions and segments. It helps blend internal viewpoints and calendars. It also reduces red tape and waiting time, and lowers risks, such as costs associated with noncompliance, conflicting messages, and missed deadlines. By including mission-critical functions, this collaborative marketing model engages people inside and beyond the organization. It ties together information from company teams and speeds the brand message through the organization and out to clients, and back again.

A marketing manager should become familiar with organizational business drivers beyond the marketing department, such as staffing issues, training concerns, sales requirements, and operational needs. Attention to an integrated platform will provide the information needed to ensure smooth rollout of your marketing plan. It also reminds the marketing team to develop a calendar that considers the impact on all affected departments. When people don't feel excluded, blindsided, overwhelmed, or pressured, it is easier to promote a brand message and trust that everyone inside the organization will embrace it.

When all departments collaborate to drive brand marketing, the message gains substance and meaning internally. It helps pollinate and connect with internal operations and overall growth strategies. Internally, the outcome is a noticeable reduction of stress and a lasting truce in the tug-of-war between business units struggling for supremacy. When employees are less concerned with posturing and protecting turf, they have more time to devote to the ultimate goal: organizational success. Externally, the strategy results in a strong brand message and tighter, more relevant connections to customers in the marketplace.

Building Capacity as a Marketing Organization

Building capacity for success takes vision, time, and commitment to cross-functional communication. It also takes serious attention to planning for ongoing development of the human and financial resources needed to support a sustainable future. Figure 1.1 illustrates how the brand message flows through the marketing, sales, operations, client, and customer

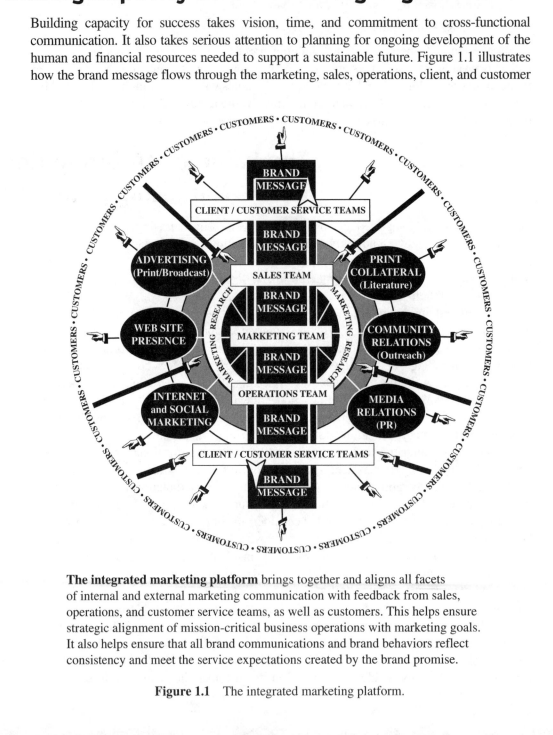

The integrated marketing platform brings together and aligns all facets of internal and external marketing communication with feedback from sales, operations, and customer service teams, as well as customers. This helps ensure strategic alignment of mission-critical business operations with marketing goals. It also helps ensure that all brand communications and brand behaviors reflect consistency and meet the service expectations created by the brand promise.

Figure 1.1   The integrated marketing platform.

service teams and out to customers. It depicts six marketing disciplines, and includes customer feedback as a form of information gathering for the critical discipline of marketing research.

QUICK TIPS TO HELP YOU BUILD CAPACITY FOR YOUR MARKETING ORGANIZATION

1. **Create an internal marketing research team.** Gather representatives from the sales, operations, finance, client service, customer service, and quality management teams to meet with you monthly or quarterly to share their insights, thoughts, and concerns regarding marketing.

2. **Schedule a regular meeting date for your internal marketing research team.** A commitment to regular meetings (but not so many that people will groan when they get your agenda in their mailbox) will convey that your new team is vital to the company's success and an integral part of the business effort. It will let other teams and departments know that you are serious about what you do and that their opinion counts. Schedule meetings and send out the dates in advance, so participants can note it in their calendars. Before each meeting, plan enough time to send out a meeting agenda and allow others to prepare for it. At meetings, take minutes and distribute them to the group.

3. **Ask for team members' input and use it.** Help your internal marketing research team feel free to relate what they see, hear, and believe as individuals inside your organization and also share what they hear back from customers. This openness will help you design a responsive marketing strategy and marketing messages that meet multiple needs. Also, assign action items, due dates, and responsibilities for everybody.

4. **Return to meetings with updates on how you used the information others had provided.** You will keep people involved when they feel that their work and contributions are valued. If, for some reason, you cannot integrate their concerns or recommendations, let them know why you can't.

5. **Build a cross-disciplinary marketing team.** In a perfect world, team members should include at least the following:
   - Copywriter
   - Graphic designer
   - Web designer
   - Digital media expert
   - Internet marketing/advertising expert
   - Event planner
   - Telemarketer
   - Direct mail specialist
   - Sales proposal writer

- Media buyer
- Press spokesperson
- Community relations specialist
- Print/production coordinator
- Print buyer

Depending on your company's size and the scope of your marketing needs, you may have a one-person shop or need more than one provider in each area. Alternatively, each of these functions can be successfully outsourced, as needed.

6. **Communicate clearly and often.** Share the marketing message internally and externally. Hold meetings in person, via conference calls, or online. Verify that the sales, operations, client, and customer service teams understand and are on board with the brand message and marketing approach. If not, explain the rationale behind your approach, and why you need their cooperation. Also, identify the internal champions who influence colleagues' opinions, and cultivate the relationships that will help you meet your marketing goals. Then, share your marketing message outside in as many ways as your budget allows.

7. **Launch customer contact campaigns in various ways, in relevant target markets.** Gather marketing research before launching campaigns. Test market before diving in. To augment paid advertising and marketing efforts, you can make use of communication tools, such as blogs, member Web sites, press releases, public service announcements, brand ambassadors (i.e., the people inside and outside your organization who are positioned to influence opinions about your company, products, and services), and low-cost to no-cost strategies, whenever possible. Test marketing helps conserve cash and provides evidence for the worth of more costly endeavors.

8. **Be consistent in how you tell your story, and inform your team as it develops.** Use the same language inside and beyond the company, avoiding jargon whenever possible so you are sure that people really get what you mean. Match the personality of your print advertising to the language on your Web site, and vice versa. Give your sales and customer support teams advance notice when you plan to change language on the Web site and in print materials; they shouldn't find out about your latest marketing approach from customers who dial in with unexpected questions.

Setting the Process in Motion

So, where do you start? The bean counter will tell you to begin with the end—your profit motive—in mind. Before investing money in marketing (or developing) products and services, savvy chief executive officers and financial and marketing officers require numbers that will demonstrate the projected return on investment. Long before a salesperson ever swings the first golf club in the relationship-building game, the marketing manager must be hard at work on substantive planning. Starting with marketing research to validate that products headed for market are relevant, needed, and primed for success, the marketer evaluates market segments, chooses target markets, recommends pricing, and plans marketing promotions. Finally, a Web presence is developed, ads are run, telemarketers, e-marketers, and networkers are sent out to prospect. Then, salespeople are charged with selling. Easy? It is, if you do it right.

Sales are easier to close when people connect with the value of your brand. That happens when marketers set the stage through strategies, positioning, and promotions that engage the senses, shift perceptions, create beliefs, communicate value, and establish connections to the people and businesses that make up targeted market segments. How do you create connections with prospective consumers?

When most people hear the word *marketing*, they first think of advertising and promotion. It is the marketer's job to build awareness, interest in, and preference for products and services. But marketing (and branding) begins way before the first line of promotional copy is ever written.

To validate your marketing effort and convince your CEO that your efforts will generate return on your marketing investment, you need to know which customers will buy and use your services and where those customers live, work, and play so you can get products to them. When you know the answers to those questions, you'll be ready to plan a meaningful message and a marketing effort for your brand.

Quiz

1. Integrated marketing principles:
   (a) Ensure that all company teams speak the same brand language and understand their roles in the marketing process
   (b) Are only for companies with marketing budgets over $25,000
   (c) Focus entirely on branding
   (d) Are taught on Facebook and LinkedIn

2. A brand promise is:
   (a) An element of the marketing mix
   (b) The expectations set through marketing and service
   (c) An example of a margarine marketing promotion
   (d) Part of a mission statement

3. The marketing team should be called in after products are developed.
   (a) True
   (b) False

4. The seven Ps of marketing are:
   (a) The marketing premise
   (b) Only as good as the CEO says they are
   (c) Known as the "marketing mix"
   (d) The most costly way to market

5. Which of the following is *not* part of pricing strategy?

(a) Calculating costs

(b) Analyzing business strategy

(c) Advertising promotions

(d) Demographic research

6. Building a cross-functional team is important because:

(a) Team members help pollinate ideas

(b) Team members facilitate communication

(c) Involved team members are more likely to support marketing initiatives

(d) All of the above

7. To *choose* the best marketing channel(s) for your products and services, you must:

(a) Conduct a cost-benefit analysis

(b) Refer to demographic research

(c) Consult with a financial advisor

(d) Ask channel representatives about their market position

(e) Both (a) and (c)

8. The integrated marketing platform:

(a) Fosters communication between business functions and segments

(b) Reduces red tape and lowers risk

(c) Identifies marketing channels

(d) None of the above

(e) All of the above

9. Brand value builds when:

(a) People are willing to pay more for products

(b) Marketers communicate in multiple ways

(c) Customers ask a lot of questions

(d) Customers experience positive outcomes

10. Reasons for doing a trade show are:

(a) To foster brand image, make sales on site, and collect leads

(b) To reduce stress inside the company

(c) To give away premiums

(d) Both (a) and (b)

(e) All of the above

CHAPTER 2

Principles of Branding

Attract customers. Build relationships. Keep them coming. That's it. "It" starts with branding. A brand is a recognizable mark, logo, or logotype designed to communicate predictable emotional and behavioral responses in the minds of prospective buyers. Branding is the action of building relationships with customers through the image you project.

Starting with your icon and ending with what people say, feel, and do in relation to it, your brand message can develop the power to engage potential customers and set even a small business apart from competitors. When your brand connects with the hearts of customers, it can launch an enterprise to the top of its field and across the globe. With the power of the Internet, e-commerce technology, social marketing, and sound marketing practices, even a small company can maximize its presence and prosper with international clientele.

Business branding combines both strategic and tactical initiatives. It requires a plan to choose the right products, build relationships around them, and get them to market. In the process, brand builders blanket the marketing mix with an overlay of symbolic, iconic, and philosophical messages—all of which influence business transactions. In line with company goals, brand marketing attends to building trust, expectations, and consistent experiences across markets. The best brand marketing develops positive experiences across the board.

Your brand logo is an external visual representation of ownership, as well as the inner message people get when they see your mark or hear your company name. As the brand icon on your business card is perceived by the eyes, ears, and touch of people you meet, your logo sends a message about you, your company, products, services, and citizenship. That message should help people understand what you represent and what they can expect from you.

Logotype

A *logo* is a company emblem that usually combines a graphic icon with text. A logotype is created with text and no icon. Whatever your logo, remember that neither logo icon nor logotype is designed to work in a vacuum. While logos represent you in print, promotional materials, and signage, they are just the starting point, akin to shouting your name. But actions speak much louder than words and pictures. Once your logo is out in public, it will symbolize the sum total of your actions and the relationships you build. Logos come to project the experience you create of strength, stability, fun, adventure, history, and/or other sentiment. Choose logo fonts and colors that match the business personality you select. Many logotypes become the formally registered symbols that identify the manufacturer or distributor of a product.

Cultivating Brand Value

Your brand, ultimately, is the value that customers sense in it. To create value-based connections, you will need to launch (or relaunch) your brand with products and services that deliver positive and meaningful benefits and outcomes for your prospects. You also will need to develop a coordinated plan for communicating those benefits, over and again, in multiple ways that speak in the right languages—culturally, emotionally, and mentally.

Every business owner, from the smallest entrepreneur to the largest global enterprise, works vigorously to capture and engage the attention of prospective customers. Doing so is not an easy task because every business, *regardless of industry and/or niche,* is actually competing for the *same* customer. You don't believe it? Take a moment to think about how you allocate your own personal or business budget. Do you spend it all on the same thing? Neither do most of the customers in your market. You make decisions and choices that often force you to trade one desire for another.

Despite that, most marketing experts still concentrate on comparisons and efforts to differentiate the companies for whom they work from other companies within a *single* industry. As an example, a smaller telephone carrier works to distinguish itself from AT&T and Verizon. A computer company directly compares its products to Macintosh, IBM, and Dell. Why? First, they do so because their target market is tuned into those brand names; second, they know that their target customers already buy those brands; and, third, they believe that prospective customers will consider the direct competition when making a buying decision.

Brand marketers also must work to help customers value what their companies offer over the myriad other products and services needed in a day, regardless of industry, because buying choices ultimately filter through each customer's mental marketplace as well as physical bank account.

Behind all the creative clutter that bombards potential customers with "buy me, buy me" messages is the hard reality that every customer only has a finite amount of money to spend, whether he or she is spending it on telephones, computers, lighting, energy, jewelry, books, landscaping, recreation, real estate, or milk. Just as important, every customer has only a limited amount of mental bandwidth through which to process those buy-me messages. Their brain calculators constantly juggle internal algorithms that shift around personal what-if scenarios: If I spend my money on a Sony television, will I have money left to vacation in the Bahamas this year? If I purchase a Land Rover, can I then pay for gas at the Hess station? If I buy a ring at Tiffany's, will I have enough left over to buy a bottle of Chanel perfume? And so on.

Buyers clearly weigh in with direct brand comparisons every day: Mac versus PC, Wheaties versus Special K, Hyundai versus Toyota; Ronzoni versus Mueller's; McDonald's versus Burger King; and so on. Decisions take place in a mental marketplace where a noisy exchange of thoughts, emotions, and judgments rumble over words and phrases like *cost, quality, ouch, no way,* and *I really, really, really want that whatchamacallit.* That mental maneuvering adjusts itself among mall walls, Web-site visits, office calls, and shops where advertisers, salespeople, and marketers all shout, "Go for it!"

To make an impact, your go-for-it marketing bulletin must appeal to and coincide with the buyers' emotional perception of value, need, pain, and the belief that they can and will enjoy life more after buying what you are selling. Emotions—not prices—rule most buying decisions, and emotions can be triggered by the impact of your communications.

In the same way that customers evaluate almost every buying decision and the wisdom of making a purchase, you may ask yourself, "If I spend money on branding, will I make enough back to pay for office space, salaries, products, lunch, and health insurance?" *You betcha!* In the long run, your brand dollars may be the best investment you make across the life of your business, especially if you tackle branding from an integrated perspective, as discussed in Chapter 1. Your bank of computers, programs, supplies, and other gizmos will wear themselves out in just a few months or years, but your brand impact will hang in for the long haul.

Getting Started

The goal of branding is to help customers recognize and believe in the value of your products and services. Brand beliefs are built in these ways:

- In the minds of employees and customers through taglines, messages, expertise, and experiences
- Through advertising and marketing strategies

- Amid internal relationships with employees and external relationships with customers, the community, and the media
- By experiences with products and services
- As customers and others share your message for you

By modeling best practices and adding your own spirit of innovation, you will get your brand ball rolling.

CASE STUDY: A Branding Flop To Avoid

Here's a story of a branding launch that could have been so much more.

This particular brand launch began inside a health-care facility and reached into the offices of local doctors, the minds of media journalists, the souls of patients seeking cures, and thousands of everyday people who read newspapers and watch television. We'll call it "The Case of Sick Branding Syndrome," or "SBS." SBS broke out in the hospital, where a new brand was about to be delivered. Administrators of this well-respected institution had written a prescription for a cutting-edge brand injection. They hoped that hundreds, perhaps thousands, of new patients (i.e., customers) would swallow a healthy dose of the institution's new health service and emerge as loyal customers. Those loyal customers, in turn, would tell all of their friends and relatives about the facility's great new miracle treatment.

The public relations (PR) department suited right up for Operation Branding. They created a new logo, wrote a new message, and then designed and printed a brochure touting the novelty and benefits of that new service. They also organized an event to engage community physicians and prospective patients in understanding the importance of that health issue and introduce them to new services the hospital had implemented to address them. The PR department created a compelling newspaper advertising campaign about the health issue. They printed up prescription and referral pads as well as direction sheets. They covered all the branding bases, visual and written, and communicated them through various media channels, including press releases and word-of-mouth marketing. They placed radio spots and newspaper ads, procured TV time, and were thrilled when Launch Day turned out hundreds of attendees for their special event—on a weekend, no less! Great branding? Great marketing? Great impact? You decide.

First thing Monday morning, the service phone lines were ringing off the hook. Unfortunately, there were not enough people to answer the phones, and callers were routed through a lengthy telephone tree. (What did the brand communicate that way?) Most of the callers who got through found out that they had to wait several weeks for an appointment. (What did the brand communicate then?) Those who got appointments found themselves in a crowded waiting room for hours before they could see the doctor. (What feelings did those customers experience?)

The reception staff was relatively indifferent. (What did customers leave believing? Just as important, what did they tell their friends?)

This campaign was a success from a marketing standpoint. It found ways to reach customers and get them to the door. But from a branding perspective—where feelings about products are involved—it flopped.

The moral of this story is that the most essential step in every branding effort is to protect your brand by giving it the attention and commitment it deserves across your service channel. When you put your money where your brand mouth is, be ready to deliver on your promise. Even a multimillion-dollar ad campaign will not generate long-term return on investment if the products and services don't deliver on promises made. Before you make the promise, make sure that the experience and quality of your products and services are every bit as good your brand message pledges. That's part of what marketing experts call "integrated marketing." That's what we call "integrated branding."

Integrated Branding: The BOLD Way

By integrating your marketing messages with operational and quality control processes, you will increase the likelihood of a successful, sustainable brand. You will create multiple connections with your customers and raise your chances of having them really like you. To create those positive, memorable connections, you'll want to organize and follow a plan for gathering the right resources in the right combination at the right time. If planning is not your strong suit, don't worry; the elements of highly sophisticated branding technology are distilled here into a simple, yet integrated, four-part strategy you can start to use right away. By weaving these four strategic elements throughout your brand effort, you will communicate in relevant and influential ways with prospective and buying customers, employees, investors, the media, and anyone else you bring aboard. Guess what? Employees, media, and investors are some of your best assets. Once they buy into your message, they can share and influence others, even if they never spend a nickel in your shop. So make sure they buy the same message you are selling!

To ease recall and help you get organized, I have developed an acronym with the power to propel your branding effort. Remember these four letters—B O L D—and the short word they form. BOLD stands for four key components of any branding strategy: (1) **b**randing identity, (2) **o**rganizational strength, (3) **l**oyalty marketing, and (4) **d**iagnostics. We'll examine each of these in turn in the paragraphs that follow.

With BOLD as the mnemonic guiding your branding process, you will excite, attract, capture, and engage people. Using this formula can catapult you to your next level of business success. Start now, by branding your business the BOLD way.

BRAND IDENTITY

Brand identity (the *b* part in BOLD) is the image you project of your company, products, and services. Visual cues, such as logo, corporate colors, images, and product designs are the obvious parts of your branding. Your brand logo is the flag you fly to announce that you have arrived. It tells the world that you are a player in the game. Whether you create your own logo, design your own materials, or work with a design professional, your job as a brand builder is to translate your business insight into visuals that intentionally communicate feelings that connect with your customers. As you build rapport, you will engage, interest, build trust, and affect the senses that evoke emotion. That psychological combination will influence branding and buying decisions.

Although design is the obvious part of brand identity, the subtle part is the thumbprint you make with each customer experience. The best way to brand your company is to really understand what makes your customers tick and then map that knowledge throughout the marketing mix into your brand message. Use your branding to communicate what you do and how you do it, in ways that make sense to your customers in *their* world. When you do, you'll be able to stay connected and build a strong rapport with them.

CAUTION

It's tempting to tell people what *you* want them to know. It is more useful to tell them what *they* want and need to know.

ORGANIZATIONAL STRENGTH

Great employees—your organizational strength (the *o* part in BOLD)—are your brand gold. They influence customer perceptions, often make or break a customer's experience, and can help you outdistance your competition. Unless you are a solo entrepreneur, your employees are usually the first touchpoint with your customers. Even when customers are shopping on the Web, employees (as well as suppliers, distributors, and contractors) are the power behind how those consumers experience your brand. By choosing and training brand-focused employees, continually developing their skills, and choosing the right channel partners, you will ensure a better brand experience. Develop employees who understand and are well prepared to communicate your brand message. Then, turn them into empowered ambassadors who create positive brand experiences for every internal and external customer.

LOYALTY MARKETING

Build loyalty (the *l* part in BOLD) by planning a marketing effort that makes sure you stay in touch with customers and keep them coming back. Nurture customer relationships so your customers will see you as their valued resource, problem solver, and fulfiller of dreams.

> **CAUTION**
>
> Stay in contact with customers, and always let them know that you have their best interest at heart. Use newsletters, blogs, advertising, Web-site updates, and customer events to tell them about items of special interest to them. Also, as often as possible, let customers and employees know that you appreciate and celebrate them with greeting cards, thank-you notes, and acknowledgments of birthdays and anniversaries.

For topical updates, choose to focus on issues that resonate with your audience. Consider writing about the environment (this is a hot topic with longstanding impact) or other business and product issues. Whatever your subject, include facts about new products, services, or pricing; special sales; added features; coupons; news; and surveys requesting readers' opinions. Send a news clipping of interest to a particular client. Deliver a product sample to a segmented market group. You can also send an occasional postcard or e-mail message. (Avoid sending a barrage of e-mail messages. If you use e-campaigns, create a permission-based list with links to opt in and opt out.)

However you do it, let your clients know you are always thinking of them and have their interest at heart. Choose print, customer appreciation, or viral marketing strategies. Tap into the power of social networks and the visual connectivity offered by YouTube. com and Webinar providers. Whether you have beer or champagne pockets, social media sites let you reach across the globe. Just *do* something. Let your customers know they are top of mind with you, and you will stay top of mind with them.

DIAGNOSTICS

You will make better branding decisions, and become better at forecasting results, when you regularly assess marketing assumptions and efforts with diagnostics (the *d* part in BOLD). Diagnostic tools, such as feedback from focus groups and surveys, marketing research, and accounting and statistical analyses, all provide insight to brand impact. As you use diagnostics to assess and measure gaps in the market, in products and services, and between targeted and actual results, you will build the foundation for responsive brand marketing. As you analyze and evaluate every part of your marketing effort and test your assumptions, you will develop marketing intelligence. The information you gain will help you make adjustments at the right times in the right places.

Building Brand Image

Brand image building begins where your R&D team left off. You've already got a business premise, you've researched your competition, you've got products, you've got services, and maybe you've got employees. You may even have a healthy dose of being overwhelmed.

Now it's time to break down your branding effort into smaller, manageable steps. Let's assume that everyone in your organization has agreed to work together toward a common vision. They are aligned with your company's mission. You've worked through operational issues. To move forward, you'll need to focus on tactics.

INTEGRATE VISUALS, MESSAGES, AND EXPERIENCES FOR IMPACT

Branding is a key marketing strategy for every business. Your brand must influence—in a positive way—what people *see, experience, say*, and *believe* about you. Your branding will have a big impact on how quickly you get off first base, attract great employees, hear phones ring, crane your neck to watch products fly off your shelves, wow your investors, and deposit checks into the bank. (Remember the profit motive.) Integrate creative visuals with succinct messages and great customer experiences to consistently reinforce brand image.

THE IMPACT OF PERCEPTION

What influences perceptions and beliefs also influences behavior. Inject your marketing fuel with strategic communication, and you will drive lasting connections. Start by crafting your message. The following thoughts and exercises will help you whip that message into shape quickly and with relatively little stress. A good first step is to think about what your customers need to see, hear, feel, and experience before they will get in sync with you. Planning, writing, speaking, and acting out your message will be beneficial for you. The more ways you process it, the more clarity you will gain.

> ### CAUTION
>
> Marketing is less about products and geography or demographics than it is about people. Focus on people strategies and you will uncover what differentiates your product or services in the minds of customers.

Creating and Communicating Value

Most customers don't care too much about a list of capabilities or your product ingredients. What they really want to know is what you and your products can *do* for them. Your communications must focus on *value*! As a result of choosing your brand, will customers save time or money? Will your products bathe them in coveted cachet? Smooth out your customers' wrinkles? Add years to their lives? Make them feel like they've just had a long vacation on a tropical island? Help them make money? Enable them to jump-start their own business productivity?

Whatever your product, service, or company message, you will communicate value by conveying the obvious benefit as well as the ultimate impact or outcome. By tuning into what your customers care about most *and exactly how they communicate and process information*, you can influence the power of beliefs and create lasting connections. The strength of those connections will depend on how well you anticipate your customers' concerns and tap into their mental wiring.

CONNECTING THROUGH SENSORY COMMUNICATION

Find out what makes your customers tick. You can learn that by observing them and listening to the words they use when they speak. Did you ever attend a seminar and afterward hear a friend say, "Wow! That was a great speech!" Did you agree? Perhaps, you thought it was only ho-hum. If so, chances are that the speaker matched language to your friend's style but not to yours. Maybe you knew a child who did great in school while the kid in the next seat flunked the test. It's likely that the teacher processed information in much the same way as the successful student, but used language that did not stimulate the failing student to recall information.

Connections happen more quickly when you make links in sensory terms that match a customer's own neural setup. For example, did some of the words in this chapter interest you more than others? Did they make you take *notice*? Did a word make you *see* a possible solution, *tune into* a strategy, or *feel* like you got the message? I couldn't possibly know about the inner wiring of each and every person who will read this book, so I may not have matched my language exactly to your own neural circuits and mental preference. But, I can show you how to increase your chances of connecting with more customers more quickly.

THE VISUAL, AUDITORY, KINESTHETIC (VAK) MODEL

The art of branding is founded on the power of personal connections with products and services. Language is founded on the power of visual, auditory, and kinesthetic connections. By communicating in different ways—using words that stimulate the right neural pathways and senses—you will make quicker connections, open more dialogues, overcome more obstacles, break through more barriers, and speed up your desired branding. That is why, most marketing campaigns use multiple marketing vehicles and approaches.

CAUTION

The language-processing rule is that people are more likely to notice words or images that come to them in their own way of processing language. Be alert to your word combinations, use as many combinations as are sensible, and you will win more attention.

When writing and communicating with your own customers, you'll get the best results if you speak in their terms, using visual, auditory, or kinesthetic (i.e., tactile experiences or actions) language that matches their preferred mode. Since you probably do not know every customer personally, choose words that reach across sensory lines, and you will have a good chance of breaking through internal communication barriers.

Think about how you describe your brand and set expectations.

What kind of words do you use? Do you use words that form mental images, sound bites, or affect feelings? For example, if you use words, like: *show*, *see*, *look*, *color*, *imagine*, *observe*, or *picture*, you may be a visual thinker and make decisions based on pictures that take place in your mind as others are talking. Other visual people will connect with those words, too. If you use words, such as: *hear*, *listen*, *describe*, *tell*, *sounds like*, or *tune in*, you may be an auditory thinker and place strong meaning on what you hear. You probably like to have things explained verbally before you make decisions. Other auditory people will tune in to similar words. If you use words, such as: *feel*, *touch*, *connect*, *experience*, or *balance* when describing your work or products, then your preferred language style may be kinesthetic, and you may need to feel experiences before you decide if they will work for you. So will other kinesthetic language processors. For them, you would pepper your communications with action words.

All communication is tied up (a kinesthetic word) in the way that people hear (an auditory word) what you say. Help customers to process your meaning by giving them words that work for them. They will be more likely to notice (a visual word) and connect (another kinesthetic word) with your brand.

Uncovering Beliefs that Influence Consumers

Brand identity is built on beliefs. Extraordinary brand identity is built on unshakeable brand beliefs. Such beliefs come from meaningful, reliable, translatable experiences with your brand. Make first impressions count. Use visual cues, and create real experiences that foster senses of respect, action, reliability, and consistency. Powerful brands emerge through perceptions as well as facts.

HELPFUL BRAND MANAGEMENT BELIEFS

1. Innovation gets you first to market and keeps you ahead of the curve.

2. Provocative imagery captures and sustains attention.

3. Concrete differentiators clearly articulate value.

4. Market responses based on customer trials, experience, and testimonials deliver important feedback about your brand.

5. Attention to customer feedback will keep your brand vital.

Connecting with Customers

As the New York Lottery catch phrase goes, "You can't live the dream if you don't play the game."[1] Get your word out across media channels. Depending on your budget, you can use social media, newspapers, magazines, Web blogs, Web sites, cross-links, radio, television, or some combination of these. Here are some helpful hints (we'll discuss this concept in detail in Chapters 9 through 15):

- Tell your story with evidence.
- Add credibility-building testimonials and references.
- Send keyword-rich articles to e-zines.
- Use sensory channels to speed up perceptions and deepen connections.

TWENTY WAYS TO CONNECT WITH CUSTOMERS

When you communicate and market your brand, make it a point to reach your audiences through different sensory experiences as well as varied marketing vehicles:

1. Create a compelling visual design, and use it on banners, brochures, and boxes.
2. Write a press release. Post it on your Web site. Add a podcast recording.
3. Contact a reporter to generate public relations interest.
4. Place ads in local papers, on radios, cable television calendars and channels, or major networks, and on the Internet, if your budget allows.
5. Build the buzz with an interactive contest on your own Web site. (Yes, you do need a Web site!)
6. Send out a newsletter.
7. Speak before a group.
8. Offer referral incentives to customers.
9. Keep employees happy, and get them talking positively about you.
10. Create a video and place it on your Web site and YouTube.com.
11. Write a blog.
12. Join a networking group.
13. Launch an e-mail campaign.
14. Host a meeting on a topic of interest for customers.
15. Write and publish a book.
16. Leave a value-driven message on your voice mail.

---

[1] This is a registered trademark of the New York Lottery. The New York Lottery obtained federal trademark registration for this service mark on August 24, 2004 (registration number: 2876899).

17. Eliminate voice mail. Speak to callers directly!

18. Attend a trade show.

19. Build a good marketing list.

20. "Reach out and touch someone."[2] (I couldn't resist.)

CASE STUDY: How a Small Business Used an Event to Build Brand Recognition

A two-year-old energy-consulting firm cultivated awareness of its company by capitalizing on the power of "green" branding. The firm invited 100 companies to attend an educational breakfast event about energy benchmarking. Doing so allowed the firm to feature its consulting team as part of a "grassroots" effort through which the team taught building owners and facility managers how and why measuring energy use in a certain way would save companies money for mission-critical projects and protect the environment at the same time. The breakfast, held at a local university, cost just a little to execute. The brand outcome for the energy group was a room full of clients who now see the firm as an educational, informative, trusted advisor, and a protector of the environment, with the cachet of university support.

This small enterprise used an event to help shape its brand image. The event execution plan that was implemented used the following methods:

- Sent letters to 100 customers and prospects inviting them to the event
- Wrote three press releases, each with a slightly different emphasis
- Issued press releases two months, one month, and one week, respectively, before the event
- Wrote and issued a "media advisory" (a simpler form of information than a press release, using bullets to tell the media the *who*, *what*, *when*, *where*, and *why* of the event) and released it the day before the event
- Listed the event on Web-based and print community and newspaper calendars
- Responded to a topical blog entry maintained by the local business newspaper in advance of the event
- Informed county legislative representatives about the event and invited their participation
- Offered a free energy audit to every company that registered for the event
- Followed up with phone calls, letters, and e-mails on relationships built through the conference
- Started planning long range for the next client event

---

[2] AT&T marketing campaign.

What made this a brand win? This client connected with existing customers, prospects, and larger entities (including the region's major energy supplier) with the power to influence thinking and preference for their brand. The event helped the group to shape and control the perceptions of event attendees, as well as people and potential customers who read about the firm in the two newspaper articles that were picked up as a result of press releases. Team members also founded ongoing relationships and closed new business. They also used their first success as the premise for submitting a proposal to speak at a major regional business conference, and won that speaking opportunity.

Employing Communication Essentials

When writing, designing, or overseeing brand communication, always strive for these things:

- **Simplicity.** Be clear and concise. Most people have an attention span of about a nanosecond for advertising. If you are writing a press release, stick to the basics, include a pertinent quote or two, and send it out. If you are writing a brochure, use short, uncomplicated sentences with bullets to organize your thoughts. Use visuals, such as photos and charts, to illustrate your meaning without words. If you are exhibiting at an event or trade show, make sure that your booth graphics include only a few words or just one compelling sentence. That's all an attendee will have time to see and absorb when passing your booth.

- **Relevance.** What customers see is based entirely within the context of what they need or are concerned with at the moment. If they don't perceive a need, your message will have no meaning. Help your brand communicate effectively by taking time to consider cultural influences, income levels, and other demographic data that will tell you about the needs and influencers in your buyers' market.

- **Sensory connections.** Use sensory-specific words (e.g., *see*, *listen*, *reach*, *touch*, and *feel*) whenever you can. Also, use metaphors to convey meaning and stimulate senses. Think of statements or questions people will quickly connect with, such as these:
  - "Have your cake and eat it, too." (Did you see the visual image here, and understand how the word *eat* can stimulate the sense of taste?)
  - "Stop chasing your tail."
  - "Waiting for the phone to ring?" (Here is an auditory connection.)
  - How about, "Reach out and Touch Someone"?[3]

- **Honesty.** Your integrity is your brand. Communicate with sincerity. Deliver on your promise. No further explanation is needed.

---

[3] AT&T marketing campaign.

By taking time to answer a series of questions about your business, you can uncover important information to use in your brand messages. To create a powerful brand identity, start by considering brand identity questions. Then weave them into a narrative to tell the story of your brand.

Home in on Benefits

Simply put, benefits sell. Sell your brand on the value of the benefits you deliver in the eyes of your customers. Clarify what use of your products or services does for customers. If you are in business-to-business marketing, you'll need to answer this question for direct customers as well as for managers and leaders of the companies with whom you work. Also define it for channel partners. You can identify benefits not only by speaking with your product developers but also by asking what your customers have to say. If you are still in the product development stage, imagine the testimonials you wish to hear. Then discuss perceived needs and benefits with your R&D people. Make sure to bridge any gap between what developers are considering and what your customers really want.

Focus on Outcomes

You can drive more value when you map benefits to their overall outcomes. Customers buy outcomes, not products. State your message in ways that will help people make the logical leap to their personal desire and ultimate outcomes—the outcomes they want most. Table 2.1 will help you drill down to what your products, services, and organization really do for your customers. Breaking it down this way will also help you clarify your thoughts.

Take a moment to think about your typical customers and what they need most from you. List their needs, problems, and pains in the left column. Next, state how your products will make a difference for them. Then list the obvious benefits customers can expect. Finally, include the ultimate impact on their lives. This will help you shape your branding so it will go right to the heart of your customers' innermost needs and desires.

CAUTION

Not all needs may be expressed; sometimes what's *not* said will tell you what you need to know. Listen carefully to your inner "customer radar" for critical insights. Taking quiet time to reflect on your own sense of customers and brand issues will increase your skill at predicting what customers are likely to see, hear, feel, taste, and smell in their own minds *before* they ever try or buy your product or service.

Table 2.1   Identifying Benefits, Solutions, and Outcomes

Customer's Problem/Need	Your Product/ Service Solution	Benefit to Your Customer	Ultimate Impact on Life
Example: The customer is shorthanded at work. Employees can't keep up with their workloads. The customer doesn't receive products on time.	**Example:** Our staffing company has employees who are ready and able to put people to work when you are.	**Example:** More hands are available in the office. Work is completed more quickly. When you use our temporary staffing solution, your own customers are highly satisfied. There is less worry and stress for you as a manager.	**Example:** You will be able to transact more business, more quickly, with fewer problems. As a result, you will rest easily at night. Company managers also may get a bonus for meeting critical project deadlines, strengthening productivity, and adding revenue.
Your situation:	**Your situation:**	**Your situation:**	**Your situation:**

CAUTION

Most customers want to save or make money, enhance their quality of life, speed up business productivity, feel better, increase morale, save time, feel balanced, and build better relationships. Every one of those benefits leads to a more enjoyable life. Do these benefits fit with your brand? If not, what do you offer? Why does a customer care?

Differentiating a Brand

Brands build in proportion to customer recognition. When consumers quickly recognize a brand symbol, they make instant leaps to the meaning behind it; for example, Target's powerful branding emerges from consistent repetition of bold art as well as a consistent message of value and fun. Your brand will build when customers understand *why* you are the best and perhaps *only* company that can give the product or service they really want. Creating that belief is the process that marketers call "differentiation." As you communicate and differentiate your brand, you will simultaneously create recognition and empower your sales effort. That is the purpose of branding. That's also how customers begin to rely on your brand promise.

DIFFERENTIATION STATEMENTS

Now, take a moment to identify what differentiates you from your competition. Try on these possible differentiators:

- We save you more money than our competition.
- We save you more money than you could save on your own.
- We help you earn more money by_____.
- We are staffed to offer you peace of mind.
- We are more accessible.
- We are close by.

Take a moment to consider these questions:

- How did they make you feel? What images did you connect with?
- What do they tell you about your company's own perspective on those issues?
- What does it make you think consumers believe?

Meeting Customer Needs

No matter what you say about your brand, or what people want to believe about it, the only way you will really make a difference is by meeting the needs of your customer better than anyone else can.

Individual consumers have many needs that must be filled in a day, which offers you many opportunities to brand myriad products and services in special ways. But when it comes to business customers, there are only three needs that really matter: (1) *money* (how you can help them save money or make money), (2) *time* (how you can help them save or maximize time), and (3) *productivity* (how you can increase productivity and enhance morale). If you can show your prospects and clients how you will address these needs better than your competitors will, you will differentiate your brand and close the deal.

Quiz

1. The four elements of the BOLD Branding Formula are:
   (a) Boldness, organizational development, loyalty, and differentiation
   (b) Branding, organizational development, loyalty marketing, and diversification
   (c) Branding, organizational development, loyalty marketing, and diagnostics
   (d) Boldness, operations, loyal customers, and differentiation

2. Sensory language is perceived in signals that are:

   (a) Visual, auditory, and kinesthetic

   (b) Differentiated from other marketing clutter

   (c) Given in several ways

   (d) Visual and verbal

3. Differentiation is:

   (a) The importance of offering different options among which customers can choose

   (b) Not a factor in brand communication

   (c) The process of setting your brand apart from your competition

   (d) None of the above

4. Brand messages that target the senses are perceived faster.

   (a) True

   (b) False

5. Which of the following ingredients are essential for good brand communication?

   (a) Channels, productivity, outreach

   (b) Simplicity, honesty, sensory words, benefits

   (c) Honesty, benefits, consumer, events

   (d) None of the above

6. Which of the following benefits are most sought by business customers?

   (a) Money, time, productivity

   (b) Time, mission, accountability

   (c) Mission, branding, differentiation,

   (d) Accountability, differentiation, mission

7. Where are brand preferences won?

   (a) In shopping centers

   (b) In a mental market place

   (c) On the Internet

   (d) Through smart telemarketing

8. To build a sustainable brand:

    (a) Develop a big budget

    (b) Call in a marketing consultant

    (c) Deliver on your brand promise

    (d) Capture attention in multiple markets

9. Your brand must influence:

    (a) What people see, say, experience, and believe about you

    (b) Buyer expectations

    (c) Employee connections

    (d) All of the above

    (e) Only (a) and (b)

10. If you use words such as *see*, *look*, and *imagine*, you are most likely:

    (a) To connect with your customers

    (b) Creative and inspirational

    (c) A visual learner

    (d) Able to create a good logo

PART TWO

Developing a Marketing Plan

CHAPTER 3

Elements of a Strategic Marketing Plan

Have you been so caught up in getting through day-to-day operations and putting out fires that you've become comfortable flying by the seat of your pants? Are you hoping that you can stay on track through willpower and guts? If so, it's time to take a break and learn how to plan. When you do, you will have mastered a key ability of peak performers.

The plan you need depends on what you want to accomplish for a particular part of your business. Strategic marketing plans set a direction for helping to achieve the mission of an entire organization. They present a future-focused view of a company, specific business unit, department, or product. They also set the stage for long-range planning. Most strategic plans focus on missions, goals, operations, and projected outcomes in key results areas, ranging from product development to customer service and financial outcomes. Tactical plans, by comparison, drill down to specific action steps needed to execute an overall strategy. Both strategic and tactical plans target predictable business revenues and profitability, each at a different level. While a strategic plan decides the destination, the tactical plan sets the sails.

Building a Strategic Marketing Plan

Most marketing plans are a hybrid of strategy and tactics. Your strategic marketing plan should define key marketing areas and results needed to ensure that your products and services will get to intended markets and targeted consumers. Your tactical plan should explain how your marketing team will do the work. Combining both strategic and tactical planning will result in a comprehensive marketing plan that addresses the marketing mix in an insightful, practical, and cost-effective way. While this chapter focuses on the first P—planning—future chapters will tackle other elements of the marketing mix in turn: products, positioning, placement, pricing, people, and promotion. This chapter will help you create a framework you can follow to achieve your marketing goals.

Getting Started

Strategic planning begins where marketing research and analysis leave off. The goal of every marketing plan is to create sustainable profits through products, services, and messages that are a proven fit for their intended markets. Whether you plan to place products in mass targets, target markets, or niche markets, your plan should lay the groundwork for achieving mission-critical objectives. Marketing research will provide the data-driven, evidence-based support for introducing and delivering a product or service to the right market at the right price.

The Planning Pyramid

Think of your plan as a pyramid. First, you build a strong foundation by gathering information, assessing market opportunities, identifying external threats, analyzing internal strengths and weaknesses, and assessing your ability to compete. When you understand market needs, desires, and personalities, you will be able to set realistic goals that help you meet your business mission. After you've outlined your goals, you can explain how you intend to achieve them. Finally, you will outline a process for evaluating your efforts, controlling outcomes, and managing for ongoing success. See Figure 3.1 for further details.

Figure 3.1   The planning pyramid.

Goals of a Strategic Marketing Plan

Not only does your strategic marketing plan show how to market for success, it can serve as a guide for prioritizing projects and making decisions. The best plans have eight characteristics in common, and those attributes are excellent predictors of success.

THE EIGHT PREDICTORS OF STRATEGIC MARKETING PLAN SUCCESS

1. Aligns with the organizational, business unit, and product missions
2. Assesses the current business environment and competition
3. Addresses the needs of consumers in targeted markets
4. Identifies current marketing projects and needs
5. Clarifies strategic goals
6. Provides a logical pathway for reaching those goals.
7. Prioritizes tactical objectives and due dates
8. Includes a method for measuring and evaluating success

Best-Practice Planning

A plan clarifies where you are going and helps you evaluate whether you have arrived. It also helps fire up the organization for success. When people at multiple levels of a company are engaged in the planning process, the likelihood of successful implementation increases. People are more committed to success when they've had a role in the planning, and they are much better at executing when they understand the game plan.

Best-practice plans emerge when planners are clear about the outcomes they want and approach planning in an orderly way. Prepare in advance so you will be clear on the goals of your strategic plan. Gather input from all areas of your company. Whenever possible, pull together a cross-functional team of employees and other stakeholders who can provide relevant, insightful information. Start by setting the intention of your plan. What is your goal? How will you know when you've reached it? Consider the current and desired positioning in the minds of your buyers. Decide where you intend to place your products. Then use the planning process to refine key branding, value propositions, and communication strategies so you can translate them into sales.

If your marketing plan were a living, breathing thing, it would have a goal of its own: to get used. Ensure that your plan doesn't grow dusty on a shelf; provide relevant, timely, actionable information that outlines both strategic and tactical objectives and assign responsibility and due dates to people on your team. If you don't have enough people on your team, you can outsource every marketing task, from research to promotion.

> **CAUTION**
>
> A strategic marketing plan helps bring stakeholders on board and gains their confidence and support for moving that plan forward. Create a user-friendly plan so that stakeholders will understand your planning recommendations, the evidence that underlies your decisions, and what results they can expect.

A strategic marketing plan maps marketing activities to specific organizational goals. Such plans acknowledge internal and external situations and goals, consider the competition, analyze opportunities and threats, address the market, and provide the pathway for getting products into customer hands.

Before drafting your plan, it helps to preplan. Start by asking, "What do we do as an organization?" That question will remind you to focus your plan so it aligns with the basic mission and competencies of your organization. The second question to ask is, "How do we do it?" Your answer will shed light on your resources and challenges. Your third question should be, "How is it working?" Your penultimate preplanning question should be, "Why do we do it this way?" The answer to the why question can help you sharpen your goals and build the buy-in, motivation, and organizational staying power you need to execute plans for sustainable success. And finally, ask, "How will we measure and control for success?"

The First Rule of Planning

Once the planning retreat has ended, people get right back into the daily grind. Keep your plan alive with the PDCA approach: **p**lan a process improvement; **d**o the improvement; **c**heck results; **a**ct to hold gains or reenter planning (see Figure 3.2).

Elements of a Strategic Marketing Plan

Planning is serious business and a strong predictor of success, but even the commitment to imperfect action is a start. For example, a plan begun on a napkin can morph into exacting success with follow-through and the right next steps. Best-practice plans follow

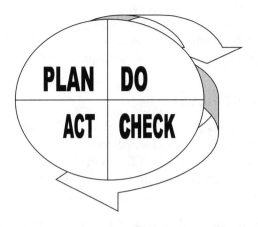

Figure 3.2 The PDCA method.

a similar structure. Figure 3.3 shows a sample table of contents; the paragraphs that follow explain in detail what content belongs in each section.

EXECUTIVE SUMMARY

The executive summary is the first section of your plan. This is a brief overview of the goals, marketing rationale, and main elements of your plan. It gives the reader a quick synopsis of what you intend to accomplish and why, where, and when. While it may help

Marketing Plan Contents

Executive summary..

Situational analysis...

Industry analysis..

Competitive intelligence....................................

Opportunities and issues analysis.....................

Goals and objectives...

Strategy and tactics..

Budget and financial projections......................

Evaluation and control......................................

Figure 3.3 Sample marketing plan table of contents.

you outline a few key points when you start out, it is often best to write this section last. As you work out all the details of your plan, you will be able to easily summarize the high points and differentiators that will make your plan a success.

SITUATIONAL ANALYSIS

A situational analysis sets the tone for your marketing endeavor by acknowledging the mission, recent history, and current situation of your company. This section includes a synopsis of your product and where it fits in the overall marketing and business plan. It provides a starting point and ends with a description of the results you are seeking. Here's how to shape your situational analysis:

- Describe the mission and purpose of your company and/or product. Include details that describe the current climate, culture, and events underway inside the company.

- List current challenges and goals. Clearly state the goal(s) you seek to achieve.

- Address current business issues, marketing projects, and needs. Identify what is needed in terms of human and capital resources, innovation, operations, and training to reach your goal(s). Describe marketing projects already underway, and comment on their effectiveness. Describe the products and/or services you will bring to market. Explain the purpose of your effort: the breakthrough outcome (i.e., big goal) needed.

- Reflect on the current and desired positioning of the company, service, and/or product. Describe your target audiences. Describe who will buy your products and on what the assumptions they base their decisions. Discuss how your intended plan will impact positioning.

- Indicate where you will place your products and services.

- Describe your value proposition and differentiators. What makes your company, product, or services genuinely unique and/or better than the competitors'?

- End with a summary discussing your decisions about how you intend to address the market. Explain how you mean to differentiate yourself in the market: price, special features, access channels, or other points of differentiation.

Finding Data for a Situational Analysis

Whether you are crafting a plan for a client, an employer, or your own enterprise, start by reviewing the company mission as well as existing marketing and business literature. If there is no written mission statement, you can start by clarifying the purpose of the organization and the project. Also review and evaluate the impact of prior plans, if any. Study your company's Web site and those of your competitors. Look inside the press rooms on their Web sites to get a handle on current issues and activity. Talk to people inside the organization, whenever possible. Ask questions: What have you done before? How has it worked for you? What would you do differently now? If you can't ask a competitor, ask someone who uses their products. Gather impressions and feedback. We all know what we know. The trick is to identify what we don't know. Listen closely, and incorporate what you learn from feedback into your plan.

INDUSTRY ANALYSIS

Preparing your industry analysis is an exercise in due diligence and offers evidence for decision making. Here's how to construct your industry analysis:

- Gather information about your industry to reveal relevant history, size, and scope.

- Contact your local Small Business Development Center or search the Internet for census data relating to your industry sector. You can gather census information by using Google or other search engines and plugging in the keyword *SIC* [Standard Industrial Classification] *code* or *NAICS* [North American Industry Classification System] *code*, or visiting www.census.gov. If you don't know your industry code, you can do a search for that too. The SIC/NAICS information (some of which is free) will give you general data on the number of establishments, revenues, paid employees, and aggregated annual payroll, within an industry sector. Trade and professional organizations also gather data and share it with their members. Check the Web sites of the organizations to which you belong.

- Discuss industry trends (historic and current) as well as recent innovations and how they impact your plan.

- Describe industry products: what's on the market now, what is needed, and how you know it. Cite your sources, and explain your methods of research and analysis.

- Note geographic markets, target market segments, and relevant niches.

- If you are in a regulated environment, address that too. Note how the regulations impact product development and marketing in your industry.

- Provide an overview of industry leaders.

- Describe the opportunities you see.

- Note trends or industry issues that may pose a threat to your success. Indicate how you will address threats, if any.

COMPETITIVE INTELLIGENCE: DIGGING INTO DETAILS

Every marketing plan should demonstrate understanding of the competition. By analyzing your competitors' action, you will clarify issues of interest to consumers, areas of opportunity, and points of differentiation. If you've researched your market, you should know a lot about your competitors. Use that research in this section by explaining what you know about direct and indirect competitors.

> **CAUTION**
>
> Like the U.S. Central Intelligence Agency (CIA), you can gather business intelligence about your competitors by studying their advertising, products, key personnel, Web sites, customer base, and industry and consumer blogs. If you don't know how to get the information you want, try phoning your competitors' sales reps and asking questions, or hiring a firm to do that for you. The information you gain can help you determine the best strategies for getting your products to the markets you want to reach.

To get a handle on where you stand relative to your competitors' offerings, you'll also want to know about their products, services, media attention, business volume, profitability, and customer base. Having that information will help you see how you stack up by comparison. You can do this by creating a competitive analysis grid that allows you to visually compare competitor strengths and weaknesses relative to your product. Then you can evaluate your findings, determine your best differentiators, and decide on tactics to help you stand out from the competition. Table 3.1 shows a sample competitive matrix created for a doll manufacturer. When designing a similar matrix for your needs, choose categories and features that are relevant to the company, products, and/or services addressed in your marketing plan.

OPPORTUNITIES AND ISSUES ANALYSIS

One way to identify marketing (and other business) opportunities is to use a simple tool called a SWOT Analysis (see Table 3.2) that considers strengths, weaknesses, opportunities, and threats (SWOT) with the power to influence your business and marketing success. Your planning goal is to identify your strengths, weaknesses, opportunities, and threats in the market.

- **Strengths.** Strengths may be special characteristics, features, benefits, differentiators, and/or areas in which your company, products, or services provide a competitive advantage (or equal standing) by comparison to your competitors. Strengths may be product based or process based, such as a new innovation or an unusual plan for how to get your product to market. Strengths also may include features such as ease of purchase or assembly or even the ability to be first to market with desirable colors. Remember how Macintosh influenced customer behavior by offering computers in purple, blue, orange, and green? Before they knew it, they started a trend. Appliance manufacturers began offering everything from toasters to vacuum cleaners in bold, day-glow colors.

- **Weaknesses.** Weaknesses are disadvantages. Among other things, they can range from low budgets to untrained staff, long product-development cycles, or

Table 3.1   Sample Competitive Matrix Used by a Doll Manufacturer to Help Establish Market Positioning

Product Dimension	Company Doll	Competitor 1	Competitor 2	Competitor 3
Price				
Size of doll				
Stitching quality				
Texture quality				
Image reproduction quality				
Use of audio chip				
Quality of audio chip				
Outfits or other products available				
Quality of outfits or other products available				
Anticipated opportunities for expansion				
Identified target markets or niche markets				
Messaging				
Literature availability				
Literature quality				
Web-site design				
Web-site ease of use				
Delivery time				

insufficient access to reliable marketing research. By addressing your weaknesses, you will better be able to assess the risks associated with marketing actions or inactions, and consider plans for strengthening those areas.

- **Opportunities.** Opportunities can be found in unsatisfied client and market needs, assuming you have or can develop the capability and resources to meet them. One way to find your opportunities is to observe trends. Trends will tell

Table 3.2   Sample SWOT Analysis

SWOT ANALYSIS	
Strengths	Weaknesses
Opportunities	Threats

you what consumers and the media are most interested in. For example, Martha Stewart noticed the spike in green product buying, so she launched a line of green cleaning products and used the slogan, "Finally Green Means Clean." Another way to identify opportunities is to read and interpret customer feedback. Watch for customers' requests. Pay attention to what's discussed in social media, at cocktail parties and on television. Watch what larger companies are introducing and talking about in their ads. Perhaps you can introduce a similar product or benefit. By identifying the right channel partners, you may be able to move into a new market. Also, pay attention to what small businesses advertise as their key product features and differentiators. Their ads may point to an opportunity for you.

- **Threats.** Threats can include competitor encroachment, regulatory changes on the horizon, bad publicity, an economic slump, a political lobby, or a trend that negatively impacts your business, such as mounting collection issues. Unless you find a strategic marketing action to combat threats, they may have the power to erode your market positioning or impede your product launch.

The goal of a SWOT Analysis is to identify issues and provide guidance for strategic decision making. To reap as much information as possible, begin with a brainstorming session. If you can, gather a group of individuals to brainstorm with you. Then develop a list of strengths, weaknesses, opportunities, and threats relating to your company and its products and services. Depending on your group and your list, you may find it easier to use separate flipcharts for each element of the SWOT Analysis. You also can use a whiteboard, and have someone transcribe the data for follow-up. Planning in this way will help you bring issues to the surface, identify opportunities, and focus on realities.

GOALS AND OBJECTIVES

A clear goal is important to every marketing plan. So, think about what breakthrough, when reached, will provide the results you need. To justify your time on task, your marketing plan must help you create marketing breakthroughs, go beyond the pale with new products, reach into new markets, and promote innovative ideas or proven concepts in new ways.

A strategic marketing plan may be comprehensive or simple, depending on your needs. You may include either big goals or smaller goals, as needed. No matter how many goals you set, you can maximize your chance of reaching them by following SMART goal-setting guidelines: make your goals **s**pecific, **m**easurable, **a**ctionable, **r**ealistic, and **t**imebound (see Table 3.3).

STRATEGY AND TACTICS

Strategy doesn't need to be complicated; it does need to be clear and detail the steps for reaching your goals. Strategy will either capitalize on opportunities or help you battle

Table 3.3   Sample SMART Goal-Setting Grid

☐	SMART GOAL SETTING		Our Example	Your Goal
	Specific	What will we do? Exactly?	Educate female heads of household, with incomes above $25,000, and residing in Topeka, Kansas, about the rise in dental caries and how our new toothpaste prevents it.	
	Measurable	How many people will we reach? How much product will we sell? (Or use another relevant measure.)	We are targeting 10,000 women with samples of our new toothpaste.	
	Actionable	How will we do it? By what percentage do we expect to increase sales? How will we evaluate our results?	We will use direct mail to provide 10,000 women with samples of our new toothpaste and coupons they can redeem for another tube. We are targeting redemption of 10% of coupons.	
	Relevant and Realistic	How do we know it is needed? Why is it needed? Is our plan realistic? Can it be accomplished with our resources?	Studies of the American Dental Association and new research indicate a rise in prevalence of dental caries. Clinical trials show a 94% success rate in preventing caries in people who brush twice a day with our toothpaste. We have allocated $32,000 to advertise, produce samples, ship, and track results. We also will partner with local dentists and preschools.	
	Timebound	When will we start and/or complete this goal?	We will launch the mailing on December 1, 2010, and measure coupon returns March 1, 2011.	

identified threats. Either way, your main strategy must align with your business purpose and guide goal setting so you will be able to improve business performance by expanding existing market penetration, developing new markets for existing products, or designing new products in response to identified market opportunities, conditions, and trends.

For most businesses, strategy will be tied to your business philosophy and product or service positioning. Once you have determined a market need, your strategy will set the direction for your marketing tactics. For example, how will you get your products into the hands of customers? When considering strategy, think about whether you need a mass marketing approach or a target marketing approach. Will you target customers across a specific industry vertical or go after various markets? Can you maximize your resources by focusing on a particular niche market? Will you differentiate based on price, features, or brand reputation? Once you've answered these questions and others like it, your next step is to detail how you will manage elements of the marketing mix—products, positioning, place, price, people, and promotion—to accomplish your goals.

The following section is a sample of a tactical marketing plan. Notice how it blends various elements of the marketing mix such as planning, product development, and placement with disciplines of marketing promotion, including public relations, advertising, and publications and training.

Public Relations Tactics (Phase 1)

- Identify target consumers, companies, and/or markets.
- Establish a public relations budget to cover personnel, media subscriptions, conference attendance, wire services, and so on.
- Write a script to present the right messages for each target audience.
- Research and identify the media outlets. (Create a list of newspapers, TV and radio stations, Internet sites, and social media in wellness market.)
- Allocate sufficient time to cultivate journalists and gain articles in papers, magazines, blogs, and the like.
- Prepare a media outreach implementation plan. (Decide whether to restrict all media outreach to corporate personnel or allow other employees and affiliates to reach out to media under the brand. If affiliates will be empowered to manage their own media outreach, then develop and provide a media training program for them.)
- Develop and disseminate communication guidelines to ensure professionalism and consistent branding. Include standards for use of logo, trademarks, language, and graphics.
- Develop a *Graphic Standards Manual* with guidelines for printed materials that use the logo image or logotype.
- Conduct media outreach.
- Track media placements.
- Evaluate PR outcomes and budget allocation.

Advertising Tactics (Phase 1)

- Establish advertising goals, and choose appropriate markets.
- Determine the advertising budget, and plan accordingly.

- Assess appropriate media vehicles in target markets (e.g., national, regional, local, trade, and professional associations).
- Gather ad pricing information from media in top target markets and verticals.
- Plan a strategy for viral marketing to help contain ad costs while still getting the word out (e.g., with blogs, Facebook, LinkedIn, Twitter, etc.).
- Prepare copy and creative art for each vertical market.
- Gather ad deadline information, and create an ad placement schedule.
- Submit ads as needed.
- Develop ad templates that branch offices and affiliates can use in their own markets.
- Track ad responses. (Insert a tracking mechanism for each ad, e.g., a separate landing page.)
- Cosponsor a branded minute on one radio station in the top three geographic markets. (Solicit pricing, and add that to budget.)
- Reach out to cable television stations to interest them in running a branded public service tip once a week on TV. (That objective is not easily accomplished, but it's not impossible.)
- Develop appropriate, sticky Web-site content.
- Develop Web content guidelines and/or links as needed by employees and affiliates.
- Track advertising responses, and evaluate results.
- Determine what changes are needed to sustain or enhance success. (Follow the PDCA model.)

Community Relations (Phase 1)

- Define community relations goals for penetrating the wellness (or other) market.
- Establish a community relations budget to cover personnel, media subscriptions, conference attendance, wire services, and so on.
- Gather information about community groups and professional associations in the target markets (e.g., meeting dates, times, speaker bureaus, and keynote needs).
- Identify target consumers, companies, and/or markets we intend to reach.
- Create a speakers bureau in each region and/or niche, then publicize with the goal to get bookings for information sessions and keynote addresses. (Track results.)
- Develop talk tracks and PowerPoint presentations that employees and affiliates may use to conduct community talks in their own markets. (Standardized presentations will promote professionalism and branding.)
- Design specific stock ads for community talks that can be placed as public service announcements (PSAs).

- Develop radio scripts for PSAs announcing free community talks.
- Provide newspaper and online calendar announcement formats for employees and affiliates.
- Develop and distribute guidelines for conducting a successful community talk.

Publications (Phase 1)

- Complete the training manual and/or other needed publications.
- Write a book for a worldwide audience.
- Create smaller books for targeted niches.
- Design templated sell sheets for each vertical that can be downloaded and customized by affiliates.
- Design stock ads that can be downloaded and customized by branch offices and affiliates.
- Create stock articles that can be submitted to community publications. Create a "managers monthly" publication—a simple, easy to write and lay out, two-sided publication and/or e-blast with tips each month. This information will be sent monthly to keep the brand name top of mind with potential client companies. In the first year, develop 12 one-page articles. The back page may include background information about the program or brand, and it will be the same every month. Reformat articles for Web posting.

Social Marketing (Phase 1)

- Set up and maintain separate blogs to focus on separate niches.
- Monitor and update the LinkedIn page. Respond to LinkedIn queries.
- Continue expanding the LinkedIn network.
- Set up a fan page on Facebook.
- Create online joint ventures with colleagues who can refer to the program.
- Offer an affiliate marketing program with a bonus structure.

Operational Tactics

- Develop customer service standards for "corporate" office and associates.
- Create a continuous quality improvement (CQI) team. Meet quarterly or as needed to review program and service quality.
- Tie in with research and development teams as needed.

> ### CAUTION
>
> The feature that sets integrated marketing apart from less comprehensive marketing efforts is operational alignment. Involving members of your operations team during planning stages will help ensure that your marketing dovetails with efforts across the organization. Place operations at the heart of integrated marketing to bring your marketing effort full cycle.

BUDGET AND FINANCIAL PROJECTIONS

Building a budget and projecting revenues is part of success planning. Whether you are allocating money to cover the costs of overhead, staffing, media buys, print collateral, and/or other promotional programs, a simple spreadsheet program is probably all you need. Budgeting will be discussed in more detail in Chapter 19.

EVALUATION AND CONTROL

Every plan really should begin with the end in mind, so start with what you'll need to complete the final element of your marketing plan: evaluation and control. Once you've decided what you intend to accomplish and how you are going to measure it, you'll be able to develop a plan that packs real punch. Like the dashboard on your car, benchmarking tools provide at-a-glance views of success targets. While a car dashboard indicates speed, revolutions per minute, and fuel resource, a management dashboard provides mission-critical performance data and continual updates on strategic goal achievement.

Increasingly, management consultants are helping companies look at their business dashboard and output "scorecards" with ratings in primary results areas (pars) that affect profitability, such as financial goals, business processes, customer service, learning and growth, and energy management. Once key results areas are defined on the dashboard, scorecards are evaluated through a strategic lens to provide insight to critical issues. That insight can help managers track results, plan for adjustment, or monitor to make sure they hold achieved gains. Here are some questions to consider:

- How can we meet current and future goals?
- How can we retool for stronger cost efficiency?
- How can we alter work flow and processes to streamline efficiency?
- Does our human resource strategy meet current and future needs?
- What needs to change so that our company can become more profitable?
- What is the best way to measure and track outcomes?
- How can we create stronger stakeholder/shareholder value?

A Balanced Scorecard (BSC) program helps companies set and monitor performance expectations and results. A BSC demonstrates a comprehensive business approach in which all business components contribute as needed, and enables the company to deliver high value to clients while achieving bottom-line profitability. Through ongoing reviews with assigned accountability, managers can monitor and help improve productivity and efficiency across areas from financial performance and operations to manufacturing, training, and customer relations. By gathering data, managers can track alignment of business actions with goals, and activities across departments or business units, and achieve measurable objectives across the organization.

Primary Result Areas

Decide how you will evaluate your own efforts and choose your primary results indicators. Create a grid with three columns. In the first column, list the top three to six primary result areas that will support the strategic goals you need. In the second column, list the issues that may influence your success. In the third column, state your target goal. In the fourth column, list what steps you will take to address those areas/issues. In the fifth column, list how you will measure results. Also add columns to indicate who is accountable for results and the time period in which progress is to be evaluated. This will set the stage for your strategic marketing plan and also will provide insight for tactical planning. Good luck!

Table 3.4 Primary Results Areas

Primary Results Area (PRA)	Issues/ Influencers	Goal to Reach	Specific Next Steps	Measure(s) of Success	Person(s) or Departments Responsible	Time Period under Evaluation

MILESTONE PROGRESS REPORT

Use the following spreadsheet format to help you plan and track tactical execution of strategic marketing endeavors. Distribute and collaboratively update the spreadsheet with your marketing team or with cross-functional team members, as needed. Use the red flags column to call attention to dependencies or circumstances that can derail success. This will facilitate accountability and ensure that all team members are aware of potential obstacles to success. Awareness will reduce mishaps.

Table 3.5   Milestone Progress Report

Action Item	Person Responsible	Due Date	Project Status	Issues/ Needs	Red Flags	Time Period under Evaluation

Quiz

1. Strategic marketing plans:

    (a) Set a direction for achieving the mission

    (b) Set the stage for long-range planning

    (c) Present a future-focused view of a company

    (d) All of the above

2. Which of the following is more action-oriented?

    (a) Strategic plan

    (b) Tactical plan

    (c) Hybrid plan

    (d) Organizational plan

3. The planning pyramid process consists of:

    (a) Control, strategic planning, process planning, and market analysis

    (b) Market analysis, strategic decision making, process planning, and control

    (c) Strategic planning, market analysis, process planning, and control

    (d) Long and complicated procedures

4. The goal of a SWOT Analysis is to identify issues and provide guidance for strategic decision making.

    (a) True

    (b) False

5. Alignment with goals, environmental assessment, and evaluative planning are predictors of:

    (a) Strategic marketing plan success

    (b) Vision-based planning results

(c) Data-driven planning

(d) None of the above

6. When people at multiple levels of a company are engaged in the planning process:

(a) The likelihood of successful implementation decreases.

(b) The likelihood of successful implementation increases.

(c) The likelihood of conflict increases.

(d) The process takes longer.

7. A strategic marketing plan:

(a) Is scheduled during implementation planning

(b) Maps marketing activities to specific organizational goals

(c) Helps bring stakeholders on board and gains their confidence and support for moving the plan forward

(d) Both (b) and (c)

8. The first rule of planning is:

(a) Don't overplan.

(b) Use it.

(c) Make it as complicated as it needs to be.

(d) Start at the beginning of the calendar year.

9. PDCA is:

(a) An acronym for plan, do, check, and act

(b) A process improvement model

(c) Part of quality management

(d) All of the above

(e) Only (a) and (c)

10. The executive summary:

(a) Is the first section of your strategic plan

(b) Is not part of the plan

(c) Belongs at the end of the plan

(d) None of the above

CHAPTER 4

Applying Marketing Research

Marketing research is the process of gathering and evaluating information that sheds light on market opportunities and provides data for assessing marketing strategy. Research can reveal everything from consumer attitudes and competitive intelligence to the interaction between specific product dimensions, price points, and the best distribution channels. With data in hand, marketers can

- Evaluate marketing scenarios and assumptions
- Monitor performance in market segments and target markets
- Assess competitive threats
- Synthesize information for ongoing business decision making
- Go to market with relevant products and campaigns

Research helps decision makers predict customer response and gauge potential return on investment. Fine-tune your marketing research by asking the right questions and you will make effective use of your marketing time and dollars. Start by thinking about what information, resources, and evidence will increase your chances for success. Then collect information and impressions from people who think and behave like those you would expect to purchase your products (i.e., your target market). Use that data to guide your strategy. And, plan to reassess perceptions along the way. This chapter will show you how to do that.

If the prospect of marketing research scares you, ask yourself: why? My guess is that you have just ventured into unfamiliar terrain. To help you overcome your fear of marketing research, you need to take a few simple steps and locate information you don't have yet. First, you'll need to identify potential resources, then gather information, and develop a plan to meet your needs. By breaking down your research needs into smaller, successive steps, you can then execute your project in stages until you achieve your research objective. How do you learn what you need to know? How do you even know what you don't know? Ask lots of questions. Asking even five other people how they would handle a similar problem will help you shape your answer. As you move forward, step by step, you will gain the knowledge and confidence needed to choose a wise course of action.

Marketing research concentrates on collecting and understanding certain types of data:

- Demographic information about specific consumer groups
- Observations on industry segments and trends
- Factors influencing buying behavior

It can take several forms. *Descriptive research* provides a picture of what is happening in a particular market, such as who is buying what, where they are buying it, and from whom. Primarily a search-and-gather exercise, *exploratory research* is inquiry based and helps researchers and companies learn about and understand issues they know little about by collecting various types of information about a topic or market phenomena. Typically informal in scope, exploratory research questions and answers serve as the foundation for establishing a more structured research design. *Causal research* is a research approach that assesses the impact of one variable or multiple variables on a specific outcome.

Research designs can be qualitative or quantitative. *Qualitative research* is largely anecdotal, helping companies assess consumers' feelings and perceptions through probing questions. While qualitative research typically deals with impressions, *quantitative research* deals with specific numbers. But even qualitative responses can be categorized, tabulated, and quantified.

Once you decide on an overall research approach, you need to consider what kind of measurements will give you the answers you need. Quantitative research is designed to provide specific measurements based on data gathered from single or multiple samples. Quantitative researchers tabulate data, such as recording the results of a telephone survey, counting traffic in a store, comparing the numbers of cars sold on weekends to the numbers sold on weekdays, or comparing the prices of hothouse flowers to the prices of field-grown ones.

Understanding Demography

What, exactly, is a demographic? Think of a demographic as a slice of population pie. That slice gives you a taste of what you can expect throughout the entire pan. Populations can be sliced in many ways. Demographic data may be collected about consumer groups, industries, or business segments to ascertain market growth and contraction rates. In short, a demographic is a snapshot in time.

From the marketing perspective, *demography*—the science of collecting vital and social statistics that provide relevant information about various groups—reveals characteristics that influence the behavior of consumer groups: age, size, gender, population density, geographic distribution, and other vital statistics (e.g. births and deaths). The U.S. Census Bureau and state and local bureaus of vital statistics gather and record specific demographic information.

Demographic research provides a useful framework for revealing buyer preferences. But research doesn't stop with demographics. Researchers must define the questions that will help them interpret data in a meaningful way as well as determine the best ways to obtain information that will guide them. Data specifically gathered for a particular research endeavor is *primary data*, while data that already exists in an accessible database, such as census data, or the multitude of business databases available for purchase is *secondary data*.

It is important to evaluate the quality of data before and after purchasing. Mailing lists and other databases may contain incorrect, outdated, or inconsistent information that must evaluated and/or purged. It helps to consult a data analyst or research analyst for insight into data quality and ways to maintain the integrity of a research sample.

Styles of Marketing Research

There are several ways to collect data to help you evaluate ideas and preconceptions about your positioning, branding, or marketing strategies. Depending on the size of your business investment, you may choose a massive and complex data collection project, followed by complex statistical analysis. Or, you may choose a simple system for gathering feedback about products and services. Marketing research typically takes one of two forms: informal and formal.

Informal Marketing Research

Informal marketing research is the less costly alternative to hiring a marketing research firm to collect and analyze data for you. You can hire a team to conduct informal research for you. Alternatively, you and your team can do some research on your own. Costs to hire a firm vary, depending on the type of research needed. A simple interview tool and phone or Internet survey can be created and evaluated with minimal expense, while complex studies of large or multiple markets may cost hundreds of thousands of dollars. There's no cause for worry, because there is a lot you can manage on your own. For example, one largely untapped and highly cost-effective research strategy is to head to your local library. Many libraries have business centers dedicated to business research, and their

services are free. Similarly, professional trade organizations often offer free marketing research information to their members.

Informal research can be as basic as observing people who are standing near you on supermarket lines or sending a small band of clipboard-toting college students to the mall where they can interview consumers. Another informal research method is to send your products, pictures, brochures, and ideas to 10 friends or business associates and ask them for comments. If you take that approach, structure a standard set of questions so that you can more easily compare responses. Also, make it clear that you are looking for honest feedback. It won't help if people just tell you what you want to hear.

How formal or informal you get with your research will depend on how much money you plan to invest in your products and product marketing. Either way, you'll want to get up to speed on reliable research strategies.

Research Strategies

One pitfall to avoid is trusting that your gut instinct is enough to define your brand and target a market position. If you don't have a professional branding team aboard, or even a marketing coordinator, try creating a focus group. All you need to do is assemble a few friends, a board of advisors, a couple of colleagues, your spouse, investors, customers, and/or prospective customers into a gathering of 8 to 10 people. When you get them together, you can present marketing ideas or campaigns, ask them questions, and listen to their feedback. Since your goal is to create a successful business venture, be sure to encourage them to speak freely and not worry about hurting your feelings. You also can ask someone with an interest in your business to help you brainstorm the answers you need, or you can turn to more formal research methods. Once you have decided on your own product or marketing concept, your next step is to gather the information you'll need to confirm how welcome and successful your products will be once they hit the market.

Information Gathering

Focus groups, telephone surveys, anecdotal information, direct mail reply cards, Web-site surveys, e-mail requests, contests, and even responses to free offers can help you obtain important marketing insight. They can help you learn about buyer preferences, buying culture, and what processes are most likely to influence buyers' behavior.

FOCUS GROUPS

A *focus group* is a small group of individuals assembled for the purpose of providing feedback on a marketing issue or campaign. Focus groups can clarify ideas and provide suggestions that may influence your thoughts on positioning, branding, or marketing strategies. Focus groups can be formal. They may be held in rented conference centers or restaurant meeting rooms, and they may be organized and run by a trained facilitator with the skills to present concepts in an unbiased way and elicit relevant feedback. Or you may turn to a small group of individuals who represent your target market and are willing to provide feedback on your brand concepts directly to you. To avoid influencing the group's feedback and skewing the results you are paying for, you can opt not to attend the focus group session. Some focus group venues offer one-way mirrors, so that you can observe responses and listen to dialogue, or you can arrange to record focus group sessions.

It also is customary to provide participants in focus groups and other marketing research surveys with a small gift, such as a free meal, e-book, or coupon, or with monetary compensation for their time and feedback.

Before finishing the process, you will need to evaluate the results. For that, you may need a statistician to determine whether your results are significant enough to generalize beyond your small sample. You also may want to run multiple focus groups and compare the data.

SURVEYS

Surveys can be conducted in person in offices, stores, and shopping malls, by telephone, e-mail, or Web site. You can add structure to your research by asking each interviewee standardized questions, and including a simple numerical rating system (1-2-3-4) for cataloging and quantifying answers. Notice that the rating system above offers an even number of numbers. Using a scale with even numbers eliminates the middle value and forces respondents to let you know their true leanings (love it more or hate it more). While some statisticians prefer an odd-numbered ranking system with a middle value, I believe you can learn more by pushing respondents to decide one way or the other. A middle value, however, will tell you when something doesn't really matter to a respondent. Today's online tools make survey design, dissemination, and collection easier than ever. You'll find a sample at surveymonkey.com.

ANECDOTAL INFORMATION GATHERING

Not all answers need to be strictly quantifiable to be valuable. Collecting comments, thoughts, and stories about your products and services from your target customers can provide a good sense of how people perceive proposed or existing products, and where they position your products in their minds. Anecdotes can result in excellent testimonials, too. While verbal and/or written comments may be more difficult to quantify than numbers on a rating sheet, you can turn those comments into data by sorting anecdotal responses into categories that help you assess preferences within your

- Market segments (e.g., geographic ranges, industry, or government sectors)
- Target markets (e.g., gender, culture, or military personnel)
- Niche markets (e.g., wellness suppliers, accounting firms, or people with tennis elbow)

THE MISSING LINK

Paying attention is often the missing link in marketing efforts. Business leaders frequently press forward based on their own beliefs rather than rely on feedback from other sources. Listening with a third ear—for what is said and not said in marketing discussions and research sessions—will help you decide whether your business positioning or concept is on the mark. Watch for any gap between expectations and needs. Look for what's missing, as well as the obvious, and you may uncover hidden opportunities.

COMPETITIVE ANALYSIS

Marketing research includes gathering intelligence about your competition. You can get pertinent information about your competitors from salespeople, customers, databases, news media, annual reports, company literature, Web sites, and blogs. A little competitive sleuthing can be revealing, too. Listen to what others are saying in public, in meetings, and while networking. Or, post questions in online chats, and review product ratings on interactive Web sites. Pay attention when you hear business colleagues, friends, or family members mention whether they are delighted or disgusted with a customer experience. You'll then have to assess what the information gleaned really means. Not every bit of data is reliable.

DIRECT RESPONSE RESEARCH

Maybe you called your Web-site host for tech support and later received an e-mail message asking you to take a brief survey about its services. Feedback is critical research data. Direct-mail reply cards, Web-site surveys, e-mail, LinkedIn queries, contests, and even free offers can fill your research pipeline with information about customer demographics, preferences, lifestyles, buying behavior, and more. Just think about what you need to know, put it in the form of a question, and send it out. Then monitor your replies.

CONTESTS

If you are like me, you have you received a call saying, "Congratulations! You've just been chosen to receive a seven-day, six-night vacation to Orlando, Florida, and free tickets to Disney World. All you have to do to claim the prize is sit in on a presentation and answer a few questions by our sales reps." Run a contest if you believe that customers need motivation to respond. Perhaps they don't know you or your product, are part of an overworked market segment, or would welcome some money or a special perk. Once you engage them in conversation or filling out a form, you can ask the questions you need answered.

Formal Marketing Research

To ensure reliable results you may choose a more formal research project. If your firm doesn't have a research department, you can hire a research firm to gather, document, and evaluate information using accurate statistical measures. Formal research can provide you with important insight to your markets and consumer behavior. Studies can reveal information about consumer needs and preferences, competitors and competitive products, perceptions and preferences, responses to positioning strategies, or whatever you and your marketing team decide to study. You can drill down to the types of purchases made in particular hours, days, or months in given locales with access to the right databases, and/or consumer observations.

Professional marketing researchers are skilled at assembling focus groups, formulating surveys and/or feedback sessions, conducting telephone interviews, and other forms of information gathering. Their services can be expensive, starting as low as $2,500 and running into millions of dollars, depending on the scope and longevity, and location of your projects. Nevertheless, even simple marketing research conducted quickly and reliably can provide you with information you need to make sound business decisions and marketing budget allocations. That is, it will if you pay attention.

SWOT Analysis

To learn about their market potential, many companies use the simple tool called a SWOT Analysis to assess company strengths and weaknesses and identify opportunities and threats in the market. SWOTs are typically conducted in brainstorming sessions. Results are used to identify issues of importance to the strategic marketing process. See Chapter 3 for a sample of a SWOT Analysis, which was described in the context of the planning process.

Market Segmentation

Location, location, location. Finding your best market fit is a lot like choosing a neighborhood. Maybe you ask a friend; maybe you search real estate listings on the Internet; or perhaps you just get in your car and drive to a neighborhood that looks good. When you arrive, you probably want to meet people who know the area and ask them a few questions. If, while driving around that neighborhood, you spot a house that looks good from the outside, what would you do? Write a check to the Realtor whose name is on the for-sale sign outside? Probably not. Before buying, you would ask the Realtor to set up a tour of the house. You would ask for information on comparable sales and look for evidence that you will enjoy the quality of life you desire in that home. It's the same with marketing. To find the best location for your products and services, you need to ask questions with the power to reveal where your products and services will get the most action and the best business outcomes.

Market segments are selected based on common demographics. Choose the market segment with the desire and money to buy what you sell. For that, you need to get at the perceptions, patterns, and capabilities of the people in your demographic segment.

Your goal is to evaluate whether potential sales volume in a particular market is worth the price of entry.

Segmenting, or separating, potential markets into groups helps businesses identify and target buyers cost-effectively. To learn which segments will work best for you, consider which factors are most likely to affect purchasing. You may study market segments based on per capita income, geography, zip code, age, gender, religion, and/or ethnic group. Or, you may look at their lifestyles and buying behaviors. Gather information about how similar target markets have responded to similar brand and product offers by your own company or your competitors. Then you can further group those markets according to more specific buying habits—if you collect the right data.

Every company makes strategic decisions about how they will reach customers and which of those customers to pursue. By segmenting your audience into the most likely buyers and/or buyers you wish to cultivate, you can direct your resources effectively. New technologies have made it possible to target segments as small as individuals. Variable data printing, for example, makes it possible to personalize outreach to a customer of one. By contrast, globalization, Internet marketing capability, and fulfillment technologies make it possible to reach a massive audience. We now can take orders, track inventory 24 hours a day, seven days a week, and ship worldwide. We can even service customers immediately with online payment for downloadable products. With all those choices, it becomes really important for marketers to adopt the right segmentation strategy, and align operations and resources appropriately.

Impact of the New Economy

Understanding how the current economy impacts buying behavior is very important. Categorizing buyers based on the kind of purchasing they do now will help you decide which channels to invest in and where to promote products most heavily. According to Harvard researchers, the challenging economy has added a new psychological dynamic to the buying process. Buyers' emotions have changed, and marketers must adapt their behavior, in turn.

Buying Patterns Predict Next Purchases

Amazon.com segments buyers based on their online search and buying patterns. If you log on to Amazon and search for a certain book, the site returns a page with information on more than just the book you entered in the search field. Based on Amazon's knowledge of buying habits of other customers who had previously searched for the same book you did, Amazon exploits that data to sell more products. In essence, Amazon segments what would otherwise be a massive buyer audience into specific pockets based on actual buying behavior. They then target specific customers, based on similar search behavior.

Zooming in on Target Audiences

After marketers segment their audiences, they zoom in with a tighter scope to determine the most relevant and motivated buyers within those market segments, and then focus their marketing campaigns accordingly. For instance, if you are marketing the services of a personal shopper, you might be interested in learning more about women buyers within the geographic reach of your personal shopper(s) who have young children at home and can't get out to shop, or who work all day and have no time. You also might look for information on corporate-based males, who really don't like to shop. To learn about those groups, you need to gather data on people of the right sex, with the necessary disposable income, living in nearby zip codes, and matching the age range that your personal shoppers excel at serving. You also should find out who, if anyone, is already buying services from a personal shopper—and how that personal shopping service is doing.

As you gain information about your competition, you can use it to decide how to differentiate yourself in the minds of potential customers. If the competition offers nine-to-five weekday service, you might advertise weekend and evening services, positioning yourself as the most convenient choice. Or, you might consider a different positioning entirely and brand yourself as the working woman's shopper, the statesman's shopper, the elegant shopper, or the fun shopper. Now, you are getting into market positioning, which can plant you inside the minds where you can grow a particular presence.

Suppose you are marketing a day-care center. You might target single-parent households or households with two working parents; households with incomes of $20,000 or more, or with incomes that meet qualifications for child care vouchers; families with children living at home; or households within a certain zip code. You may also compile a list of school districts without prekindergarten programs. Whatever business you market, it makes sense to create a profile of your target customers; then place and promote your products where those customers reside or where they can access you.

Assessing Market Potential

When you invest time, talent, and treasure, you want to be sure that consumers will welcome and purchase your products and services. Rather than guessing, savvy marketers test their research premise. Much like the hypothesis testing learned in high school science, marketing researchers conduct experiments of their own.

They establish a hypothesis (e.g., that a target market will generate 500,000 product sales in one year). Then they test the hypothesis by studying market activity and launching a test run. They might test different products in different markets and compare sales data. They might track sales of the same product by color, zip code, store outlet, or chain. At the end of their test run, they would compare data and decide which product attributes resulted in highest sales, which markets generated the most sales, and which outlets generated the best return on investment.

Researchers can test the hypothesis that a specific group of consumers will find a particular product attractive for a specific reason, such as access, affordability, quality, texture, or convenience. They can test overall product utility with attitude surveys and purchasing data. Results would clarify assumptions on whether products are good to have or essential to consumers. As researchers vary and test product dimensions, marketing assumptions, and strategies, they will learn more about customers' perceptions. They also will identify which variables are most important to individuals in a specific market. As marketers use their learning to refine their approach, they can increase the accuracy of their market predictions.

Identifying Opportunities through Market Segmentation

As with any relationship, understanding comes with information. The more you know about people, the better able you are to predict their behavior. With marketing, prediction is the name of the game. *Market segmentation*—the process of dividing groups of consumers into predictable groups—will help you decide whether specific types of consumers are likely to purchase your products and services.

Once you know the number of consumers meeting your criteria, then you need to dig into your business plan and determine how much revenue you need to support service delivery (and marketing!) to consumers you intend to target within those segments. This is where your marketing must align with your operating and sales plans.

Marketing trainers often tell the story about Henry Ford: he offered customers any color Model T as long as it was black. In Ford's eyes, customers simply wanted transportation, and a basic black car met that bill. That philosophy worked because there weren't many options or competitors in those days. In today's highly evolved market, consumers are more demanding. Companies must work harder to differentiate themselves and merit customer loyalty.

Increasingly marketers are turning from mass marketing a one-trick pony to a tighter focus on targeted markets with niche-oriented products. While mass marketers go for the cost efficiencies associated with minimal customization and one-size-fits-all campaigns, others contend that well-researched target markets are more predictable and profitable because they enable marketers to concentrate budgets and messages for greater efficiency and build stronger rapport with customers.

Determining Your Market Fit

While market segmentation begins with understanding the behavior of your target customers, your market positioning strategy is your chance to impress your own products' personality into the minds of your target customers and begin the process of cultivating their desire to buy. Positioning helps guide consumers. It also helps set expectations in the minds of consumers and allows them to see where you fit in their lives, according to their own inner framework for cataloging information. Positioning is a mind game in which the goal is to control perception. Perceived value changes, however, based on a consumer's changing needs. To position correctly, you need to understand your customers' views and their perceptions of your competitors.

Demographics may be sorted by political affiliation, interests and hobbies, income (family or individual), type of work (blue collar/white collar), and a variety of other dimensions (see Table 4.1). After you learn about your customer, you'll need to make decisions: Which factors are flexible? Which do you have the power to influence? What will you need to do to alter your prospects' buying preferences? How much money can you allocate to accomplish that? Review the table below and complete for yourself with descriptions of your own targeted market segments.

Table 4.1   Sample Market Segmentation Worksheet

DEMOGRAPHIC SEGMENT	BEHAVIORAL INDICATORS	PSYCHOGRAPHIC INDICATORS	YOUR SAMPLE
Gender	*Example:* May access information through the Internet, social networks, chat rooms, newspapers, and magazines	*Example:* May be sports minded, fashion conscious, or highly spiritual	M/F Describe the behavior and lifestyle preferences, activities, interests, and values of your market segment. What time of month or year are they most likely to purchase your product?
Age range	*Example:* May be early adopters of new technology or may be cautious buyers	*Example:* May be financially comfortable and looking for new experiences, or worried about the future and more likely to repair products they already own.	Describe the age range of your target sample and how that group behaves, what values or lifestyle circumstances influence that behavior relative to your product or service offering. What benefits are they seeking?

(continued)

Table 4.1 Sample Market Segmentation Worksheet (*Continued*)

DEMOGRAPHIC SEGMENT	BEHAVIORAL INDICATORS	PSYCHOGRAPHIC INDICATORS	YOUR SAMPLE
Type of household or business segment (if you are marketing business to business)	*Example:* May be families, with two parents in residence caring for minor children or may be single–parent households; may be companies with more than 100 employees.	*Example:* May require childcare, and/or financial planning services for college-bound children; may have cultural beliefs about use of daycare services, and/or trust issues relating to advisors; may be young or mature company dealing with issues along business growth continuum.	Describe household and/or business behavior and major concerns that influence that behavior relative to your product or service offering. When do consumers need your products or services? For how long will they use them? At what rates do they consume products? Which brands do they buy now?
Geographic locale	*Example:* Consumers and/or businesses that purchase through retail stores, malls, discount chains, or the Internet.	*Example:* Consumers prefer to shop within walking distance, shop within 10 miles, or use mass transit; consumers may prefer regional foods or a more cosmopolitan menu.	Create a profile of the consumer groups you intend to reach in the geographic local you are targeting. How do holidays and special occasions influence buyers in these segments?

Using Marketing Research to Postpone or Validate Market Entry

The purpose of marketing research is to substantiate business and marketing decisions. For example, one family I know was looking to start a landscaping business in a warm climate. They asked questions of a number of landscapers, consulted with business development experts, and relied on a family member's corporate background for guidance. Following the well-known marketing principle that it is less expensive to satisfy existing customers than to find new ones, this business group found a way to capitalize. Rather than postpone market entry until the economy picks up, they chose a geographic market segment where there is a high demand for landscape services—Florida. They learned through marketing research that there are more than 13,000 competitors in a targeted area of Florida. Grass grows and properties need landscape services all year. They also used the data they collected to assess landscape rates in commercial and residential markets.

Through ongoing research, they located landscapers willing to sell their books of business, and immediately acquired a direct business channel. Rather than spend money on scattershot mailings, coupons, and advertisements to grow a landscape enterprise painstakingly over time, the family bought functioning businesses, kit and caboodle. Using acquisition as a marketing strategy, rather than attempting slower organic growth, they entered a profitable, mature market immediately, with *bona fide* accounts in hand. They also maintained staff from the companies they had purchased. The takeover was transparent, and market presence was captured without a hitch.

Research Resources

Research resources take many forms. You can find research-related news feeds and podcasts via an online search. Or you can subscribe to databases offered by well-respected research firms, such as Forrester Research, Hoovers, U.S. Census Bureau, Dun & Bradstreet, and Gartner Group. Also, McKendrick & Associates is a smaller research team, based in Pennsylvania, that concentrates on research in the technology sector.

Evaluating Research Information

Whether evaluating focus group outcomes or major research initiatives, you'll want to know what your data means and how reliable it is. You also may need more sophisticated statistical analytics to make sense of data collected and help you decide how to use it (i.e., inferential analysis). Consult a seasoned research specialist for advice or learn about statistical software programs that can help you evaluate data samples and determine statistically significant variations.

Quiz

1. Marketing research is used to:

   (a) Evaluate marketing scenarios and assumptions

   (b) Monitor marketing performance in market segments and target markets

   (c) Assess competitive threats

   (d) Synthesize information for ongoing business decision making

   (e) All of the above

   (f) Choices (b) and (c) only

2. _____ research provides a picture of what is happening in a particular market.

(a) Causal

(b) Qualitative

(c) Exploratory

(d) Descriptive

(e) Primary

3. Qualitative research is not measurable.

(a) True

(b) False

4. Primary research is:

(a) The first step in every research initiative

(b) Data in an official database, such as the U.S. Census Bureau or a bureau of vital statistics

(c) Mostly qualitative

(d) Data collected for the study at hand

5. Causal research differs from descriptive and exploratory research in that it:

(a) Requires more information

(b) Provides information on the interaction of variables

(c) Is easily explained

(d) Integrates price and shopping information

(e) Is less formal

6. For research to be meaningful, researchers must define _____ that will provide insight to marketing issues that are not clearly understood.

(a) Focus groups

(b) Demographics

(c) Variables

(d) Perceptions

(e) Questions

7. Segmenting, or separating, a potential market into groups helps businesses _____ and _____ target buyers.

(a) Budget/promote to

(b) Identify/cost-effectively

(c) Scope/research

(d) Understand/analyze

8. To encourage survey responses:

   (a) Keep questions short

   (b) Ask only college graduates

   (c) Offer a contest, payment, or gift

   (e) Learn about your market in advance

   (f) Use an Internet survey tool

9. Two common research approaches are:

   (a) Formal/informal

   (b) Complex/statistical

   (c) Active/latent

   (d) Primary/secondary

   (e) Cause/effect

10. Target marketing helps companies:

   (a) Build rapport with customers

   (b) Concentrate budgets

   (c) Control market variables

   (d) None of the above

   (e) Choices (a), (b), and (c)

CHAPTER 5

Positioning Brands, Products, and Services

You've decided there is a market for your products. You've researched that market and chosen the segments you intend to target. Before finalizing your marketing plan, you'll need to decide how to position your brand, products, or services. Positioning is a strategic component of the marketing mix that helps you determine

- Where you stand in the minds of consumers
- Where you stand when compared to your competitors
- How you will differentiate your company and/or products in the marketplace

Positions are closely tied to reputation. When a company goes after a particular brand reputation, its positioning efforts would follow suit. But there is a distinction to be made between the brand itself and the brand position. A brand is a reputation, assumedly built on facts; it likes to stand on its own, without comparison. A position is always relative. It is absorbed in the minds of consumers, based on comparative marketing and brand or product differentiation.

In line with business objectives, companies attempt to capture a position based on brand or product dimensions, including but not limited to

- Service reliability
- Innovation
- Leadership
- Cost sensitivity
- Quality
- Social responsibility
- The biggest and the best

Once a desired position is identified, companies market accordingly. The process of positioning begins with a strategic choice influenced by a company's business objectives. When positioning, you need to consider your brand and product potential and how you will tease out the response you need from the people who make up your market. As you make headway, you must follow through with continual analysis of market factors, consumer perceptions, and competitor actions.

Establishing Market Position

When positioning, a good first step is to decide what you want consumers in specific markets to see, hear, feel, think, and believe about your brands, products, or services relative to those of your competitors. This chapter provides insight to market positioning and positioning strategies.

When you *develop* a brand, you create an image for your company, products, and/or services. Then you act in ways that reinforce that image. When you *position* a brand, you decide how to influence consumers' beliefs about your brand, products, and/or services by comparison to others. To capture a specific slot, you need an action plan that will shape perception, build demand, capture the market position you desire, and build name recognition in your intended bracket.

Think of positioning as marketing psychology. Marketers Al Ries and Jack Trout, defined *market positioning* as "the space products or services occupy in the minds of customers."[1] This dynamic element of the marketing mix lays the foundation for the emotional appeal behind every sale. It also is a highly volatile component of the marketing mix, since it is continually targeted by competitor action.

When you choose a position that resonates well with your targeted market, everyone will think you are a marketing genius. Reinforce that position—with sound business

---

[1] Al Ries and Jack Trout, *Positioning: The Battle for Your Mind* (New York: Warner Books, 1982).

strategy, effective branding, creative promotion, the right market placements, competitive strength, and relevant pricing—and you will position for profitability.

Strategies for Market Positioning

The goal of every positioning process is to capture top-of-mind status in the mind space you choose. How you position depends on five things:

1. Your overall business goals and corporate strategies

2. What you want to be known for

3. Whom you intend to influence

4. Whom and what you are positioning against

5. Your resources for snagging the slot you want

Successful politicians are masters of positioning. Campaign managers conduct polls to learn which issues are most important to voters and how those issues interact to influence a voter's feeling about a candidate. Based on research, candidates and their campaign managers develop positions they believe will engage the good will of the electorate and garner the most votes. Marketers work the same way when attempting to capture brand or product positions.

THE FIVE-STEP POSITIONING PROCESS

1. **Choose your market and study your competition.** Consider industry size and scope, geographic reach, accessibility, market maturity, and market opportunities and competition. Learn what motivates buyers and influences brand, product, and service preferences. Assess the hold that competitors have on the market as well as their strengths and weaknesses.

2. **Choose your positioning strategy.** As a marketer, you can position your brand and products against competitors' along a number of dimensions: price, place, product, promotion, people (i.e., service), and quality. You can position based on features, benefits, and purpose (i.e., use). You can position directly against another brand name (e.g., Avis says, "We try harder" when positioning against Hertz and other rental agencies). You can make a direct product comparison (e.g., Burger King says they've got more beef in their Whoppers than competitors have in

their burgers). The important thing to remember is that successful marketers communicate value on dimensions proven to be important to their target customers (see Table. 5.1).

3. **Communicate your position.** Give your market position a mouthpiece through marketing communication. Use words that communicate your value in the space you choose. Reinforce your position using the power of sensory integration, whenever possible.

Table 5.1 Value Selling Matrix Illustrating Sample Issues, Solutions, and Impacts that Underscore Brand Positioning

Sample Issue	Sample Solution	Impact/Value	Possible Positioning
Getting the best price on items when you have little time to shop.	One-stop shopping *Example:* Wal-Mart Costco Sam's Club	V = Price savings Customers go to one location and get everything they need: food, electronics, clothing, business and household supplies, etc.	The brand you can rely on for economy pricing
There is too much emerging technology to stay current with changing information.	Consolidate access. Make information available in a portable format. *Example:* Apple iPhone, with many downloadable applications, including a new application that lets you program applications	V = Time savings, portability, and problem solving A diverse consumer base can quickly find solutions to myriad problems through cell-phone-based Internet access. The customer can use one device to check e-mail, make phone calls, schedule appointments, find locations, surf the Web, or access thousands of applications.	The brand that brings you innovative, life-changing technology
The need for increased access to banking personnel and branch services, given that consumers often cannot get to a bank during their regular business hours.	Extend branch hours. *Example:* TD Bank	Value is convenience. Branches are open seven days per week with extended hours, so customers can interact with live people as well as call the 800 line.	The brand that means convenient, neighborhood banking
What issue(s) concern(s) your targeted customers?	What is your solution?	What value do you add to the market?	How do you want to be viewed in consumers' minds?

4. **Evaluate your positioning effort.** Marketing is an ongoing process and needs monitoring. Gather data that will help validate that your positioning is on track, or identify variables that will guide you to the right strategic advantage. Collect information about customer perception of value-based product features, price, accessibility, quality of experience, and/or other relevant dimensions. Measure results. Determine mind share relative to your competitors. Analyze where you stack up. Decide where you want to be.

5. **Review and respond as needed.** Are you at the top, middle, or bottom of your positioning bracket? You need to create competitive advantage and then hold the gains. Remember that positioning is a process. The FOCUS approach to quality management will help you monitor that process. Quality managers, influenced by the work of Dr. W. Edwards Deming, implement the FOCUS approach.

The FOCUS Approach to Quality Management

- **F**ind a process to improve.
- **O**rganize a positioning process improvement team, as needed.
- **C**ollect data.
- **U**nderstand the variables influencing perception.
- **S**tart the adjustment process.

If you've determined that an adjustment in your positioning strategy is needed, then shift into the PDCA gear, as described in Chapter 3.

Positioning to Your Best Advantage

Positioning begins with choosing the best fit for your products. That means doing marketing research. Marketing research tools, such as surveys and focus groups, can help you decide which issues carry the most weight. The information you gain will help you choose and promote the right position, based on analysis of your own strengths as well as those of your competitors and your resources.

For example, look at basketball. Imagine you are a college basketball coach. You've recruited your players and set your sights on the division championship. You believe you have a good team, but your team needs to prove its capability in real-life competition. As a coach, you need to learn everything you can find out about every opposing team in your division. So, you scout out the field, watching play-by-play videos of your competition in action. You also watch play-by-play videos of your own players to evaluate internal strengths and weaknesses. Then you structure a game plan to give your players the best competitive advantage.

As a marketer, you need to gather competitive intelligence—meaningful information about your competition. You can start by researching and identifying the features and benefits of competitive products. Like the basketball coach, you'll start by assessing their strengths and weaknesses relative to those of your team. That will help you decide what you may need to do differently.

When it comes to positioning, the goal is to stake your claim. To stay top of mind, you must master market positioning. Uncover which aspects of your product influence perception of value in the minds of targeted customers on which dimensions. Then, turn that knowledge into a unique value proposition.

CREATING YOUR VALUE PROPOSITION

In the sales world, folks know a few things. First, people buy from people and companies they like and trust. Second, they buy based on the perceived benefit that a brand, product, or service will deliver. Your value proposition should explain, in just a few words, why a prospective buyer should choose you over your competitors. You must communicate what the buyer can expect when doing business with you. As you uncover what consumers consider valuable, you will find clues to a meaningful position. Here are some questions to ask yourself:

- What makes us different from our competitors?
- What unmet needs can we fill?
- How can we gain the best competitive advantage?
- What else can we do to increase perceived value of our brand, products, and services?
- Is there room for innovation, and will innovation make a difference to our prospective customers?
- How important will changes in our products, brand, and services be to our customers?
- How can we quantify that?
- What can we do to prove our value and/or justify our price?

When you identify the most valuable aspects of your brand, you will develop a pathway to increase both mind share (i.e., positioning) and market share (i.e., sales).

COMPETITIVE POSITIONING STRATEGIES

If you are positioning on the dimension of volume (e.g., the biggest and the best), you might want to be the number one hot dog seller in the world. Alternately, you might claim the position of top-selling hot dog provider in a significant market (e.g., all hot dog stands in North America); the largest seller in a smaller market segment (e.g., all hot dog manufacturers selling in the Northeast); the top seller in a smaller target market (e.g., in the five boroughs of New York City). Perhaps you are more interested in being the best provider in a particular market niche (e.g., those selling organic or kosher hot dogs). Whatever your market, your task is to decide what position will give you the best competitive advantage, and then work to stay top of mind.

If you are marketing a small retail shop, you probably want to be known as the best place for customers to get the specific products they want. In that case, you might position based on your specialty items or your breadth of stock. You can make your sales case by offering classy stock or reliable volume. You might communicate value based on pricing or service, convenient hours of operation, or the most accessible location, depending on which dimensions are most important to your customers.

Marketing research can help you determine which brand, product, and service attributes are most valuable to prospective customers. Use that information to strengthen your plan, communications, and actions to fill that mind space.

CALCULATING YOUR MARKET POSITION

Positioning strategies measure awareness as well as perceived value. Use the positioning grid shown in Table 5.2 as a guide to measuring consumers' awareness of your brand, products, and/or services. Use it also to calculate the perceived value you have developed in the minds of consumers as compared to your competitors. Correlating consumers' views about your brand in relation to those of your competitors will help you calculate best-fit market positioning.

In Table 5.3, three staffing companies compete for market share on dimensions of name recognition and brand value, as measured by customer perception of candidate quality, turnaround time, and cost of temporary staffing. The grid shows dimensions measured by companies A, B, and C, rated on a scale of 1 to 4, with 4 being the highest mark.

Communicating Value

Positioning is designed to stimulate the senses and tease out inner responses that make people want to buy. For example, thoughts of sports cars can elicit fantasies of freedom, speed, control, and attraction. When a car is positioned as a luxury through glossy ads in

Table 5.2   Positioning Grid with Brand Attributes

Brand Attributes Influencing Positioning Premise	Nearest Competitor's Estimated Mind Share	Top Competitor's Estimated Mind Share	Your Brand's Estimated Mind Share	Percent Change Targeted
Prestige				
Service reliability				
Product quality				
Ease of use				
Convenience				
Safest				
Best price				
Socially responsible				

upscale magazines, fancy accessories, placements on movie sets, and expensive ad campaigns, they command a high-end price tag. Yet, a car also can be positioned as a cost-effective alternative to other forms of travel, or as an environmental change agent. It can be packaged to appeal to the practical buyer's cost-saving instincts and marketed to buyers who are less status conscious. The direction chosen during R&D will depend on the company's overall business strategy, the markets it intends to serve, and the costs of production and marketing.

High-end positioning can command a higher product price, but it also will mean more costly media buys in venues that target wealthier consumers and markets. Low-tier positioning may seem less appealing, but it can open access to a much broader consumer base, enabling you to increase volume-driven profit.

Table 5.3   Positioning Grid

Dimension	Company A	Company B	Company C	Positioning
Candidate skill	4	4	3	Quality
Response time	2	3	3	Service
Low cost	2	1	4	Economy

UNDERSTANDING THE CUSTOMER MINDSET

Product and brand position is tightly linked to sensory and emotional connections, as discussed in the introduction. Remember to use sensory-specific words—such as *see*, *hear*, and *feel*—in your marketing communication and positioning efforts. In the 1970s researchers Richard Bandler and John Grinder conducted pioneering studies that shed light on how people process information. Their work evolved into a science called "Neuro-Linguistic Programming" (NLP). NLP studies demonstrate that that every bit of information we absorb through our five senses—sight, sound, touch, smell, and taste—is processed first through a layer of internal filters in the form of sensory data, then through long-held beliefs. We then process that information into thoughts, feelings, and perceptions as codes, or patterns, that influence our behavior. In turn, our behavior and experience generates additional feedback that goes back into our mind-body system. (See Figure 5.1.)

Now, you've got a new tool in your marketing arsenal. Knowledge of sensory data helps marketers connect more quickly, and on multiple levels, with consumers. It makes marketers more credible communicators and can speed up marketing results.

To employ NLP strategies, use sensory words, as explained in Chapter 2. Also search for cues about how people perceive messages. (You can do this through focus groups.) Once you've picked up on the cues, you'll be better able to influence people's perceptions.

STOP AND THINK

NLP strategies carry the power to shift beliefs, perceptions, emotions, and behavior. Putting yourself into the mind frame of a potential consumer can help you establish a psychological advantage. Imagine that someone is standing by and listening to people talk about your products or services. What might that person be wondering or believing

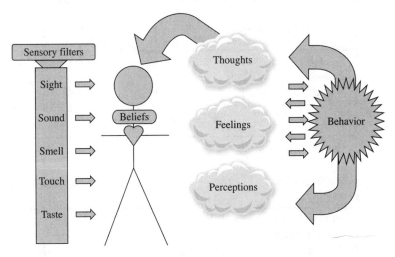

Figure 5.1   Integrated sensory, beliefs, perception model.

while listening? What words, thoughts, and feelings would they experience? What would that information tell you? What can you do to influence the beliefs of the potential customers who come across your products in advertising, online, or in stores? Pay special attention to beliefs that potential customers might hold about your product or service and where they believe it might fit into their life. Address those beliefs as you work to claim your chosen position.

VALUES AND BENEFITS

Explain the value of your products and services in benefits and impact that consumers understand. Trout and Reis designated three types of benefits—functional, experiential, and symbolic—that can be communicated through positioning strategies (see Table 5.4).

POSITIONING AND MARKETING

Positioning is not only about what goes on in someone else's head. It reflects the thoughts and beliefs of organizational leaders. Positioning strategies must relate to overall marketing strategy as well. Depending on company objectives you can

- Position for broad appeal instead of boutique appeal
  (A mass marketing strategy)
- Position as a luxury provider (or product) for wealthy consumers
  (A target marketing strategy)

Table 5.4   Benefit/Value Matrix

Type of Benefit	Sample Value Indicators for Customer	Your Product Benefits	Ultimate Impact (Value)
Functional	What will this product or service do for me? How will it fit in my life? What need will it fill? What benefit will I achieve?		
Experiential	How will I feel when I use it? Will it excite me? Will it relax me? Will I have fun?		
Symbolic	Will I feel better about my life if I use it? (lifestyle priorities) Will I feel better about me if I use it? Will I fit in better with a social group?		

- Position as a luxury product for wealthy women consumers who play golf
  (A niche marketing strategy)
- Create a position that is likely to generate high-level return on investment
  (A sane marketing strategy)

Repositioning an Ailing Brand

Brands ail for all sorts of reasons. Companies that limit business to a particular geographic locale encounter new competitors through online networking and globalization. Newer, more desirable products enter the market. Competitors' public relations strategies trump yours. Consumers respond to economic factors. Tastes change. Crises emerge. Priorities shift. Expectations vary.

When companies notice that their brands, products, or services have taken a hit in the market, they have several options. They can adjust sales strategies, reallocate resources, and/or consider a brand repositioning. Before embarking on new strategies, they must get to the reason for change, by conducting research that helps uncover and understand the sources of variation.

With every brand repositioning, you must explore and assess the market and identify as many repositioning options as possible. Then gather data that gives a clear picture of positioning options before jumping to conclusions or attempting to shift customer perceptions in a particular direction. After analyzing all options, chart the course that maximizes your relationship in targeted market segment(s). Identify the resources you will need to support your repositioning endeavor. If you are unsure about costs, options, markets, or strategies, interview and consider hiring a brand consultant specializing in your market. If you don't know a consultant, inquire through your business networks or do an Internet search. (Also see Chapter 16, Executing Special Projects.)

Depositioning a Brand

A final option in the positioning world is an out-and-out attack on your competitor's position. While most brand experts do not recommend attacking competitors, depositioning is the strategy used in the television ad campaigns between Apple's Macintosh operating system and the PCs using Microsoft systems. Each has attacked the other's position as a user-friendly product. Similarly, Verizon and AT&T have butted heads in a contest attacking position based on signal reach. To deposition another brand, you will need to understand the value drivers in customer minds and have access to resources capable of supporting and sustaining a head-to-head campaign.

Quiz

1. Positioning is a strategic component of the marketing mix that helps you determine:

   (a) How you will differentiate your company and/or products in the marketplace

   (b) Where you stand when compared to your competitors

   (c) Where you stand in the minds of consumers

   (d) All of the above

   (e) None of the above

2. A position is always relative.

   (a) True

   (b) False

3. A good first step in positioning is to:

   (a) Assign an intern to conduct market analysis

   (b) Decide what you want consumers in specific markets to see, hear, feel, think, and believe

   (c) Create an action plan

   (d) Evaluate competitors

4. The goal of every positioning process is to:

   (a) Provide market analysis

   (b) Segment the audience

   (c) Find the right niche

   (d) Capture top-of-mind status in the mind space

5. Marketers work the same way as _____ when attempting to capture market positions.

   (a) Politicians

   (b) Researchers

   (c) Pricing experts

   (d) None of the above

6. The FOCUS Approach is designed for:

    (a) Statistical analysis

    (b) Quality management

    (c) Positioning strategy

    (d) None of the above

7. A value proposition refers to:

    (a) Your company's pricing strategy

    (b) Employee benefits programs

    (c) Why a prospective buyer should choose you over your competition

    (d) All of the above

8. _____ can help you determine which brand, product, and service attributes are most valuable to prospective customers.

    (a) Competitor analysis

    (b) Market analysis

    (c) Marketing research

    (d) Online marketing strategies

9. Studies in Neuro-Linguistic Programming demonstrate that information absorbed through the five senses is processed first through internal filters and influence:

    (a) Positioning

    (b) Beliefs

    (c) Perceptions

    (d) Results

    (e) Only (b) and (c)

10. Three types of benefits described by Al Ries and Jack Trout are:

    (a) Functional, psychographic, and experiential

    (b) Profit, time, and productivity

    (c) Functional, experiential, and symbolic

    (d) None of the above

CHAPTER 6

Placement Strategies

Placement is the process of choosing the right distribution system for delivering products and services to target markets. A critical element of the marketing mix, placement decisions impact brand presence and market share alike. How you get your product to market can influence your positioning and make or break your budget. Depending on your resources and your demographic mix, the right placement strategy may include single or multiple channels.

Channel Marketing

Channel marketing—employing other business entities as part of a sales, delivery, or service effort—increases your ability to reach and influence targeted markets. Think of a channel as a pathway to customers. When planning your placement strategy, choose channel partners based on their connections with those customers whom you cannot reach or influence yourself.

TYPES OF MARKETING CHANNELS

Channel partners are a necessity for penetrating markets that are difficult to enter, due to geographic spread, physical and/or financial resources, human resources, or time constraints. Channel partners reduce overhead burdens while facilitating sales. Think of them as your outsourced distribution team for sales, delivery, and service needs.

Wholesalers

Wholesalers are often the first point of entry for products on their way to market. They purchase and resell goods as they are, rather than transforming them into other products. Wholesalers typically deal in high-volume orders and mark up the products before selling them to retail operations.

Retailers

Retailers purchase products, mark up pricing to cover their costs, and then distribute those products directly to consumers.

Brokers and Merchants

Brokers bridge relationships between buyers and sellers. Print brokers, for example, use specialized print industry knowledge to build relationships with a variety of print manufacturers (i.e., their vendors) and sell those vendor services directly to other businesses (i.e., their customers), in exchange for a commission. Brokers do not themselves purchase the inventory, as is the case with a wholesaler. Instead, they serve as middlemen. Merchants, by comparison, buy goods and resell them to other wholesale or retail buyers.

Joint Venture Partners

Joint venture (JV) partners are strategic collaborators who expose your products and services to their own customers. As opposed to wholesale and resale agreements based on pay-for-purchase arrangements, joint venture partners are typically paid a share of the sale, with profit sharing relative to the strength of their contribution.

Joint venture partnerships have become highly popular among Web marketers, especially sales trainers, coaches, and wellness experts. Later in this chapter, I will give you more information on building a joint-venture partnership.

Strategic Allies

Channel partners who are strategic allies may provide additional resources, such as a sales team, related products, distribution network, and financing. Think of GE Money Bank, which provides financing for contractors making in-home sales. Strategic alliances work best when there is a synergy between ally needs and clear terms outlining expectations, responsibilities, terms, and risks.

Affiliate Marketers

Affiliate marketers are usually e-retailers who help expose products and services, via their Web sites, in exchange for a reward, such as cash or gifts, when a sale is made. Tracking software and buying codes let companies know which affiliate referred which customer for which purchase. Affiliate marketers help drive traffic from one site to another, using special offers and product links.

Fulfillment Houses

After products have been ordered, fulfillment houses play an important role in executing delivery. This combination warehouse, order management, storage, and/or pick-and-packing service is often the last stop in the product-to-consumer continuum. Fulfillment houses may offer everything you need from literature and direct-to-individual print options on such things as branded premiums and promotional items, sales literature, and hard merchandise. Some fulfillment houses are industry specific, stocking food products, health and medical supplies, clothing, electronics, and preprinted and/or customizable literature. Fulfillment houses may concentrate on a specialty, such as direct mailing or shipping. More robust fulfillment operations stock large quantities for customers, track inventory, and mail on demand.

E-procurement

An e-procurement channel facilitates almost instantaneous exchange of goods, services, and merchandise for consumer markets, business markets, and government markets. This technology-driven supply chain covers the full product-placement cycle, from online requisitioning, bidding, and payment systems to vendor management, sales help, online shopping carts, electronic order fulfillment, and inventory management. E-procurement offers cost efficiency and can speed up the fulfillment cycle. However, the vast exposure of products in the e-marketplace may push down pricing. E-procurement strategies, including competitive online auctions, shift the driving force from buyer emotion to seller action, in which vendors must cut prices to win the job. E-channels also include online stores, such as E-bay and CafePress, where sellers can set up shop in minutes.

Network Marketing

Also known as direct marketing groups, network marketing organizations serve as channels in themselves, hawking their own products. Network marketing companies, such as Market America, Shaklee, and United First Financial (UFirst), create a downline of independent product distributors, who each earn income by selling company products directly to customers, and from commissions earned based on sales of other distributors they bring into the channel. The multilevel compensation plan typically is pyramid shaped, with early entrants receiving higher-level commissions and later entrants providing the base for commissions sent upline.

RSS Feeds

RSS (Really Simple Syndication) feeds are a recently developed marketing channel, used on the Internet and broadcast electronically. They help marketers share content and reach more consumers by making it easy for others to plug your content into their own Web sites.

If you manage unique, in-demand content that is updated in a regular, timely way, RSS feeds can link you to the visitors at other Web sites. Set up an RSS widget on your Web site, and other companies will be able to share your text, video, and audio content as soon as it is uploaded, in real time.

CAUTION

Before keying in or recording hours of content to stream worldwide—or posting someone else's feed on your site—clarify your expectations about how it will drive visitors to your own Web site and, ultimately, help you market and sell your own products.

Sales Force

Internal sales teams, telemarketers, and direct marketers tie your company to channel partners, business buyers, retailers, and/or consumers. Manufacturer's representatives, who sell various products for multiple vendors, also can extend the reach of your sales force. Their broader product range and location mix can increase exposure to potential customers.

TRACK YOUR INVENTORY

Whichever marketing channel you choose—conventional fulfillment or electronic procurement, Internet based or brick-and-mortar outlets—protect your brand with rigid inventory management to ensure stock availability. Brand management demands that you do not disappoint customers.

Choosing Channels for Success

The key to successful channel marketing is unlocking value. To market products cost effectively, you may need to test drive or juggle alternative ways to create high value for your customers as well as your company. Integrate key members of your sales team in channel marketing discussions to pollinate strategies, pragmatize ideas, and gain buy-in on management decisions.

Big firms with global product capabilities deal in multichannel markets, with international brokers, buyers, wholesalers, shipping companies, and fulfillment houses. Smaller firms often create more direct supply chain networks. Regardless of the size of a business, technology has reshaped marketing channels, with the Internet driving commerce, and sophisticated electronic data systems used for order management and inventory control.

Whether you are targeting Internet shoppers, local retail shops, convenience stores, buying clubs, or warehouse outlets, your job is to maximize throughput in the most cost-efficient, brand-building way possible. Simply put, you've got to get your products to the right place at the right time for the right price. Marketing channels help companies build product visibility in ways that both attract retailers and build demand from end buyers. Once you've gotten your products into a store, catalog, or Web site, the final placement challenge is to arrange for a great in-store location. When making deals, work to secure shelf placement, end-cap, and/or point-of-purchase displays to maximize visibility. With online channels, strive for Web site advertising banners and link placements that best meet your needs. You'll find more about this in the Chapter 10, Marketing in a Digital World and Chapter 14, Advertising and Media Placement.

Virtual Placement

Placement isn't just about physical locations or even online venues. Virtual placement, for example, uses advertising and promotion as the marketing channel. While wholesalers, jobbers, and retailers all concentrate on push marketing to excite demand by placing products directly in front of customers, virtual placements operate on pull marketing strategy. The goal of pull marketing is to create emotional connections that encourage customers to actively look for and request a product. Tapping the power of virtual placement, marketers pay to insinuate branded products in television and broadcast storylines, as well as concert halls, convention centers, and other venues. People, such as celebrity artists can be venues in themselves when they are seen using products, such as clothing labels, sneakers, and cars. Choose venues and artists based on their appeal to your target market. You've seen it yourself when Macintosh laptops, Pepsi cans, and Breyers ice cream cartons are strategically placed in full view on television shows. You've seen athletes flaunting product emblems on their sports apparel, and television stars driving BMWs. You also may have heard radio announcers discussing their personal experience with specialty products, from Lasik eye surgery to botox treatments.

Marketers define placement options in terms of the marketing channels they use as a conduit to customers. For example, virtual placement is used by the advertisers to connect with specific target customers in a viewing demographic. Each member of a distribution channel provides access to a particular customer base and/or serves a logistical role in helping move products from manufacturers and service providers to the buying public. Each member of the marketing channel serves a purpose. Marketing research will help you uncover the best options.

Integrating Marketing Research

Marketing research is the driving force behind every element of the marketing mix, including where to place your products. Research outcomes help shape decisions on the most logical conduits and locations for connecting with your customers.

Depending on your research questions, a review of hard data and anecdotal evidence can reveal whether customers show a preference for accessing products in stores or through Web sites and print catalogs. Research also can help you decide where to locate physical stores, which Web sites offer the best traffic, and where the best target markets are located. More is not always better.

Niche Markets

Sometimes small micro-markets, known as "niche markets," make the most sense. Niche marketing focuses on meeting the unique preferences of a small market with very specific needs. Niche markets make it easy to concentrate resources and home in on sharply targeted groups with strong product interest. For example, the lingerie market is huge. But the market for breast prosthetics is small. Prosthetics manufacturers may target only hospital and health-care providers—or an even smaller niche of breast surgeons—reducing both advertising costs and the need for a huge sales team that calls on cross-country and/or lingerie buyers. At the same time, prosthetics manufacturers will reach exactly the right customers for their products—people with a real need. In this case, breast surgeons would serve as a niche marketing channel, providing direct entry to patients in need. Targeting small micro-markets can deliver higher per-capita return on time, talent, and financial investment.

Targeting Qualified Placements

Less is also more when considering Internet-based pay-per-click programs. They can generate hundreds, thousands, or millions of hits, each of which will cost you your pennies. However, you can choose the number of clicks you are willing to pay for in a given time period, thereby controlling your budget, but also limiting your advertising views. In this case, though, the critical measure is actual sales, not voluminous prospects. Before choosing any channel, assess its capability for bringing you qualified buyers who have an interest and the means to purchase your products.

Before collecting data, assemble a team that can help surface placement issues, Consider which marketing channels have the best potential to deliver the outcomes you need at a cost you can afford. Ask the kind of questions(s) that will lead to the information (research outcomes) you need. Start by determining what you hope to accomplish in a given market. Next assess the challenges you face. Once you have identified the first potential challenge, always ask, what else? And keep asking until you've listed all logical possibilities. Then set your planning priorities.

Once you've made your list, the next step is to decide how you will get your answers and where they will come from. If you don't already have that information, you can locate marketing research firms by checking with your local office of economic development, Small Business Development Center, or searching on the Internet.

Test Marketing

Before leaping with a major budget allocation, study how that market has worked for your competitors. If there's no one else in the space, you may be on the leading edge with new products or technology. In that case, your challenges will be finding and cultivating relationships with early adopters. There's also the possibility that your targeted demographic really has no interest in your product. Learn as much as possible about your targeted customers, and then toe into that target market slowly, when it looks promising. Test with small product runs in limited locations, special offers, coupons, and product giveaways. Simultaneously, work to build a viral buzz that drives demand. Then track results before jumping in whole hog. Also, keep in mind that markets change. Stay current with your market. Test and retest.

Identifying Opportunities

Individual consumers have different wants and needs. They buy based on their personalities, their perceptions of basic needs, physical and emotional desires, and a dose of pocketbook reality. Individual markets also have personalities. Marketers define them by building market profiles, or personae, that reflect characteristics of market segments, based on knowledge of that group's buying history, trends, and predictability. Once you have created a picture of your market, you will better understand how to address its needs, habits, and buying behavior. When focusing on a more narrow market, you will be able to create a sharply targeted marketing message. For that, you will want to segment your potential customers into logical groups. Even when targeting a diverse customer base, you can sort customers based on the differences, such as, geography, preferred shopping locales, and shopping habits (Internet vs. physical shopping).

Sorting Market Capabilities

The goal of market segmentation is to create the best fit between you and your channel partners and/or end consumers. Think of market segmentation as criteria sorting (see Table 6.1). Your job is to select the criteria that make the most sense for your business based on your mission, values, goals, resources, and business process.

Barriers to Entry

Barriers to entry may include overwhelming competition, lack of geographic reach, cost considerations, outdated technology, cultural buying patterns, and access to decision makers or influencers. When conducting a SWOT Analysis or other market assessment, considering barriers to entry will help you avert costly mistakes. But remember that many barriers can be broken with a thoughtful approach. For example, you may need to establish a connection

Table 6.1 Market Segmentation Opportunity Assessment

Market Issue	Good Fit—Easy to Access and Implement	Bad Fit—Strong Barriers to Entry
Geography	• The buyer mix is concentrated. • Buyers are in close proximity to one another and to business locations.	• The customer base is broadly dispersed. • Buyers are difficult to reach.
Technology	• It's readily available and affordable. • It's already in place, or it can be purchased and implemented easily. • User-friendly interfaces offer easy compatibility and exchange with current business information systems.	• Major, costly software conversion is required. • There's a long implementation cycle. • It requires a lot of training or retraining of staff. • It does not easily interface with customer portals.
Cultural Fit	• There's a proven buyer affinity for the products and/or services. • The language used matches current operations. • There's strong values compatibility.	• Resources are needed to introduce product and build preference. • Significant time is needed to break through cultural influencers and boundaries.
Finance	• Pricing is favorable. • Payment terms are reasonable. • There's easy access to credit. • The channel partners have excellent credit histories.	• Set-up costs are high. • There are no volume discounts available for required parts and labor. • Immediate payment is required. • Situation does not offer credit options or financial partners. • History of profitable market endeavors is not evident.
Implementation	• Goals are clearly set. • The timetable meets turnaround needs. • Turnkey processes are in place. • The team is professional. • Excellent support services and communications have been demonstrated.	• Plan articulation is nonspecific. • A long implementation cycle would delay market entry. • Massive technology updates are required. • There is little-to-no internal communication support. • There is lack of logistical integration with other delivery partners and other support services.

to the people who influence community opinion (such as a church leader, business leader, parents, teachers, newswriter, columnist, or a popular blogger.) The keys to breaking through a barrier are to assess the costs involved and resources needed, then to plan your effort in small successive steps, while keeping focused on your end goal.

Building an Internet-Based Joint Venture Partnership and e-List

With the proliferation of e-business opportunities, Internet-based joint ventures are increasingly common. A joint venture is a collaborative marketing opportunity that can increase your exposure over the Web and help you build your e-marketing list—a key Internet channel to buyers.

FINDING POTENTIAL PARTNERS

You can find joint venture partners by scouting experts at professional conferences, through business networks, and by searching the Internet for people whose product offer is similar to yours. When it comes to joint ventures, it's time to turn off your competitive mindset and turn up your collaborative spirit. By working together, you can drive more traffic to a single event or location, and to each other's Web sites than one person usually can do alone. You can use joint ventures to:

- Position yourself or your company as an expert resource with relevant content, and grow new relationships with your partners' contacts.
- Increase product or service accessibility.
- Schedule and fill seats for an Internet event.
- Use event to present yourself as a subject matter expert and expand your e-list.

CREATING DEMAND FOR YOUR JOINT VENTURE CHANNEL

Free Web events are proven draws, when multiple partners market the same event to their qualified prospect lists. Here's how:

- Pull together a roster of experts, and invite them to participate in a free educational Webinar or teleseminar series that you coordinate on a topic of interest to buyers in your respective markets.
- Ask each partner to advertise the seminars on its respective Web site and through e-broadcast lists. Ask the partner also to place a link to your Web site on their Web site—and reciprocate.

- Use the telesessions and e-blasts to promote both giveaways and the sale of other products—typically downloadable audio or video files, and books.

- Create multiple product offers, with content from various partners. Because not all attendees will be able to make all sessions of a teleseminar series, also sell access to the full telesession series on DVD or podcast, for user convenience. Research market pricing for similar promotions on the Web when planning your own offers.

- Gather e-mail addresses from visitors "channeled" to you by your JV partners. When visitors come to download your content, ask them to register by providing their e-mail addresses. Most visitors will supply an e-mail address, although they may be reluctant to supply their name, address, and phone numbers until you have built a relatively strong relationship with them. If they see value in your first offer, they will probably opt in to your ongoing e-newsletters. Over time, they will gain comfort with you and your philosophy and be more willing to divulge personal contact information.

- Collect data about your new visitors, analyze their buying patterns, and move them into an auto-responder program. (See more about this in Chapter 12.)

- Expand your e-list to extend your Internet marketing capabilities.

Let's say you know 10 experts. Each would blast out information about the series, potentially a free 10-session program, where each expert would present information for one hour. For people who are intrigued, but can't attend, you can offer the opportunity to buy a copy of the entire event or a single session. Thereby, you would generate additional income. One particular list-building coach recently brought in $65,000 on the sale of one DVD series over an eight-week period. After sharing proceeds with other list builders on the expert panel, she profited $37,000. She based that income distribution on how many people from each list bought the products, and took for herself an additional stipend for serving as the conference coordinator. You can start building your own e-list today by offering a gift, such as an e-book, white paper, or a free MP3. Later, you can transform those giveaways to sustainable income by choosing the right joint venture partners and adopting effective Internet marketing strategies.

Quiz

1. The process of choosing the right distribution system for delivering products and services to target markets is:

   (a) Placement

   (b) Channel marketing

   (c) Positioning

   (d) Promotion

2. Employing other business entities as part of a sales, delivery, or service effort is called:

   (a) A marketing vertical

   (b) Channel marketing

   (c) Service marketing

   (d) Target marketing

3. Channel partners are necessary for:

   (a) Penetrating markets that are difficult to enter

   (b) Reaching geographically dispersed markets

   (c) Maximizing physical and/or financial resources

   (d) All of the above

   (e) Only (a) and (b)

4. Companies that purchase and resell goods as they are, rather than transforming them into other products, are known as:

   (a) Retailers

   (b) Merchants

   (c) Wholesalers

   (d) Channel partners

5. Companies that help expose your products and services to their own customers are:

   (a) Retailers

   (b) Joint venture partners

   (c) Affiliate marketers

   (d) All of the above

6. _____ is a supply chain system that covers the full product placement cycle, from online requisitioning, bidding and payment systems, to vendor management, sales help, online shopping carts, electronic order fulfillment, and inventory management.

   (a) A joint venture

   (b) A fulfillment service

   (c) An inventory system

   (d) E-procurement

7. Joint ventures are a _____ marketing opportunity that can increase your exposure over the Web and help you build your e-marketing list.

  (a) Collaborative

  (b) Expensive

  (c) Time-limited

  (d) Forward-looking

8. _____ are proven draws for joint venture marketing prospects.

  (a) Networking events

  (b) Free Web events

  (c) E-mail lists

  (d) None of the above

9. When you collect data about your new Web visitors, and analyze their buying patterns, you can:

  (a) Qualify them as prospects

  (b) Sell to them

  (c) Move them into an auto-responder program

  (d) All of the above

  (e) None of the above

10. _____ will help you reflect on the potential of each market segment, assess market segments, and target segments that will work best for you.

  (a) Developing a market profile

  (b) Building an e-mail campaign

  (c) Creating a joint venture

  (d) None of the above

CHAPTER 7

Pricing and Profitability

By now you know the foundational principles of integrated marketing and branding. You have uncovered your competitive differentiators and can segment a market. You can select target audiences and channels that will deliver the business results you need. You also know what's needed to draft a strategic marketing plan.

When loaded with maps, a satellite-guided global positioning system (GPS) can tell you exactly where you stand relative to your destination while you are traveling. But without data on road and weather conditions, you might find that your trip takes longer than planned. When driving a car, you need to be able to stay the course or change course quickly. When it comes to pricing, you need a type of GPS, too, along with real-time data to assist in course correction. Consider this chapter your GPS, otherwise known as your "guided pricing system."

Pricing, however, is not as cut and dried as it might appear. Although price is largely based on mathematical calculations, a simple formula may not tell all you need to know about how your decision will affect your bottom line. Formulas are only as good as the data and research assumptions are. First, when calculating prices, you must factor in the cost of product development and purchases, infrastructure and operating overhead, and advertising and sales expenses. You also need to consider what it will cost to address branding issues and influence customer perspectives. You may have financing costs to add, and must estimate the impact of time to value from sales, as well as the financial impact of accounts receivables—payments outstanding (sometimes known as "DSOs" or days-of-sales outstanding).

Second, your price must align with your overall business strategy. For that, you really must understand what drives your own business as well as what's happening in your market. You will want to consider industry maturity, product cycle and longevity, and the percentage of market share you expect to capture. You will need to research how the economic climate and regulatory environment may impinge on product and pricing expectations. You'll need to assess market characteristics, competition and competitive pressure, prospect criteria, investor requirements, and management demands, as well. Finally, you must consider current and projected market supply and the availability of comparable, substitute products. Figure 7.1 reveals the many considerations, strategies, and options that impact pricing decisions.

Third, remember that price makes a psychological as well as mathematical impression. Regardless of your market—individual consumers, businesses, not-for-profit organizations, and/or government entities—your price must reflect your understanding of market needs, buyer awareness, buying habits, and the varied psychographic factors influencing buyer demands. And you need to assess your cash availability and projected cash flow. Armed with that information, you will gain a better handle on your pricing thresholds based on estimated time to sales and profitability. But pricing is not just about outside forces. Pricing strategies depend on where you are in your business life cycle and whether you are introducing a new product or managing a product you've been marketing for a while. Choosing the right price requires the right information.

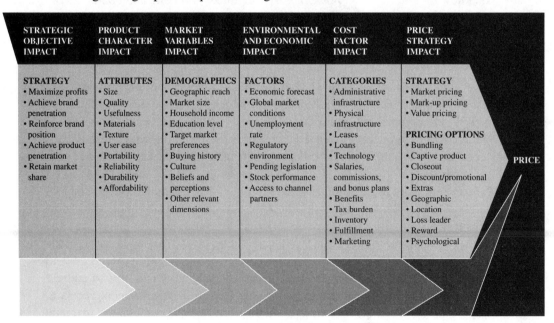

Figure 7.1 Pricing filters.

> **CAUTION**
>
> Remember that information trumps instinct. Pricing requires attention to detail and facts as well comprehensive knowledge of your product and your market.

Integrating Cost, Pricing, and Marketing Strategies

To set your GPS, you must input your cost structure, pricing strategy, pricing method, and pricing option. To choose what will work best for you, consider how the price you set will interact with other elements of the marketing mix and create the desired perception and demand for your product or service. Here's a quick overview of my four-part guided pricing system (GPS):

1. **Align pricing decisions with your overall business and branding strategies.**
   - Determine how your product fits with overall business objectives.
   - Decide what your chosen price will communicate about your products.
   - Make sure your pricing strategy aligns with your brand strategy.
   - Build your required return on investment into your price.
   - Consider the ways in which company departments will be impacted by price and sales.

2. **Identify what information you need to make the right decision.**
   - Gather information on competitive products. Identify current market pricing for competitive or similar products.
   - Gather market intelligence, including relevant demographic information, available sales outlets and their associated costs, and buyer preferences.
   - Consider what factors will influence product perceptions.
   - Decide on a pricing strategy, and, when costing, estimate the markup needed to turn a profit.
   - Calculate your costs to manufacture or purchase stock, introduce and advertise your product, manage inventory, and ship, track, and control for profit.
   - Consider how pricing options will influence short-term and long-term profitability. For example, a special introductory rate or coupon may cost you profit in the short term, but it can develop customer connections for long-term relationships and profitability.

- Estimate the number of products you expect to sell in the first quarter and first year; then track your results and adjust accordingly.

- Decide what numbers you need to be profitable at the end of those periods.

- Review and assess the validity of assumptions supporting your decision. If you offer discounts, prepare to assess costs against sales gained.

- Check your confidence in your decisions, based on your expectations. Assess your finances, and decide how much risk you can handle.

3. **Test the market.**

- Choose a representative target market.

- Estimate the cost of product runs in test markets.

- Establish a budget for test marketing across the product cycle, from inventory through shipping.

- Also consider the costs of not running tests in a target market. What might it save you in upfront expenses? What might that cost you in profit avoided?

- Outline your test process and goals. Decide how many customers you want to reach and at what price in which markets.

- Implement testing. Vary your pricing in test outlets, and collect data for analysis.

4. **Evaluate the results.**

- Did sales meet expectations? How much did you sell, when, and where?

- How did sales vary from outlet to outlet?

- How did sales vary with special promotions?

- How did sales vary day to day, month to month, and year over year?

- What factors influenced those variations?

- What can you learn from the new data about your pricing decisions?

- What might you need to change?

- If everything went as you had hoped, what will you do to hold the gain?

Assessing Your Cost Structure

Regardless of business strategy, at some point pricing comes down to a calculation of the following factors:

- The cost of bringing your product to market

- The cost of protecting or shifting your market position

$$V = \frac{Q}{C}$$

Figure 7.2   Perceptual pricing ratio.

- Assessment of perceived value in the minds of customers
- The cost of creating value in the minds of customers

While pricing is generally calculated based on a combination of fixed costs and variable costs, it must closely match perceived value and perceived need in the minds of customers who can afford it. In its simplest form: value equals perception of quality divided by cost (see Figure 7.2).

Estimating perceived value requires an understanding of the people who make up your target markets. Marketing research will give you clues about perceived value based on product attributes and what you've learned about buyer behavior. Your goal as a marketer is to maximize perceived value in the minds of your *suspects* (potential buyers who have not yet been qualified), *prospects* (potential buyers with an interest in your product), and *customers* (people who already buy from you.). With reliable data to fuel understanding, you can vary elements of the marketing mix to create the emotional and perceptual shifts that will match your business needs. This is the point where ethics and pricing meet. Socially responsible marketers will ensure that profit is the likely result of understanding the people who make up a market and serving consumer interests rather than manipulating them. We'll discuss this more in Chapter 16. Now, let's concentrate on costs.

Fixed costs typically reflect infrastructure costs, such as mortgage or rental rates, lease arrangements, inventory and inventory management control, fixtures and furniture, license and permit fees, compensation programs, loan repayments, technology costs, and salaries. Variable costs may include office supplies, telephones, expense reimbursements for gas mileage and cell phones, insurance, taxes, equipment purchases, advertising and promotion, and training and development. These costs may vary with production, seasonal variations, and the caliber of employee and sales teams.

Calculating Costs

Listing all anticipated expenses will help you determine your product launch budget. Budget-based planning will help keep your business on track. Be sure to include all potential expenses, fixed and variable. See Table 7.1 as a model for cost assessment.

Pricing Strategies and Methods

As a consumer, you know that prices can fluctuate dramatically from one day to the next. Sale price changes can reflect inventory loads, competitor actions, and market fluctuations.

Table 7.1   Probable Cost Worksheet

Fixed Costs	$ Per Month	$ Per Year
Mortgage or rent		
Leases (cars and equipment)		
Salary		
Commissions (projected)		
Benefits programs		
License and permit fees,		
Computers/technology		
Fixtures and furniture		
Loan repayments		
Start-up costs/R&D		
Technology requirements		
Internet services		
Other		
Variable Costs	**$ Per Month**	**$ Per Month**
Office supplies		
Telephones		
Expense reimbursements		
Insurance		
Taxes		
Postage		
Shipping and fulfillment services		
Training and development		
Advertising and promotion		
Marketing research		
Other		

The key is to determine the right price for your particular market at the right time. Your pricing strategy should reflect high-level business goals as well as specific product line objectives. While there is no hard-and-fast rule, your price should generate sufficient profit to warrant your business risk. Whether you are selling directly to consumers, other businesses, or government entities, your price should be guided by the objective to stay in business, drive sales, and profit in the process. Most companies choose one of the following strategies.

PROFIT-BASED STRATEGY

Profit-based strategies are governed by the desire to maximize financial performance. With profit as the motive, prices are set to deliver fast return on investment. But, when market factors are not controllable, even high price points and the ability to realize a profit does not guarantee long-term solvency. The economic debacle that commanded worldwide attention, beginning in the fall of 2008, was a reflection, in part, of profit-based strategies that exceeded the market capacity to sustain them. To achieve success with a profit-based strategy, you must be capable of understanding and influencing consumer demand. To maintain it, you must position yourself to respond to market forces across time. You can do this through sound planning, ethical governance, trend monitoring, and research that provides relevant evidence for decision making and reliable forecasting.

Government and nonprofit organizations represent an alternative position to profit strategy. While they strive to cover costs and maintain a sound operating fund balance, they are not bound to deliver profit to investors or shareholders.

PENETRATION STRATEGY

To gain market share, companies introducing new products or seeking to best their competition often turn to penetration pricing. In this case, sellers set pricing low enough to encourage customer trials and to stimulate sales. Penetration pricing works well in markets where buyers are very price sensitive or don't have an affinity for the product. One benefit of this low-price strategy is that profit margins do not typically inspire competitors to run head to head against you, while the lower price also helps move inventory.

SKIMMING STRATEGY

When products enter the market at the highest price consumers are likely to pay, the management objective is generally to skim the cream—taking as much profit as quickly as possible in what appears to be a lucrative market. Skimming strategies work well for innovative, leading-edge products with strongly perceived benefit. But skimming is often a short-term pricing strategy. Profitable markets draw fierce competition; as competitors catch up with technological innovation, prices eventually drop. In the 1980s Macintosh computers entered the market at a much higher price than personal computers from IBM and other companies. With a 160-*megabyte* hard drive (yes, Macs once were that small), my first Macintosh Performa desktop and monitor set up cost more than $3,000. I recently bought another i-Mac with a much faster processor, a *terrabyte* of memory and a 21-inch monitor, for less than half what I paid over ten years ago. Each new Mac product or version carries a top-of-the-industry sticker price, and buyers still pay the price. Customers have responded to Apple's strong value proposition, based on its aesthetics, user-friendly technology, and high-level application reliability.

As you see on holiday season newscasts, many customers will stand on lines overnight to get products, such as Xbox and Wii, as soon as they are released, despite high price tags. Consumers pay them because of the products' high emotional appeal and because they have come to believe that they "need" these products to feel happy or satisfied.

POSITIONING STRATEGY

Price is another way of communicating your brand positioning. When marketers vie to capture markets based on reputations of innovation, reliability, leadership, or social responsibility, they often command higher prices. On the other hand, Wal-Mart positions itself based on value, with its "Save Money, Live Better" slogan. Other companies set price based on easy access and friendly service, without frills. For example, Southwest Airlines has captured the market of price-conscious travelers. The airline makes up for its lack of luxury by featuring friendly, approachable staff and affordably priced flights.

To maintain profitability, companies often make price accommodations. Premium airline carriers, for example, may attempt to differentiate their brands through an exceptional customer experience. When setting ticket price, they would consider service variables as well as anticipated fuel costs. They would factor in the cost of wider seats, more legroom, premium food and beverages, entertainment systems, and varied passenger loads. Then, they could predict and continually recalculate pricing based on buying patterns, flight patterns, business expectations, and needs. But, no matter how well they plan, if the cost of jet fuel suddenly rises, they must either reduce service levels or increase ticket prices (or both) to cover added costs. While Southwest and Jet Blue have maintained their economy pricing strategy, they also have raised baggage and beverage pricing. (We discuss "extras" pricing later on; see "Extras Pricing.")

PREMIUM STRATEGY

To maintain the prestige of unique products and services, premium pricing is effective when directed at tightly targeted, sustainable high-end markets where significant discretionary spending occurs for products such as luxury spas, yachts, travel, entertainment systems, and cars.

ECONOMY STRATEGY

Similar to a market penetration strategy, an economy strategy is useful when the goal is to move inventory quickly; in such a case, product costs are set relatively low per unit. Positioned as economy models, these products may be lower-priced "generic" derivatives of more prestigious brands offered by the same manufacturer. This strategy is appropriate for price-sensitive markets or when there are few product differentiators.

MARKET PRICING

Many businesses set their price based on what competitors are charging, and the cost they think customers will bear. This strategy can work in two ways: it can eliminate price as an obstacle and open the door to a relationship sale. In other words, when prices are consistent from brand to brand or vendor to vendor, customers must compare product and/or service features to see the value of one brand or vendor over another. And, when companies recognize that market pricing is no longer the determining factor in a buying decision, they must look at other ways to build relationships with prospects and customers, such as guarantees, warranties, and more convenient service options. On the other hand, market pricing can turn your product or service into a commodity shopped by price rather than reputation. In this case, as vendors bring their prices into closer alignment, it becomes more difficult to differentiate your brand, particularly when the price cuts make it more difficult to find money in a budget to enhance product features and services that might attract customers, or to increase spending on marketing and sales efforts.

> ### CAUTION
>
> All businesses are not created equal. Overhead varies, as do customer relationships, business volume, and overall business capitalization. If you plan to match competitors' going-rate prices, take stock of your firm's financial wherewithal, cost, and markup issues. Also make sure you have done a good market analysis and can reliably forecast sales volume at your preferred price.

MARKUP PRICING

Many companies set prices by calculating total costs for developing and bringing a product to market, dividing it by number of units to be sold, and adding the percentage they believe will deliver acceptable profit. Sometimes, in a bid to win business, companies reduce their markup. Unless they factor in all their costs and risk accordingly, those reductions can severely cut or eliminate profit. Remember that if you don't add in enough profit, or if you cut too deeply with discount plans, you may not last long enough in business to continue providing those products.

VALUE PRICING

Perhaps you are planning to introduce an innovative product. If so, you must balance cost criteria with perceived product worth in the eyes of customers. On one hand, value pricing can mean high prices for products that deliver special benefits or offer a unique experience.

This method works well when you are targeting niche markets with high emotional connection with and demand for your products.

On the other hand, you may use value pricing to justify low prices. You may structure special deals to overcome economic conditions or when business assumptions demonstrate that lower costs will impact buyer preference and help you move inventory or gain market share.

CAUTION

How you set your price depends on how you approach your business and your beliefs about the market.

Choosing among Many Pricing Options

How do various pricing approaches influence customers? The paragraphs that follow show some options to consider, based on your overall strategy, cost analysis, pricing strategy, and pricing method.

LOSS LEADERS

Sometimes companies offer certain merchandise or services at an intentional loss to drive traffic to stores, service locations, and/or Internet sites so customers will come in contact with the higher-priced options in their product lines. For example, despite the exceptionally high operating cost of a burn unit, maintaining such a service would demonstrate commitment to the community firefighters and emergency personnel, and gain loyalty from such groups when it comes to choosing more profitable hospital services, such as cardiac care, general surgery, and/or maternity.

GEOGRAPHIC PRICING

When geography and/or cultural differences impact the economy, you may need to price based on differing sets of expectations and market capabilities. In that case, you can vary your price based on your product locations. Retail and boutique shops, for instance, generally support higher prices than outlet stores, Internet sites, and buying clubs, based on customer perceptions and expectations.

EXTRAS PRICING

Depending on your product or service line, you may find it advantageous to offer basic products and services at a "standard" rate, with an added price for upgrades. Restaurants frequently use this approach. As an alternative to the prix fixe menu, they may charge extra for salads and desserts. A hair salon may offer a low cost for a cut and blow dry, but may charge extra for hair conditioner. This strategy enables buyers to purchase from a moderately priced product line while the vendor capitalizes on profit from the sale of extras. Customers motivated by prestige are highly susceptible to extras pricing. When choosing among pricing options, make sure you understand the mindset and financial standing of your customer mix.

BUNDLING

If you have surplus inventory and/or carry multiple items, you may choose to package the items together. You may factor in a lower price for the inventory you most want to move and pair it with a higher priced or more desirable product as a sales incentive. You can bundle different products together or package the same item in multiples. You can also try this approach in collaboration with offers from your channel partners; for example, cable and telephone companies have turned to bundling service packages (e.g., telephone, TV, and Internet, with special monthly prices extending across a promotional time period).

CLOSEOUT PRICING

Another promotional pricing strategy, closeout sales, offers deep discounts in an effort to sell off stagnant inventory. This approach is typically used when new models are about to be introduced or items on the shelves have outlasted the season or are nearing expiration dates.

CAPTIVE-PRODUCT PRICING

Some products require other products to provide ongoing value. In that case, you would probably offer the original product at a lower price. You can then earn your profit on supplies. For example, Dell offers promotional pricing on printers ordered along with computers. But, the company earns additional money over the printers' lifecycle from repeated customer orders for ink and specialty paper and/or service plans.

PSYCHOLOGICAL PRICING

Do you believe that customers have a set price in mind? Or do you think that they are more likely to buy an item priced at 99 cents instead of a dollar? Some companies set their prices based on their knowledge of how customers' mental perceptions and beliefs impact their buying behavior.

PROMOTIONAL PRICING OR DISCOUNT PRICING

Promotional pricing takes multiple forms, such as special sales and seasonal pricing. You may choose to reduce prices for senior citizens, not-for-profit organizations, members of professional associations, business groups, buying groups, or channel partners. Before deciding on promotional pricing, think about what you hope it will do for your company:

- Will it bring in revenue more quickly, helping you in the short term?
- Will it entice new customers for the long haul?
- Will it help you empty an overstocked warehouse? If so, what will that save you in space and overhead costs? Will it make room for a better seller next month?
- How much will it cost you to run the promotion or discount?
- How will this affect overall profitability?
- How will this pricing strategy align with your overall brand positioning and business strategies?

REWARD PRICING

Reward pricing can take many forms. Airlines offer frequent flyer miles. American Express offers reward points for credit-card purchases. Starbucks offers punch cards entitling the bearer to a free beverage after 10 other purchases have been made. You can offer rewards for ongoing or multiple purchases. Or you can offer favorable payment terms with special purchases. Furniture stores and car dealers offer delayed payment options as well as no-interest promotions to entice and/or reward customers for doing business with them.

COUPONS

Coupons are a proven option for generating product interest and purchases. When offering a coupon promotion, remember that there are costs other than the discount you offer. You'll also have costs for coupon preparation and printing. You may have mailing and distribution costs, as well, and you'll also have to predict and track redemption rates.

No matter which pricing option you choose, always remember to track costs and factor in a percentage of your overall business burden when calculating the true cost of your price promotion.

TERMS AND CONDITIONS AND PRICE ADJUSTMENTS

If your product carries a warranty or your service a special guarantee, you need to estimate the return rate and know what that will cost you. If you offer a discount based on prompt payment, you may be able to offset the discount with the fact that money will be in your hands sooner, enhancing your cash flow and enabling you to negotiate better terms with your own vendors.

DISCOUNTING AS A STRATEGY

You may choose to offer price adjustments for not-for-profit organizations, small disadvantaged businesses, or businesses owned by women, minorities, or veterans. If you do, calculate how much business you expect to do in each category and how those decisions will impact cash flow and profitability. After all, if you are working for one customer at a discount, you may not have time or resources to serve another client at full price.

When lowering your price, be aware that if you discount too heavily, it may be difficult to justify bringing the price back up. When one company lowers its price, and another follows, customer expectations around product pricing may adjust downward as well. Once customers learn that prices drop at certain times of year, or according to product cycles (as is the case when new technology is on the horizon), many customers will wait for sales and special deals or the marketing push to offload out-of-date inventory.

Every pricing decision has the potential to alter consumer behavior. Expectation of sales in retail stores, for example, have left customers with the jaded perspective that products are overpriced and, if those customers wait long enough, prices will come down. In some cases, pricing pressure may be irreversible. Marketing teams then would be challenged to introduce stronger value propositions, while R&D teams may be sent back to the drawing board to add product features that will command upward price adjustments.

Beware of the temptation to reduce pricing just because you are competing with a neighboring business. See to it that you know exactly why you are reducing your price, and be sure that the strategy will add to your long-term business solvency.

Market Variables and Comparisons

As with every other variable in the marketing mix, setting the price requires you to understand what's happening with your competitors. When comparing your products to others in the market, remember to compare your prices not only to others for similar products but also to product alternatives. Think about what your product does, whether it can substitute for something else on the market, or whether something else could substitute for yours. You must determine whether adding or removing features, or packaging in a different way, will affect product value in the eyes of customers.

Remember, it's the impact of total experience that counts for the customer. Because most products are bought based on visual cues, be sure to inspect competitors' products as well as your own for looks, size, features, color, style, and feel. Use the information you gain to help you analyze how product attributes affect price tolerance.

Customer Perspective and Market Value

Perhaps you've already got your pricing locked in. You've done your research, and you're ready to sell. You may be wondering what other factors will influence your success.

Differentiation is the key to price strength. When product offers are highly similar across the market, those products can be viewed as undifferentiated commodities. This is one of the greatest dilemmas facing sales departments in a competitive global economy.

That's why your brand positioning strategy, promotion, placement, and other aspects of the marketing mix play an important role.

Pricing also is about flexibility. You may need to assign separate pricing strategies for bricks-and-mortar selling and online selling. Test your price options along the way to see what works best for you. Treat every aspect of the marketing mix as part of an ongoing experiment, in which you continually study the results and feedback. The world and market will change around you. You must stay nimble—in business and pricing strategies, methods, and opportunities—to succeed for the long term.

Sometimes flexibility is about speed. Being first to market often translates to having a strong hold on market share. If you are lucky enough to produce or introduce an innovative product, and if your product is not easy to replicate, you will more than likely enjoy at least a brief lead time to build rapport with your customer base. That lead time can infuse your cash coffers, giving you a jump on market penetration.

As markets change, strategies must adapt; your business actions must connect with realistic market assumptions and information. Before launching a new product, jumping into a new market, or shifting strategy, think about what you expect to happen. Brainstorm about possibilities with your team. Run numbers for the options you identify, and then project potential outcomes. This type of price inquiry presents an opportunity for you to "ghost"—study and predict— the competition and competitive action before it even exists. Consider who your potential competition would be under various scenarios and how they might respond to your own market entry or maneuvers. For example, if you drop prices, and they respond by dropping prices, too, you may lose the low-price differentiator. Or, if you advertise in one magazine, and your competitor shows up on the next page, it may impact differentiation or confuse customers about the difference in value between your products and services and those of your competitor's. Once you've analyzed your anticipated competition and crunched some numbers, you'll be better positioned to choose the right price points and reflect your value proposition in your marketing endeavors.

Pricing Models

All companies set prices based on an estimate of fixed and variable costs. *Product pricing* is easy for a customer to understand. When a product price is decided, it may be listed in a wholesale or retail catalog, on a price tag, or in an Internet shopping cart. *Service pricing*, however, may not be the same across all transactions, even in the same company. Service fees may be set by the hour, service, or project. The advantage of *project pricing* (a single price for all services leading to a completion of a job) is that it lets your customer know what to expect and enables you to more easily project your income. For example, when services may be purchased a la carte or hourly, it may be more difficult to project cash flow at project inception. You can control that by specifying the time required to complete the project, as well as all aspects of individual service pricing.

The goal of pricing is to make a sale that represents a win for your company and a win for your customer. Once your price is official, you can track sales and use that information for ongoing forecasting and decision making.

Quiz

1. Pricing calculations typically include:

    (a) Cost of product development

    (b) Cost of merchandise

    (c) Salaries

    (d) All of the above

    (e) Only (b) and (c)

2. Industry maturity, product cycle, and longevity represent:

    (a) Market analysis

    (b) Cost indicators

    (c) Branding factors

    (d) Factors influencing pricing strategy

3. A market-based pricing strategy may include:

    (a) Market needs and competition assessment

    (b) Buyer awareness and buying habits

    (c) Factors that influence buyer demands

    (d) Cash on hand

    (e) All of the above

    (f) Only (a) and (d)

4. A profit-based pricing strategy is:

    (a) Governed by the desire to maximize financial performance

    (b) Always established based on a fixed markup percentage

    (c) Equivalent to fair market value

    (d) None of the above

5. Strategic objectives, product attributes, demographics, and cost factors are examples of:

    (a) Strategic price planning

    (b) Filters used for calculating pricing

    (c) Factors in calculating fair market value

    (d) None of the above

6. Punch cards and frequent flier miles are examples of:

    (a) Captive product pricing

    (b) Loss leaders

    (c) Inventory control strategies

    (d) Reward pricing

7. Choosing a representative target market, estimating the cost of product runs, and establishing a test budget are methods for:

    (a) Testing the pricing strategies

    (b) Marketing principles

    (c) Cost-factor analysis

    (d) None of the above

8. Penetration pricing strategy is characterized by:

    (a) Competitive analysis

    (b) Low pricing

    (c) Strong customer relationships

    (d) Wide profit margins

9. The downside of skimming strategies is:

    (a) They have a low profit margin

    (b) That skimmable markets attract competitors

    (c) They take a long time to return value

    (d) None of the above

10. Special sales and seasonal pricing are examples of:

    (a) Economic strategy

    (b) Fire sale strategy

    (c) Promotional or discount pricing

    (d) Captive pricing

CHAPTER 8

Incorporating People and Culture

No matter how strong your market planning, pricing, placement, and positioning, people are your magic bullet. How they behave internally and externally speaks volumes about your brand promise and business culture. Young companies have a unique opportunity to consider the expectations, attitudes, and rules that will govern the way people relate inside and beyond the organization before beliefs and behaviors even take root. Mature companies can seize opportunities along the business continuum to assess and shape people attitudes and behavior. Regardless of a company's age, the goal of the organization is to make sure that people accurately and positively reflect the brand. Gaining brand momentum means tapping into people power. That requires attention to the rules that govern relationships and expectations.

Employees, in particular, are purveyors of your brand message. They build products, manage automated technologies, and deliver service. Their performance affects every outcome. While their personal preferences and behavior also are rooted in cultural and family values, their performance reflects your company's culture and beliefs about accountability and results. Both the people who power your organization and the customers who patronize it operate within a framework of cultural and social beliefs as well as personal experiences, perceptions, and preferences. Your job as a marketer is to identify and influence behavior in line with your own corporate culture. Respectful, reliable, and consistent interactions build trust inside organizations.

Branding as a Key Recruitment and Retention Strategy

Why talk about recruitment and retention in a marketing book? Because companies that integrate and align their branding strategy with human resources and operations perform at higher levels. From the broadest perspective, your goal is to maximize opportunities for achieving appropriate matches between your firm's business needs and its employee qualifications.

When a company takes active steps to identify, assess, articulate, cultivate, and communicate a high-performing culture, it builds resilience for long-term success. Every company has a distinct culture that binds its employees through shared vision, knowledge, and experiences. The discipline of anthropology can provide valuable insights into an organization's culture and how a company can apply these concepts to create a culture of high performance.

An organization's culture defines how it sees itself, its relationship to others (e.g., customers, prospects, and strategic partners), and how it conducts its activities on a day-to-day basis. If someone were to ask you to describe your company's culture, what would you say? What images come to mind? What does it feel like to work there? What words would you use? These are not questions for idle contemplation. The answers have serious implications for employee recruitment and retention, brand identity and marketing, as well as daily operations.

A company identifies and communicates what it expects—financial and operational results, as well as the employee behaviors and attitudes necessary to achieve those results—within the context of its unique business culture. The same behaviors in different companies may yield different results. Because employee recruitment is a huge upfront investment of time and resources, and high turnover drains productivity and diverts resources, companies must align their business culture, business objectives, job-specific responsibilities, and skill sets.

It takes a strong brand culture to make people happy. Happy employees are more productive and they reflect well on the brand. In turn, brand performance impacts outcomes for your employees. With surveys, ask employees what they would change about your company and company management. Then integrate their feedback. There are few things worse than asking for advice and not implementing relevant feedback.

Infuse culture-based people strategies into every aspect of employee engagement—from recruitment and hiring, orientation and training, job responsibilities, and account-abilities through performance management and celebration of employee success. The result will be a collaborative mindset built around your core objectives.

Developing People as a Core Marketing Resource

Every employee is a marketing resource for your business, regardless of job title, function, and reporting chain. Every person in your organization can feed the revenue pipeline as a source for business referrals, networking contacts, information about contracting opportunities, and feedback from friends, family, and neighbors.

With every interaction, people create tangible branding impact and consequences for the ultimate success of your business. Every time an employee answers the phone, responds to an e-mail, or interacts in person with a customer or prospect, he or she represents your brand and entire operation. With the power of social media, an unsatisfactory (or unexpected) experience can quickly unravel even a strong brand, leading to organizational crisis. Consider these facts:

- People are often the product in themselves.
- People serve as the bridge in customer relationships.
- People's behavior is felt more strongly than advertising.
- People's passion for the brand (or lack of it) is evident and easily communicated.
- Your people are an important resource for brand differentiation and competitive advantage.

In short, people are a critical component in the marketing mix.

Make your employees a valuable, core marketing resource by educating them on your brand, marketing strategy, and overall business objectives. Armed with information, your people will better identify what type of customers, prospects, and contacts are most appropriate for referral and connections. They also will know exactly what to say about your business to prospects and how to treat and care for your customers.

Engaging your people as problem solvers can create the massive momentum you need to drive organizational mission, culture, and positive change. Here's how:

- Assess the present situation.
- Identify and explore the presence of any gaps influencing success.
- Identify the cause(s) of variation in business or employee performance.
- Close those gaps.

It's your job, as a marketer, to influence organizational success and communication. Help your team communicate the expectations, programs, and processes capable of creating success. Finally, monitor the change process and encourage the organization to adapt as needed.

Culture and Communication

Culture is communicated formally through policies, memos, and business meetings. It is shared informally through behavior. While CEOs and presidents lead company visions, people across the organization make it real. Managers communicate expectations and goals that support strategic directions. Team members implement the daily actions required for success.

Culture is transmitted through mission statements on Web sites and brochures. It is described in sales proposals and discussed at meetings. The most important cultural marker, however, is behavior. Action translates statements, visions, and values into the beliefs, expectations, concrete behaviors, and shared attitudes that reflect real organizational culture. Culture is company behavior in action. Companies must walk the talk for desired culture to take root.

If a company prides itself on a culture of risk taking and innovation, its organizational system and action must be structured to support that cultural value. For example, despite presenting itself as an innovative company, leaders may become so focused on controlling internal systems that they squelch employee creativity. That disconnect between message and action is noticeable to employees and may be perceived outside the organization as well. Without commitment to expressed values, culture begins to erode. When employees perceive changes they don't understand, or when those changes don't match expectations, a culture of pride may shift to one of indifference. That atmosphere affects market results.

Why focus on culture? Business performance depends on it. Whether merging multiple brands, strategizing to grow organically, or working to reinvigorate an ailing brand, your business and marketing decisions must center on performance. People and culture impact performance across the board.

Warning Signs of a Brand Disconnect

Most companies strive to engage and satisfy customers. Some strive to satisfy employees, too. Sometimes they miss the mark. Communications may reflect the level of engagement with your brand. To guard against a disconnect between your brand message and its reality, watch for these signs of impending trouble:

- Every employee you ask about the brand says something different.
- Your customers get the impression that your employees have something more important to do than respond to their needs and requests.
- Employees don't understand how marketing is relevant to daily operations.
- Your prospects have begun to respond to your product or service as a commodity, demonstrating more concern for price than features and benefits.

Assessing Your Own Business Culture

Your company's culture influences competitive advantage. Rather than operate by default, you have the power to choose and nurture a business culture that gives life to your brand, reinforces your marketing messages, and helps employees deliver on your brand promise.

Your first step is to observe business culture in action. Once you know what's happening, you can apply lessons learned to shift people's beliefs, attitudes, and behaviors. Meaningful cultural assessment and development focuses on understanding and controlling the following variables, according to business anthropologist Stephanie Leibowitz.

MONITOR BEHAVIOR

Observe written and unspoken rules governing employee behavior and customer interaction relating to:

- Structures around reporting and communicating
- Internal gatekeepers who control schedules and access
- Open-door policies
- Power hierarchy—top down hierarchy or democratic decision making?
- Emphasis on policy and procedures
- Attention to training and development
- Formality of job descriptions
- Effort to qualify employees or prospects

The behavioral approaches guiding a company are often reflected in their business outcomes. What does your organization's own behavior tell you?

OBSERVE COMMUNICATION

Communication varies in terms of openness, accepted language, frequency of communication, and vehicles for sharing. Observe and monitor the following communication protocols to determine how they influence your business culture:

- Internal newsletters and e-blasts
- Phone conference calls and department meetings
- Instant message programs for internal communicating
- Town meetings with employees
- Shareholder meetings

Companies that don't communicate send a message of indifference. What does your organization communicate about its culture?

NOTICE BELIEFS

Everyone holds beliefs. Inside organizations, people are influenced by what they believe about these things:

- Company vision and goals
- Definition of success
- Standards of ethical and acceptable behavior

They are also influenced by family and social beliefs. Beliefs permeate and perpetuate culture. Beliefs color perception and affect behavior. What beliefs drive your organization?

ASSESS BUSINESS ORGANIZATION

Beliefs and attitudes about business structure define how work is accomplished. In a high performing business culture:

- Individual performance is prized.
- Teamwork is expected.
- Department and division managers clarify expectations around responsibilities, accountabilities, and interactions.

Observing and documenting business organization and workflow will reveal how business mechanics and cultural dynamics relate. How does your company structure exhibit your culture?

ANALYZE BUSINESS PROTOCOLS

How a company operates defines its culture. Business anthropologists look for evidence that a culture has:

- Clarity of expectations about behavior and results
- Examples of the criteria governing goals and processes
- Performance management programs that support strategic and departmental goals
- Protocols for hiring, management, compensation planning, marketing, customer procurement, customer service, and litigation

Assessment of business protocols can help uncover the driving messages, beliefs, and attitudes behind company outcomes. What do your company protocols reveal about your culture?

Meeting the Needs of Internal and External Audiences

Everyone wants the best possible customer base—people and companies who need your services, value your products, and have the wherewithal to pay for them. It's your job as a marketer to scope out the markets with the right companies, market segments, or ethnic cultures to match your business goals and direction. Next, you have to allocate resources to reach the potential clients, channels, and alliance partners that are most likely to respond to your messages and/or buy your products or services.

To assess marketing fit with potential partners, capture information that tells you

- About what your prospect is most concerned
- How your prospect makes buying decisions
- What criteria your prospect uses to evaluate its own customer service
- How your prospect treats its customers
- How your prospect resolves problems
- How your prospect communicates with customers and suppliers (and how often)
- What your prospect values most
- The benefit of doing business with your prospect

When targeting business-to-business (B2B) contracts, make sure that your company's culture and business proposal effectively mirror (or enhance) that of your prospect. Doing so is especially important when sales proposals are being prepared. When in buying mode, decision makers look for evidence of a good fit between the suppliers under consideration and their own company. By researching a prospect's culture, history, and operations, you will be better prepared to present a proposal that demonstrates your commitment to similar values (assuming you hold similar values), your business ethic, and your compatibility with the prospect's processes and operations.

Cultural Marketing

Cultural marketing is the application of knowledge about a culturally defined market to strategies for reaching and influencing the people inside. Cultural marketing may target external groups (e.g., prospects, customers, strategic allies, channel partners, and industry groups) as well as internal groups (e.g., employees and shareholders). Most people associate cultural marketing with strategies to reach specific ethnic groups. However, cultural marketing principles extend to every market segment, because each segment is characterized by the unique attributes that would make it a good fit (or not) for your value proposition.

Whether your target is defined by ethnicity or demographics like age, gender, or economic status, the success of your marketing effort will depend on how well you understand why that segment behaves as it does. When you understand your audience's cultural beliefs, values, and behaviors, you have better information for making marketing decisions.

The Impact of Training on Culture

A brand reputation is shorthand for how people perform. Brands are expressed in product quality, variety, and cost. They communicate values, such as leadership integrity, social responsibility, and philanthropy. Brands also tell your story through customer service, which should be friendly, rapid, and focused on solutions.

Your marketing department may *define* your brand, but your people *control* your brand! Customers relate to brands of companies whose employees treat those customers well, accurately answer their questions, quickly resolve their concerns, and communicate how important each and every one of them is.

> ## CAUTION
>
> Keep in mind that employees are customers, too. Not only do they often buy company products, they also require service from other company members. When your internal service culture is as important as your external reputation, you develop positive internal branding.

INTERNAL BRANDING AS A PEOPLE STRATEGY

Internal branding is an important people strategy that establishes and strengthens your competitive positioning from within. The objectives of an internal branding program are to:

- Connect employees to your brand.
- Cultivate a passionate, highly engaged workforce that helps connect customers to your brand.
- Create a seamless, differentiated experience for internal (and external) customers.
- Maintain your edge in the market (at a minimum), or surpass your competition (if you can).

Positive internal branding yields dramatic results. When employees meet service expectations, customers reward you with business. Consistent, professional behavior is perceived as competence. If you want repeat business, you had better be sure that your people know the process and execute correctly and consistently.

In today's multicultural work environment and global marketplace, internal education is a critical marketing maneuver. Better-informed employees provide better service to customers, prospects, and business partners. This is important not only from a marketing perspective but also from a cost consideration. Money is wasted when employees don't have the education or time to do a job right from the start. Corrective efforts are costly in time, money, and prestige.

Formalized training is a best practice that plays a vital role in establishing, communicating, and reinforcing correct behavior and cultural standards. Training can build the skills of new hires and veteran employees alike. At a minimum, implement the following into your people marketing formula:

- **Orientation program.** In addition to specifying job duties, introduce new hires with a guide to company history and key milestones, business vision and goals, the company culture, expectations, scope of departments, roles and responsibilities, an overview of the business brand, and how the company culture impacts the brand. Teach them their role in branding company culture.

- **Training and development program (for existing employees).** Teach veteran employees how your business defines superior customer service and how that relates to "living the brand." Inform and educate with just-in-time training initiatives about what new products and services are being introduced and how those relate to the employees' jobs. Show them what you need from them to make the endeavor a success.

- **Training need not be costly.** E-learning technologies make training affordable and flexible. Train-the-trainer programs can help ensure that your company continues to evolve as a learning community. When approached strategically, training will help your business to do these things:

  ○ Synchronize brand personality, value, and organizational culture.

  ○ Get employees behind the brand through actions that demonstrate alignment with company, vision, and brand.

  ○ Reinforce and repeatedly explain the brand values and behaviors you want and need for business resilience and sustainability.

COMMUNICATING BRAND INFORMATION TO EMPLOYEES

Communicate about your brand regularly in layered ways, so that messages, language, important facts, and desired outcomes are understood and reinforced. Because people learn and absorb information in different ways, vary your means and methods of communication to ensure that your message will be heard and understood, and encourage learning. Communicate via the following:

- Employee handbooks
- Orientation and training
- Departmental, cross-functional, and/or town hall style meetings

- Literature, Web broadcasts, conference calls to introduce new services and products, or other mission-critical information
- Company intranet
- FAQs (frequently asked questions) on topics including how to answer phones and customer questions (or questions from other team members), and how to resolve customer problems

Keep in mind that when you create opportunities for discussion and questions, you reduce the potential for errors. Open lines of communication help you learn what your employees, prospects, and customers are saying and thinking. When people understand the brand and their impact on it, they become a great resource for market intelligence and building customer loyalty.

Cultivating Employees as Brand Builders

A major marketing goal is to cultivate (and train) your employees as brand ambassadors for your business. The term *ambassador* connotes goodwill and positive dialogue, adding value to your marketing currency. Your employees can better serve as informative ambassadors to the public when they know what's going on, understand the brand personality, and are empowered to share that information in the community. You can help your employees become brand ambassadors by doing these things:

- Engaging your employees in the process as soon as they are hired
- Tapping into employees as a focus group for ideas and insights
- Establishing brand communication standards, and monitoring them
- Communicating clearly, consistently, and often
- Empowering employees to resolve customer problems while demonstrating the appropriate brand behaviors
- Creating a culture of trust and empowering employees to build long-lasting relationships with customers
- Creating and sharing a policy on employee use of Twitter, LinkedIn, Facebook, and other social media tools
- Demonstrating the brand-serving behavior that you want
- Providing success stories that document how and why follow-through on the brand promise grows the business
- Acknowledging and rewarding employees who exhibit your best brand behaviors

Strategic communication strategies break down barriers. Blended with your overall human resource strategy, these tactics will support cultural competence across the organization and beyond.

Quiz

1. Business culture:

    (a) Is always intentional

    (b) Is evidenced by beliefs, attitudes, and behaviors

    (c) Is passive and reactive

    (d) Costs a lot of money

2. Culture is demonstrated through:

    (a) Leadership and employee actions

    (b) Mission, vision, and values statements

    (c) Communication methods

    (d) Business protocol

    (e) All of the above

3. Companies that set a course, assign accountability, communicate, focus on quality, and build morale are:

    (a) Marketing geniuses

    (b) Organized

    (c) Mission centered

    (d) Employee-centric

    (e) Preparing to merge

4. Cultural marketing is:

    (a) Something that belongs in diversity training

    (b) The application of knowledge about a target market's culture to strategies for reaching and interesting target audiences

    (c) Always focused on ethnicity

    (d) None of the above

5. You can make employees a core marketing resource by:

    (a) Educating them on your brand, your marketing strategy, and your overall business objectives

    (b) Sending them outside with sandwich boards

    (c) Adding them into the marketing budget

    (d) Embracing telemarketing

    (e) All of the above

6. It is important to assess cultural fit with another business because:

   (a) It will help you qualify your prospect.

   (b) It will provide information on what your prospect values.

   (c) It will save money in the long run.

   (d) Only (a) and (b)

   (e) All of the above

7. People are considered part of the marketing mix because:

   (a) They contribute to a company's bottom line.

   (b) They use training and development resources.

   (c) They work for the marketing department.

   (d) They are a source of differentiation and competitive advantage.

   (e) All of the above

8. When customers experience results based on expectations you have set, you have:

   (a) Made your marketing case

   (b) Infused money into your marketing engine

   (c) Delivered on your brand promise

   (d) Asked for customer satisfaction ratings

   (e) All of the above

9. Because employee recruitment and high turnover drains productivity and diverts resources:

   (a) Companies should develop benefits programs

   (b) Managers should regularly review employee profiles

   (c) Employers must communicate about products

   (d) Employers must choose business protocols

   (e) Companies must align their business culture, business objectives, and job-specific responsibilities and skill sets

10. Sales revenues, the ability to meet financial goals, divisional results, market share, customer feedback, employee morale, time to value, and return on investment are:

    (a) Important aspects of a marketing plan

    (b) Bottom-line goals

    (c) Topics marketing professionals must teach to employees

    (d) Key performance indicators to reflect the impact of people and productivity

PART THREE

Mastering Marketing Communication

CHAPTER 9

Promoting Products and Services

Product development and promotion are linked by the same rationale. Product development hinges on the desire to fulfill unmet needs in the marketplace or to fill those needs in new ways. Promotion publicizes products, services, solutions, and events that address perceived needs and provide consumers with an incentive to buy.

Product design often involves expansive research and development teams, reams of marketing research, and millions of dollars. Or it may be the brainchild of a single "wow" moment in the mind of an everyday inventor. Either way, promotion helps bridge the gap between product concept and purchase. A strong promotional campaign can influence product life cycle (i.e., how long it stays relevant) by swaying customers' preferences. In turn, that can impact sales volume and sustainability.

This chapter focuses on the most essential ingredient of product promotion—marketing communication—while providing insight to the kinds of promotions that get results. Communication promotes products and services to mass markets as well as tiny niches, over the Internet, in print, and by word of mouth. Grasping the spoken, written, and visual rules of marketing communication will help enhance your marketing promotion, whether it is a free gift, reward program, coupon, special event, or sale.

Product Marketing

Whether your company is developing a new product, choosing products to carry, or using marketing information to adapt features and messages about products already on the market, your goal is to boost sales. As a marketer, you need information on actual quality, perceived quality, pricing comparisons, features, options, and packaging needs. You also need to know how your product performs after purchase and its overall impact on buyers' lives.

Your marketing choices depend on where your product sits on the life-cycle continuum between product entry and decline. Your efforts to generate product demand and boost sales require knowledge of economic conditions, buyer mindsets, industry actions, and technical innovation. The information you gather will help you differentiate your products. Focusing on communication and promotional strategies will help you differentiate and maximize your marketing of products and services.

Influencing Buyers

Marketing promotions are designed to influence opinions and move people through the buying cycle, as shown in Figure 9.1. Advertisers, celebrities, journalists, community leaders, friends, and family all have the power to sway opinion. You can influence consumers through novel promotions that capture attention, or you can build brand buzz virally. Here's how:

- Define your target market.
- Choose words and graphic images relevant to them.
- Identify where and how they get their information.
- Choose the marketing vehicles used most by your audience (e.g., Internet, word-of-mouth strategies, newspapers, television, radio, brochures, and/or newsletters).
- Craft and package a relevant message.
- Test, evaluate, and confirm your message.
- Promote, promote, promote.

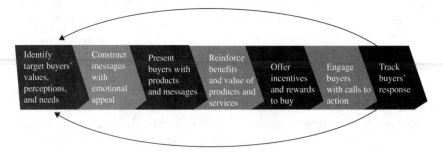

Figure 9.1 Buyer promotion cycle—action steps.

Influence Communication

The purpose of marketing communication is to share information or to influence others in some way. Hypnotic suggestion is perhaps the most prominent example of influence communication.

Savvy salespeople and marketers also have mastered techniques that tap into belief systems and figure out what motivates buyers. These marketers shape their messages in relation to both the prospective buyer's mindset and his or her needs.

When marketers set out to influence others through communication, the goal is to help them see things through carefully chosen filters. Everyone notices what they are trained to see based on their own needs, perceptions, and beliefs. Consumer marketing experts exploit this knowledge to capture attention and tap into the emotion of potential buyers. As a marketer, your job is to fire up brand relevance and command notice; you've got to connect with your prospects' senses, needs, and desires in ways that will influence their choices.

Marketers create perceptual frameworks that train brains to attend to brands and products. Choose information and images that will help your prospective customers connect the dots. For example, the Pepsi Refresh Project uses sparkling bubbles. York Peppermint Patties, a Hershey product, are wrapped in silver foil, with blue lettering, which conveys the icy-cool sensation the product sells. A restaurant may give every guest a York Peppermint Pattie along with the check. This promotion (giving a gift) is very effective. People love food promotions, and this little extra item leaves customers remembering a homey, friendly dining experience. In this case, the promotion has come after the sale. It works as a reward, providing incentive for a return visit.

Influencing Perception through Creative Design

Visuals, metaphors, product stories, and testimonials all create mental maps. Once you know what to look for, you'll become a pro at choosing visuals that will influence buying patterns. You can do that with effective design. The tips in the following paragraphs will provide a guide for assessing your design, whether you are working on your own or with a graphic designer.

When faced with designing a logo, brochure, print ad, or Web site, it often helps to look at other Web sites and print designs for inspiration. Take time to note how others use fonts, color, size, photographs, illustrations, and overall organization to reinforce their brand image. In the meantime, use the following tips as a guide for thinking about and creating designs with impact.

STANDING OUT

Unlike a chameleon, whose best trick is blending in, a good brand's magic is to stand out. For example, when scientists revealed that children attend better to contrast and bright colors,

R&D teams in the toy industry sparked a whole new trend. Baby items previously designed in pale pinks and blues, pastel greens, and soft yellows suddenly sported bold black-and-white patterns and brightly colored dots, lines, and swirls. These new products stood a world apart from gentle pastels. By acknowledging the natural power of contrast, companies such as Baby Einstein hit the ground running with products designed to engage babies.

What kicks your own brain into high gear? Is it meeting with the unexpected or the unusually sublime? If you are, say, a graphic designer, your choice of fonts, shapes, colors, headings, subheads, and column width will trigger reactions. So will your choice of sizes, photos, illustrations, and style, such as straight-edged photos or silhouetted montages, paper choices, and the angle of graphic elements. You can cultivate your own visual flair to stand out in a unique way. It just takes practice.

ELEMENTS OF A GREAT LOGO

One terrific exercise for developing a brand logo is to observe what works for other companies. Open almost any magazine and you'll find an ad that includes multiple logos that represent product sponsors or affiliate partners. What do those logos tell you? How do they make you feel? What story do you hear in your head when you see each one?

Before designing your own logo, write down the message that you want people to get when they see it. Take it a step further, and tap into the minds of colleagues, clients, and even former clients. Ask them what comes to mind when they see or hear your company's name. Take that information as a foundation for creating (or revising) your logo.

The following design tips will help you judge not only your logo but also other print designs. After you decide on your message, choose design elements that will communicate accordingly. Your logo must be easy to interpret, and it must contain enough contrast to catch the eye. It also has to match the personality of your brand.

Not every logo requires a visual icon. Some logos contain only a name with a strategically chosen font. As brands become very well known, an icon alone can communicate who they are; for example, look at Target, IBM, and Apple. I also recommend a logo that conveys what you *do* as well as who you *are*. Sometimes, you can do that through the art itself or with an accompanying tagline.

When creating from scratch or tweaking your existing logo, start by thinking about how you want to be seen in the market. Do you want your product or service to be perceived as fun and current, solid and stable, creative, strategic, expensive, durable, casual or formal, lean and green, sumptuous, health-conscious, or decadent? Whichever image and position you choose, make sure your logo design is a good match, as seen in Figure 9.2. Give it a lot of thought. The logo will be with you for a long time.

EVALUATING CREATIVE DESIGN WITH CONFIDENCE

With experience, you'll build confidence in your design awareness. Confidence is learned, one small step at a time. With each new success, you will come to decisions more quickly,

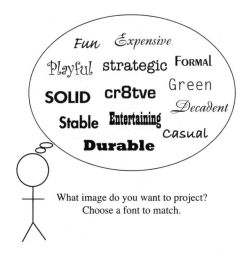

Figure 9.2   Logotypes.

with less angst. I have yet to meet a small business owner who has not agonized to some degree over logo decisions and creative representations. Because logos are a company's most recognizable icon, it pays to get it right the first time. Very few people welcome the idea of having to revisit their logo designs. Besides the considerable expense of reprinting materials, uniforms, signage, menus, and promotional materials, as well as revising Web sites and other informational sources, every logo project is wrapped in considerable emotional energy. For most companies, going through the logo design once or twice is enough.

INFLUENCING PERCEPTION

Sometimes market factors are out of your control. But how you are perceived in the market is your choice. Instead of bemoaning the economy, take an extraordinary step forward by choosing to focus your time, energy, and resources on just the marketing factors that are under your influence or control. All you need is a plan of action, a resolve to keep learning what you need to know, a fire in your belly to find the resources you need to grow your company, and the vision to choose and mold the perception you want for your brand. Start planning now with the right steps.

WORKING WITH FONTS

When you are designing a logo, brochure, print ad, or Web site, the fonts you choose give your artwork personality and meaning. A *font* is the full character set of a typeface. Each typeface has a specific style, such as roman or plain, bold, heavy, italic, and bold italic. To decide which fonts are right for your project, ask yourself what you are trying to convey.

Be aware that some fonts that look great in print can be difficult to read on the Web. You can find hundreds of fonts on the Web; for example, visit www.fonts.com or www.adobe.com.

Fonts may vary in image quality, and not all fonts are standard in size across the alphabet. Examine fonts you are considering to make sure that they are consistent in height and width, and that they have the special characters you need (some fonts don't have quotation marks or exclamation points!). Font consistency will help ensure overall graphic integrity between your logo and print collateral.

There are two types of fonts: *serif* and *sans serif.* Serif fonts are embellished with fine lines or curves that finish off the main strokes of each letter. Straight fonts, without serifs are called sans serif fonts. Serif fonts (e.g., Times New Roman and Palatino) are the easiest ones to read in large blocks of text, which accounts for their frequent use in books and documents with long text passages. They are also considered to be relatively formal, making them popular for academic publications, invitations, business announcements, annual reports, and the body of press releases.

HEADLINES

Many graphic artists choose sans serif fonts for headlines and subheads, because sans serif fonts work well in short doses. Combining a sans serif headline with a serif body text makes for the kind of contrast that stimulates the eye and guides the reader by signaling a difference in subject matter or importance. You can use the same font family for heads and subheads, and signal variations in the levels of your message by varying font size or using italics; typically, headline size varies with level of importance and detail. Choose fonts that match the mood of your brand, and inspire the brain to respond in the way you intend. Going for an elegant look? Choose a thinner font. Looking to communicate strength? Choose a thicker font.

CAUTION

Limit the number of fonts you use in a design. Too many fonts make artwork appear busy and cluttered. One or two fonts that vary in weight, thickness, and style will create the contrast you need for a logo or for an entire book.

USING SHAPES TO REINFORCE CONCEPTS

Shapes in graphic designs can be solid, thick, square, round, bold, or subtle. Circles, ellipses, squares, rectangles, rhombus, spirals, stars, and custom designs can be created with vector art programs. One such program, Adobe Illustrator, is designed for drawing and enables a trained user to create custom shapes. Some word-processing programs, such as Microsoft Word, also have a drawing toolbar that allows you to select predesigned shapes. You can find shapes to use in your designs in clip-art books and compact disks or at Web sites that carry stock images. For example, visit www.istockphoto.com for affordable, royalty-free art.

Table 9.1   Common Shapes and What They Convey to Readers

Shape	Representation
Square	Solid, conservative, practical
Rhombus	Forward momentum, directional
Wiggly line	Creative
Diamond	Royal
Spade	Good luck, death, direction
Heart	Compassion, love, connection
Link	Networking, connectivity

Shapes can enhance your artwork by calling attention to columns of text. You can place a round- or hard-edged rectangle of color behind text to highlight it as a sidebar. You also can use a shape as the basis for a logo design. When choosing a shape, think about what that shape conveys to the readers (see Table 9.1).

As you consider your graphics, pick a shape that will clearly convey your intended concept or emotion. Once you've merged it successfully with type, and you have a design concept or selection of concepts that satisfy you, you may want to give your designs to a focus group and collect feedback on what your design means to them.

COMMUNICATING WITH COLOR

Use color judiciously and often. One effective tool to help you select color is the Pantone Matching System, or PMS. The Pantone brand, which supplies printing inks, has become the industry standard for color management. The PMS color system enables graphic artists to communicate about color using a standard language. Pantone offers a selection of more than a thousand precalibrated colors. Using this system, Macintosh and other computers can render predictable colors for designers to evaluate. Your printer can show you PMS charts, as well as charts from other ink companies.

Color and Culture

As with language, colors take on varying meanings in different cultures. When marketing to specific ethnic communities or worldwide, learn what colors mean beyond the borders of the home country. In the United States, for example, blue exemplifies trust. Red and orange convey passion, power, sun, and fire. Yellow helps express light and optimism. Purple is used to connote royalty or mourning. Black communicates power, and green has come to represent the environment—but also money, life, and jealousy. These colors can mean entirely different things in other cultures and countries, so choose colors carefully. Yellow may express caution in American culture, while in China, it may connote royalty. While red depicts danger in western culture, it is used to convey purity in India.

COLUMN WIDTH

Column size makes a difference in a graphic presentation, too. A change in a column width, for example, signals the eye that something has changed. It can indicate that a totally different story is beginning or just a different perspective is being given. Glance through a newspaper and notice how relatively narrow the columns are. Narrow columns expedite reading because of the low number of characters per line and the perception that there is less to read. Wide-set columns are reserved for more leisurely reads. Create contrast by sectioning your page. Try a three-column article above a four-column article, or a double-column article over a triple-column article.

SIZE

Size can indicate importance and influence perception. In your graphic media, use fonts, photos, and text in unexpected ways to attract attention and add that special wow factor. Grand scales can give even a traditional font or image a very contemporary look.

PHOTOS AND ILLUSTRATIONS

The art you choose for your publications, icons, Web site, or other media says volumes about how you see the world and how you want the world to see you. For a traditional look, try a border around photos and illustrations. If you're shooting for a cutting-edge presentation, try silhouetted images (i.e., trimmed around the subject matter with the background cut out), or create photo collages by layering and composing multiple photos to look like one image.

RESIZING

Size and scale are a great way to add impact. Because photos and illustrations are rarely sized to meet available brochure and ad space, you have to resize them. Take care not to distort proportions when scaling to fit. If your space is deep and narrow but your photo is short and wide, do not stretch it to fit a different scale. Distorted images are definitely unprofessional looking. Try scaling an important part of your photo or illustration to fit your space, and crop out the rest. When scaling digital photos, remember that image size (i.e., resolution) is a major factor in print clarity. Black-and-white photos need to be printed at 150 dpi (dots per inch) at print size. In general, color photos should be 350 dpi, and line art should be scanned at 600 to 1,200 dpi for best results.

PERMISSION AND COPYRIGHTS

When including photos of employees, patients, clients, or others in business materials make sure that you have permission to use their image. Have employees sign a blanket release as part of the hiring process. Always keep a release form on hand.

The rule of thumb is that if a person has a reasonable expectation of being photographed—for instance, at a public outing—there is no personal infringement, and you should not need special permission to use his or her image. But photographic subjects observed in a private or semiprivate setting and who are unaware of the photographer have every expectation of privacy; they should not be photographed without permission. When in doubt, allow caution to reign, and use a photo permission form. Also, when using copyrighted photos or illustrations, be sure to procure permission and include proper attribution.

PAPER CHOICES

When choosing paper for brochures, sell sheets, letterhead, envelopes, postcards, business reply mailings, or invitations, you'll want to think about what you are communicating to whom and how you will look when you do it. Consider color, weight, and finish. Bright white paper stock helps ensure that your colors will translate crisply. Printing on colored papers, such as cream or green, can make your photos appear muddier than they would if they were on white stock.

The most popular coated sheets are gloss, matte, and silk. Some paper manufacturers offer smooth and super smooth options. You also can purchase recycled paper, which is more expensive than other paper, but it's a good choice for environmentally conscious companies. If you are unsure, ask your printer for advice.

For a sleek look, go for high gloss over uncoated sheets. Visit a local printer to look at paper samples. Printers keep books of paper and will send you a sample book or sheets to choose from. Uncoated paper is less expensive than coated sheets. It typically absorbs more ink, leaving colors flat, by comparison.

PAPER WEIGHT AND STOCK

Paper is measured by the pound, and represented in spec sheets (product specifications) with a pound sign (#). Most papers come in text (lighter) and cover (heavier) weights. Printers often refer to paper as "stock." Cover stocks are similar to postcard stock and typically vary from 60# to 110# in weight but can range up to 130#. Most trifold brochures are printed on 80# coated stock.

If you are offering a premium service and expect people to keep your brochures for a while, print on a heavier stock, such as 100# text, for greater durability and cachet. When printing a larger sheet, where the individual page size runs 8.5 by 11 inches (8.5" × 11"), I recommend 100# or 110# stock to give it more bulk. When your budget permits, add varnish or lamination, for extra pop. *Varnish* is a print coating that finishes and seals colors. This is especially important when printing surfaces in blue, black, and red, which tend to smudge if left uncoated. Varnish speeds drying and locks in color. Varnish is also important when you are using heavy ink coverage across most of the sheet or sheets. Another nice touch is a spot varnish or spot laminate, used only on photos while leaving the text area unvarnished. Or you can varnish the text as well. UV (ultraviolet) coating is a deluxe varnish, noticeably richer, and can be applied as either an all-over coating, or as a spot varnish, on photos and/or text.

PRINTED PREMIUMS (GIVEAWAYS)

Promotional product companies print millions of giveaways every year. Advertising promotions also contribute to logo recognition. They sport contact information for companies as diverse as defense suppliers, local hardware stores, medical practices, and doll manufacturers. Promotional vendors print on products ranging from pens and magnets to privately labeled coffee cans, mugs, garments, tote bags, portfolios, antistress balls, laser lights, and even hot-air balloons!

ORGANIZATION

It's more than text that drives a successful brochure. A well-conceived, ecologically sound framework guides your readers' eyes to move economically through your literature and speed them to the salient points.

BULLETS

Bullets and fonts in printed and Web materials guide the eye and break up large segments of text for easier visual and mental digestion. They help

- Keep brochures tight and crisp
- Capture attention and enhance comprehension

When organizing your print and Web literature, pay attention to the way eyes normally follow a page, from the top left to the bottom right.

PLACEMENT OF ELEMENTS

Consider size and placement in tandem. Whether designing a logo or an illustration, be aware that at some point an artistic element may need to fit into a small space or a narrow column. Wider logos may look great on a page by themselves, but they may be tough to fit on the front of a 3.5-inch-wide brochure. Proportion counts, too. When you make logos taller, you need to make them wider as well. If your type is small by comparison to the logo's visual icon, it may become illegible when reduced to fit on a business card, pen, or other promotional product.

WHITE SPACE

To keep your brochure looking good, remember that less is more. Use white space as liberally as possible. It doesn't have to be white, but it does have to be empty. Well-placed empty space creates natural breaks for eye relief. The trick with white space is to leave it open to the ends of a page. Be careful not to trap white space in the center of your document.

GRAPHIC STANDARDS

Planning is key. Think about all the possible applications of your artwork. Before approving your logo, decide how small or large you can print it. Many companies create a graphic standards manual to ensure consistency of logo application, fonts, headlines, text choices, and imagery across print and electronic (Web-based) collateral.

These manuals document processes and make it easy for employees, new hires, and vendors to represent your brand elements in line with your specifications. Writing a graphic standards manual need not be complicated. Simply specify the ways in which your logo can be used. For example, you may require that there always is at least an inch of clear space around it. You also can specify font and size and any rules you want to govern use of body and headline text, colors, paper, and placement.

By this point, you've got a pretty good idea of what to consider when designing graphic elements.

Communicating Across Visual Channels

Your ability to establish and reinforce your brand relies on the consistent application of your message across text and visual channels. Your brochures; booklets; sell sheets; newsletters for employees, clients, or investors; letters; fliers; e-mail; print or Web ads; videos; and blogs or podcasts should be visually consistent and convey the same message to your audience. Aim for instant recognition of all communications.

CREATING BROCHURES AND SELL SHEETS

While logos are all about capturing interest and notoriety, brochures are used to build credibility and sales. Printed materials can be expensive. A brochure distributed in a "goody bag" at a trade show is likely to land in the circular file. But a brochure used judiciously and appropriately can be effective as a leave-behind or follow-up mailing to reinforce your brand message. After you've met a qualified prospect at a networking function, providing a brochure or individual sell sheet is a nice touch. Include it in an envelope with a personal note, and you're on your way.

Copy Issues

Brochures should stimulate a conversation, phone call, or other connection. So never put everything about your company in that one document. When deciding how much content to include in a brochure, remember that your objective is to differentiate your products and services. Focus on communicating value and benefits.

Also decide how much information belongs on a page. If you are preparing a sales document, you'll want to provide compelling information, but in doses small enough to make readers want to contact you for more information. Don't write a book. After the sale, you can provide a technical manual, if needed. This will help you respect your prospect's time. But, if you partner with other companies, you can add credibility and widen your appeal by including a list of your affiliations, strategic alliances, and/or business partnerships.

If you are designing a patient or client information brochure, as is the case with today's growing base of wellness firms, think about what information your readers need most, and answer as many questions as you can. When educating clients, more may be better. When selling, less is more. But, always be sure to include these things:

- A brief statement about what you do and why it is relevant
- The benefits and value of your services
- How and why your services differ from others in your market

By differentiating yourself and clearly stating your value, you will teach readers why they should become, or remain, connected with you.

Whether planning a brochure or Web site, it's important to know something about the people who will read it. If you target seniors, consider larger, less complex fonts. Large fonts are also good for audiences who use English as a second language. Hospitals, health-care providers, and social service agencies have guidelines for communicating to individuals with low literacy. Consider the reading level of your target audience when composing materials.

When writing for sales documents, keep in mind three things:

1. People do not like the sense that they are being sold.
2. Readers want information quickly; they have limited time.
3. People are interested in what is relevant to them, not to your company.

So, the first rule of brochure writing is to make it relevant to audience needs. The second rule is to use simple, easy-to-read language. Pepper it with occasional, unexpected (but familiar) words. And finally, write to be understood. Before printing your brochures, always test them with a few people in your target audience. Integrate their feedback as needed.

Cost-Saving Considerations

If you're wondering about costs for brochures and sell sheets and need more information, call your local printer or visit an online service such as Vistaprint.com, FoldersExpress.com, or Humongoussavings.com. Ordering 1,000 copies of a simple trifold brochure may cost about $300, but the price could be more than $2,500 if multicolor printing and lamination are used. Some printing companies are more expensive to use than are others because of differentials in overhead costs. When choosing a company at which to print, ask what kind(s) of printing that firm can do cost effectively. For some, two-color runs are better; at others, better value is offered on four-color runs. For short runs (under 500 pieces) digital printing usually beats the cost of conventional printing. Also be aware that many printers may subcontract orders to other vendors to get the best value for you and for them. Knowing your print costs ahead of time will help you get the most out of your design options.

Using Your Brochure or Sell Sheet

Send literature only after determining who needs it and why. Doing so signals to prospects that you want to send them only those materials most relevant to them. Remember that you can use videos, YouTube posts, DVD formats, and Web sites as electronic brochures. You often can get more views for less money with audio and video than with print runs. Here are some suggestions:

- Distribute literature at trade shows, sales launches, new-employee orientation, investor gatherings, networking meetings, business meetings, and community events.
- Mail literature upon request.
- Repurpose your brochure into a PowerPoint presentation, talking points for speaking engagements, sales calls, or Webinars.
- Educate and inform prospects and customers.
- Stay top of mind.

Evidence

Sometimes branding is about tooting your own horn, but your message is so much more effective when you back it up with evidence. Statistics, such as how many people you've served, years in business, research results, and other metrics relevant to your industry will help you build credibility and give people solid reasons to choose you.

Call to Action

Be sure to tell people what you want them to do after reading your literature (e.g., visit your Web site, make a phone call, or request an appointment). Always include contact information for the company and key people: name, address, phone, fax, and e-mail addresses. When possible, turn literature into a direct response system by including a reply postcard or tear-off. Then evaluate, use, and catalog your feedback before entering it into a company database.

Consistency

If you create a series of related brochures, use similar layout and colors for all of them so they look like they belong to the same family. One option to consider is a service-oriented brochure that focuses on both client needs and industry standards. For example, detail the benefits of different product features, and include a table that helps readers decide how and what to choose. You might offer a brochure about how to select a company, such as a home companion agency or accounting firm, and help walk people through the decision process.

PUTTING THE NEWS IN NEWSLETTERS

When clients don't see you or hear from you, they move to the next visible source. Whether delivered by print or e-mail, a newsletter or article can help educate and engage customers. It also may inspire them to want to know more about your company or to become more involved with it. After growing steadily in the first five years, one small equipment company added a monthly newsletter to its marketing plan. Along with most small businesses, the firm was in continual brand development, working on one block at a time, according to budget and flexing with each new bit of knowledge. The newsletter helped the firm stay engaged with clients, as the brand matured.

Engaging Stakeholders with Newsletters

Newsletters are a great way to stay connected. Send them to your board of directors, investors, political leaders, potential or current strategic alliance partners, customers, prospects, and other stakeholders. To broaden your newsletter audience, try asking business colleagues and friends in other companies to contribute articles to your newsletter. This strategy creates opportunities to distribute your news in other venues (e.g., your friend's office or networking group), or to publish that newsletter or distribute it to their offices.

Naming Your Newsletter

Give your newsletter a simple name that is easy to recognize. A familiar name that arrives monthly or quarterly can position you as a resource in your community. Whenever possible, choose a name for your newsletter that reflects the work or mission of your organization.

Cost-Effective Newsletter Distribution

To make your newsletter distribution as cost effective as possible, consider the following:

- **Print run.** Cost efficiency with printing usually starts with runs of 1,000 or more: the larger your run, the lower your cost per sheet. Since printing costs are largely front loaded on print set up and overhead, paper costs represent a smaller piece of that pie.

- **Color.** Newsletters can be very effective in one-color or two-color versions, especially if they are well designed from the standpoints of organization, font weight, and space.

- **Delivery.** While the current trend is toward delivery of publications online, for many people there is no substitute for touch. Electronic media packs a punch too, and it can be cost effective—if it reaches your audience. When developing an e-mail newsletter, use a service that offers a link to opt in or unsubscribe. To stay on the safe side of Internet law, provide links that allow recipients to unsubscribe.

- **Content.** Standardize your newsletters so they become instantly recognizable and easy to navigate. Doing so will help you build a base of loyal readers. Appropriate newsletter sections include these things:

  - Relevant, big, and/or breaking news on the cover
  - Contents list; this belongs either on the cover or inside the left page
  - Special message from the president or CEO
  - Ongoing columns and features
  - Publicity of upcoming events and new business lines
  - A client-driven section; including questions posed by clients or other readers allows you to respond as the expert, and it helps you stay on top of changing client concerns
  - Calendar

Today's media market is marked by clutter. Some people receive hundreds of e-mails every day (not to mention the paperwork that lands on their desks), and even the best of clients can read only a finite amount. When distributing a newsletter via e-mail, remember that people will scroll down only so far, so distill your information for maximum attention and put the most important information at the top.

WRITTEN COMMUNICATIONS

A single communication will not work for every circumstance or cultural group. Map out your communications plan to help identify issues and smooth out rough spots before you even begin writing. Doing so will help you think through what and how you need to communicate for a particular project.

When planning, consider the action items and any dependencies that may influence the success of your communication. If your deadline depends on an undefined product completion date or the approval of a traveling executive, think about what items are in your control and how you will kick your influencing skills into high gear to make sure you meet your deadlines and communication objectives. Be clear about when and why you need information so that those on whom your project depends will be positioned to respond appropriately and in timely fashion.

It is possible that your communication will have only one key message. That's fine. But if you have multiple issues to address, always explain how they relate to one another, if at all, and why each issue matters. When writing, imagine that you are the host of a customer-focused talk radio show, broadcasting on WIIFM—the What's In It For Me station. If you always answer that question for your listeners, they will tune in to what you have to say.

So, how do you make sure your written communication has sufficient brand muscle? Use a sample communications checklist (see Figure 9.3).

WORKING WITH ADS, VIDEOS, BLOGS, AND PODCASTS, AND ARTICLES

The same rules apply whether you are writing copy for ads, video scripts, blogs, or podcasts, or whether you are submitting articles to an e-zine, blog, or Web site. Article marketing has gained in popularity, by comparison to newsletters, both for its ability to communicate information and to promote the presence of the content expert. Whatever your medium, first define your goals and set your intentions:

- Tease out a response and invite a call to action.

- Inform a client about a new product offer.

- Communicate a change in business direction.

- Educate about a consumer concern, health issue, or industry trend.

- Encourage readers or listeners to sign up for your regular e-newsletter, blog, or podcast, RSS feed or other content.

Please respond with a Y (yes) or N (no) within the box.

❏ Is my content relevant and timely?

❏ Does this publication customize information to meet the expectations and special interest of our anticipated readers?

❏ Does it reflect and respect the business culture of our organization?

❏ Is it comprehensive enough to answer questions and concerns?

❏ Is it clear, easy to read, and easy to understand?

❏ Is the sentence structure and word length appropriate to the reading level of our audience?

❏ Is the font size legible?

❏ Does it adequately reflect benefits and value wherever appropriate?

❏ Does it meet our purpose or intention?

❏ Does it support the promise of our brand?

❏ Is it creative and/or scientific, as needed?

❏ Is it accurate? Have I checked all facts and claims?

❏ Is it consistent with our other messages and communications?

❏ Did we include data and/or evidence to back up all claims?

❏ Is it honest?

❏ Is it complete? Is there anything missing?

❏ What would make this publication even better?

❏ Did I spell-check and proofread?

❏ Did I have a second person spell-check and proofread?

Figure 9.3 Communications checklist.

WRITING A COMMANDING AD

Start with intent. Do the following, whether your ad will print or post on the Web:

1. Plan your ad by deciding what you want readers to feel, think, and do.

2. Draft ad copy that communicates your message.

3. Pare down your copy to the least number of words possible to communicate your message.

4. Write your headline; headlines should be clever, clear, crisp, and short.

5. Pair your text with appropriate graphics (you learned what makes for attractive design in the previous section) that are expertly scaled for the size and shape of your ad space.

6. Check your work. Engage a proofreader, if one is needed.

PLANNING VIDEO SCRIPTS

Video can be a powerful marketing tool, and sites like YouTube have proven that even homegrown videos can enjoy an almost unlimited reach when they tee up a human emotion and serve a purpose. When search optimized, videos can help you connect with target and niche audiences and expand your options for reaching buyers with different learning styles. The right creative approach can engage young people and senior audiences alike. Knowing what will work in video comes down to knowing your audience—the heart of every marketing endeavor. When scripting your video, determine perspective. Decide whether your message is best served by a narrator or by actors. Will you write it yourself, or will you hire a script writer? If so, where will you find one? The International Association of Business Communicators (IABC) is a great resource for writers and marketing experts, and it has chapters across the country (check out www.iabc.com).

Your script should be only as long as needed to convey your message. Many business videos are three to five minutes in length. For more comprehensive educational videos, consider several short modules on the same DVD. That way, viewers can choose the segments most relevant to them, or they can watch the entire DVD straight through in one sitting. Video scripts, like all other marketing communications, need to be these things:

- Relevant to viewers' issues and needs
- Culturally sensitive (honoring your own business culture while respecting the cultural concerns of your audience)
- Accurate
- Creative and engaging

When developing your script, ask yourself: Are there metaphors that work well as anecdotes? Will they translate well visually, without seeming contrived or clichéd?

USE OF METAPHOR

Metaphors stimulate visual images and memories, and they often have the power to reveal beliefs and move people toward perceptual shifts. Therapists employ metaphor to help patients see what they may resist acknowledging consciously. While processing external metaphors, people make subconscious mental leaps to their own personal situations. Metaphors help convey meaning by telling stories that connect with the writer's intended meaning. They often communicate through fantasy. Advertising communications are designed to inspire fantasy and often employ metaphor. They help us imagine desired outcomes and connect to real ways of achieving them.

Standards of Excellence

Your communications are fundamental to how others perceive your business. The quality, accuracy, consistency, and clarity of your written and oral (presentation) communications indicate how you operate your business and meet customer needs. People will assume that if you are sloppy in communications (e.g., are ungrammatical, allow misspellings, don't fact-check, and provide low-quality visuals), you will exhibit the same lack of attention to product and service promises. In addition, the integrity and recognition of your brand depends on consistent use of your logo, tag/service lines, and association with other brands.

With the expansion of technology, you must monitor an increasingly large communications landscape. The best practice is to create a marketing standards manual that every employee uses as a reference for your company's communications. Keep in mind that consistency and accuracy in communications applies to internal (i.e., employees') communication as well. When you communicate the rules that govern content and creative materials, you reinforce appropriate application and reduce the likelihood of error and noncompliance. Keep in mind that communication occurs in a multitude of vehicles: written materials (e.g., collateral, white papers, press releases, hardcopy and electronic newsletters, blogs, and internal memos), oral communications (e.g., presentations and client service), and videos (e.g., television commercials, Internet promotions, educational films, and b-roll, which is production slang for rolling images in the background, while the narrators are telling the story. The background itself is often shot without a voice over, or is shown without the voice over that was created during the videotaping.)

At a minimum, standards of communications excellence should address the following:

- **Statement of company policy on communication standards.** Explain why the policy is important to the success of the brand and company; the role of employee compliance in brand recognition and, ultimately, the company's success; and what employees should do if they see inaccurate or unapproved use of the company's logo, tagline, or other materials by a third party (e.g., a competitor).

- **Logo.** Specify the logo's size, font, and color (some businesses have approved both color and black-and-white versions, to provide flexibility in printing choices); placement; approved use for advertising, video (including YouTube), DVDs, letterhead, posters and fliers, e-mail, sponsorships, cosponsorships, and endorsements of others' products and services, and so on; *un*approved use; and the approval process for use by strategic partners and alliances (e.g., use on truck signage, clothing, and food and beverage containers).

- **Style/word usage.** Specify use of punctuation, bullets, hyphens, footnotes, quotations, numbering system for tables and graphs, and so on; preferred words to use to describe company features, benefits, and value; and words not to use (e.g., some industries, such as accounting, do not use the word *guarantee*, which has legal implications; similarly, attorneys should avoid use of the word *specialize* in literature unless they have completed specialty certification).

- **Fonts.** For all media, list fonts to be used for the document body and headings and subheadings; mention when it is appropriate to use bold and italic fonts and other typefaces.

- **Use of visuals.** Discuss protection and use of visuals owned and designed by the company; also mention guidelines for purchase, use, and attribution of third-party visuals.

- **Document formatting.** For collateral, newsletters, and other print and online materials, indicate margins; spacing (whether single-spaced, 1.5 spaced, or double-spaced); specifications for paragraphs and headings and subheadings (e.g., font, size, color, capitalization/initial caps, underline, and bold); and placement of graphs, tables, and visuals.

- **Use of color (other than font).** Mention which colors are approved and which are to be avoided or not used.

Finally, review content and grammar, spell-check your document, and always proofread more than once. Hire a professional proofreader, if possible. When proofreading, also look at your document upside down and sideways. Watch for alignment issues, style variation, and misspellings and faulty punctuation. Compare returned proofs to originals to make sure all edits and changes have been made.

Evaluating Marketing Promotions

Evaluate how every communication works. Ask for feedback from your colleagues, clients, family, friends, and Web site visitors. Last, but not least, know how you will measure results. Think about your desired outcome, and track it. Here are things you can count:

- Calls, inquiries, and response cards
- Dollars and donations in the month (or sales cycle)
- New recruits
- Press hits

- Web hits
- Problems solved
- Time to completion
- Cost and return on investment (ROI)

To maximize your data collection, implement a process. Encourage those who answer calls (e.g., receptionists and salespeople) to ask prospects and clients what has prompted the call and whether callers have read the brochure, ad, flier, newsletter, or other communication.

Quiz

1. Product development hinges on the desire to _____ while promotion _____.
   - (a) Fill unmet needs / provides an incentive to buy
   - (b) Review the market / is less important
   - (c) Price a product for the market / procures leads
   - (d) Get to market quickly / builds testimonials

2. Gifts, reward programs, coupons, special events, and sales are known as:
   - (a) Advertising
   - (b) Marketing
   - (c) Promotions
   - (d) Communication

3. Influence communication is designed to:
   - (a) Change a customer's mind
   - (b) Hypnotize a reader
   - (c) Help others see brands and products through a selected perceptual filter
   - (d) Reduce marketing risk
   - (e) All of the above

4. Logo and advertising art must:
   - (a) Be colorful
   - (b) Be short
   - (c) Be designed by a professional
   - (d) Capture interest quickly through distinct, recognizable design
   - (e) Match a reader's language skills

5. Distinctive design incorporates the following:

 (a) Contrast and white space

 (b) Limited fonts

 (c) Columns

 (d) Shapes

 (e) All of the above

 (f) Only (a) and (b)

6. Premiums are:

 (a) Discounts on closeout merchandise

 (b) Small gifts given as an incentive or reward

 (c) Undeveloped business ideas

 (d) Expensive services offered at holidays

 (e) None of the above

 (f) Only (a) and (b)

7. Internet-based videos and podcasts enable you to:

 (a) Reach younger customers

 (b) Penetrate niche markets

 (c) Increase cost efficiency as measured by viewing impressions.

 (d) Cut through viral clutter

 (e) All of the above

8. Article marketing has become a popular strategy for:

 (a) Communicating information to a target audience

 (b) Promoting the presence of a content expert

 (c) Both (a) and (b)

 (d) Only (a)

9. The purpose of using a metaphor is to:

 (a) Create a perceptual shift

 (b) Demonstrate literary skill

 (c) Increase buyer retention

 (d) Emphasize a point

 (e) Enhance branding

 (f) None of the above

10. A graphic standards manual is used to:
    (a) Reduce errors and increase compliance
    (b) Communicate expectations
    (c) Protect logo integrity
    (d) Illustrate best practices
    (e) Increase brand recognition and perception
    (f) All of the above
    (g) Only choices (c), (d), and (e)

CHAPTER 10

Marketing in a Digital World

Which came first: the chicken or the egg? You might ask a similar question about marketing in a digital age. Did the fast-paced edutainment approach to Internet communication emerge from consumer demand, or has society's attention deficit become even more prevalent with the growth of the Internet? Either way it happened, the demand for quick-paced learning is here to stay. There's now a generation of consumers who never knew life before the Internet. When surfing the Net, millennials, along with time-constrained boomers, allocate only enough mental space for a bare-bones synopsis. Luckily, cognitive studies show that summaries aid comprehension. So, people who visit today's sites for folks with short attention spans may actually get the message.

Witness the sea change in expectations. Consumers expect to be *edutained*, so communicators need to be creative and succinct enough to engage consumers more quickly and give them the information they need to learn before they tune out. We live in a Wii world of edgy entertainment. Electronic book readers, such as Barnes & Noble's Nook and Amazon's Kindle, outperformed even manufacturers' expectations during the 2009 holiday season. And millions of Web marketers now deliver content through short videocasts, podcasts, and 140-character Tweets.

Not content with simply inveigling a change in communication preferences, the Internet has also wheedled its way into common language. We talk in bytes. We go on the Net. We LOL. We TXT. And people understand that terminology. The word *text* itself has shifted

from noun to verb. And I'm left to wonder how many people know that *google* is a mathematical term and not a synonym for *search*.

So what does it all mean? We need to shift from expansive explanations to concise content with laser-sharp sound bytes. We must incorporate media that excite the senses while staying in context. Flash introductions on Web sites might stimulate, but they also can impede quick access to the specific information people need. One solution is a prominent "Skip Intro" link that gets people right to the heart of a Web site.

Building an Internet Relationship

Once upon a time, owning a Web site was a luxury. Today, it is a necessity. After meeting you in a networking function or hearing about your product, people will hop right on the Web to check you out. Their first stop may be a Google, LinkedIn, or Twitter search for your Web site. If they can't find you on the Web, they will more than likely judge you to be technologically challenged and, worse, unimportant enough to merit cyberspace.

Is that true? Not necessarily. There is an elite group of business executives who get *all* their business from word-of-mouth referrals. These individuals come so highly recommended via contacts built through networking and stellar service over the years that they don't feel the need for a Web site. But, if you are concerned with building credentials and relationships, or responsible for broadening your company's business opportunities, make sure you have a Web site and social media presence. Individuals who don't maintain personal Web sites still can connect and foster relationships through online networks such as LinkedIn and Facebook.

Maximizing Your Digital Marketing Effort

The Internet is a critical space for bridging relationships with prospective customers and strengthening existing relationships. Web sites, blogs, and social media sites enhance your ability to stay connected with customers and prospects, provided you learn how to attract and retain Web site visitors and online relationships.

Whether using a Web site, blog, or social media to build your business, your first step is to attract attention. People need to find you to buy from you. Integrate the following strategies to draw people to your site:

- Post messages on blogs and social media sites.
- Update your own blog content frequently.
- Use keywords, search engine submissions, and optimization tools that will help you increase pickups by search engines.
- Set up links and cross-links with other Web sites.
- List your site in relevant online (and print) directories and databases.

- Capture data at every opportunity through feedback forms and other research.
- Conduct relevant, customer-centric e-blast campaigns.
- Generate new leads (e-mail addresses and contact information) by encouraging people to register for free products or news.

Then use market intelligence and track e-blast openings, purchases, and leads. Push your traffic via your e-mail and/or Web pages to landing and squeeze pages that will help convert viewers to buyers.

Setting Web Site Goals

It's simple to set your Web site goals, as there are only a few major goals in Web communication. Master these and you'll enjoy solid impact:

- Learn about the visitors you are targeting.
- Draw them to your site.
- Get them to stay on the site.
- Get them to return to the site.
- Get them to buy from your site (or if you don't offer e-commerce, get them to contact you.)
- Learn even more about the visitors you are targeting and apply that to your ongoing marketing effort.

Web site management is an ongoing job. Customers, markets, and search engine strategies all change. To get the most out of your Web effort, stay involved, and turn your site into a platform for learning about your customers, communicating with them, and building sustainable relationships. Stay abreast of search engine evolution and ranking strategies. The word on the street now is that Bing's search engine system is so different from Google's that the same search engine optimization (SEO) strategies will not work for both of them. If technology is not your thing, that's fine. Hire a Webmaster to watch it and respond for you.

Defining Your Target Market

Suppose you are a wellness coach. You might think that everyone in the world needs to be well. But you probably wouldn't have all the resources in the world to reach or serve such a large group. That's why you need to segment your market and target the most likely customer groups within it. Sharpening your market focus helps you increase return on investment. As you identify the best market—the customers with the most to gain from your products and the money to pay for them—you will increase your chance of converting them from prospects to buying customers.

Ten Steps to Building and Using a Meaningful Customer Profile

Building a customer profile is like painting a picture of the person you want to visit your shop. Take a moment to imagine the people you want to invite to your Web site and inside your door. What do they look like? How do they dress and act? What do they talk and think about? How much money do they carry in their wallets? How do they spend their free time?

Take care in choosing whom to invite. The wrong customers will eat up your time (and that of your colleagues) without ever paying for it. The right customers will not only buy your stuff but also serve as an ongoing resource for feedback and testimonials.

Here are the 10 steps to connect with the right people:

1. **Think about who would need or benefit from your products and services.** Consider what they dream about, what problems they need solved, and how they see themselves in life. Make a list of all possible customer types. (If you are thinking of specific people you know personally or would like to reach, make a second list and gather those people's e-mails for future use.)

2. **Shorten your list by choosing the type(s) of customers you most want to attract.** Base your selections on demographic information such as household income, marital status, age, sex, locale, and ethnicity.

3. **Gather information on the lifestyles of those targeted customers.** Are they athletic, wellness oriented, arts patrons, politically affiliated, parents of young children, children of aging parents, boaters, bikers, runners, restaurant frequenters, club joiners, churchgoers, and so on? Identify any and all special characteristics of your preferred customers.

4. **Decide whether there is a particular niche** (i.e., a very targeted sample) **that you want to target.**

5. **Put yourself in your target customers' shoes.** Think about where they would go for information and products now. To whom do they listen? What keywords or phrases would they use to search for information relating to your product category?

6. **Study the target customers' neighborhoods on the ground and on the Web.** Investigate those locations. Visit the Web sites and blogs those customers would visit. Get copies of the newspapers, magazines, and industry publications they would read. Research the groups in which they belong. Sign up for e-newsletters of relevant trade associations and social groups. Ask friends and colleagues what they know about these groups and information channels.

7. **Create a list of criteria** (e.g., lifestyle, locale, income, and interests) **that will let you know a perfect customer when you see one.** Using the information you have gained in steps 1 through 6, write a description (i.e., a profile) of your best customers and where you will find them.

8. **Plan how you will map your Web content to the needs of your targeted visitors.** Decide how you will reach them through your Web site with keywords, directories, and Internet marketing strategies, including search engine optimization, Web advertising, directory listings, e-mail campaigns, squeeze pages, auto-responders, and feedback systems. (*Squeeze pages* are landing pages where visitors are presented with the sales close and link to the shopping cart. They do not link back to other pages in the site. They are designed to close the sale. You will find more information on squeeze pages later in this chapter. *Auto-responders* are programs that send updated messages to your contacts list according to the process and schedule you specify.)

9. **Set your goals. Begin to implement, possibly first with a test that reaches out to a small sample.**

10. **Track your results, and adjust as necessary.** If you are reaching your traffic and conversion goals, keep it going. If not, ask why. Decide whether you need to change your message, business channels, or both.

Sticking with the wellness coach example, you might now want to focus your marketing efforts on a select group or groups, such as women seeking to grow their careers, men who run marathons, seniors who want to live longer, or skiers who want to improve their concentration. Perhaps you will choose all four. If so, you can use the information you gathered from the process above to develop individualized marketing campaigns targeted to the needs of each group, with different landing pages on your Web site as well as squeeze pages that will lead them through the sales cycle, and contact programs that will keep you top of mind across the year.

Whether you offer services or durable goods, online or in stores, creating a customer profile will help you develop targeted marketing campaigns in print, in person, and on the Web.

Maintaining an Effective Web Site

Whatever your Web presence, you need to make your site appealing and attractive. And, you need to keep it fresh to keep it effective. The following paragraphs show you how.

MAKING YOUR SITE STICKY

Offer relevant content in a compelling way. Think about what users want and how they will search for it. Create clear pathways to information embedded within your site with visible links on the home page, so you don't exhaust visitors by making them dig through layers to find the information nugget they are looking for. Also, if you have links to other Web sites on your site, set them up to open in a separate window rather than transfer the visitor out of your site.

KEEPING CONTENT FRESH

A "What's New" section will clue visitors into the fact that your site is worth returning to for new resource links, hot tips, white papers, e-books, stimulating discussions, Webinars, free offers, discounts, and other promotions. The good news is with all the interesting content already on the Web, you don't have to write everything yourself.

Widgets (i.e., interfaces that help applications talk to each other) make it possible to "dial in" content from other sources. RSS feeds (i.e., Really Simple Syndication feeds, which are Web applications that link you to regularly updated content) allow you to tie into streams of digital content created by others.

KEEPING WRITING SIMPLE

Use short paragraphs, with bulleted lists surrounded by lots of white space, so people can quickly identify and absorb your message.

Organizing Your Web Site

Think of your Web site as a lens that focuses on the value you bring to customers. That means telling your story through your customers' eyes rather than your own. Key in on the benefits visitors need. Use examples, testimonials, videos, audios, and demos to enhance comprehension.

STARTING WITH A STORYBOARD

Storyboards are a useful method for capturing what you want people to know about your company and sharing it with others. Start by thinking about how your story should unfold. Mapping out your site structure as if you were designing a storyboard will save time and money. Use index cards or Post-it Notes to help organize your thoughts, and figure out how information will flow from page to page on your Web site. Use one card or note for each topic you intend to post on your site. Below the title, list information you plan to include. Decide what titles you will give to your Web pages, and make a card or Post-it Note for each. Then, decide what information belongs on which page. Order your pages, topics, and bulleted lists on your project board. Add arrows where needed until you have determined the most logical relationship of pages. Doing so will help you create a site architecture that works for your visitors.

ADDING A CALL TO ACTION

Consider what you want visitors to do when they get to a page. What action from visitors will help you move your business forward? Add a call to action on every page: invite customers to take advantage of a free download. Include a "Buy Now" button that links to your shopping cart, or a link to an information request form or a phone number with a "Call Now" message.

CREATING A PROFESSIONAL GRAPHIC DESIGN

Incorporate a look and feel (e.g., fonts, colors, and imagery) that is consistent with your other marketing materials. Design your site for ease of use and comprehension, and organize your site to meet the needs of clients, prospects, and other visitors.

Your Web site faces the world, and it may be the first impression you make on potential clients. It reflects your organization's competence and culture. Treat it as carefully as you would treat your best client account.

INCLUDING A SITE MAP

Placing a site map—a section with a link to each page—on the bottom of every page is a best practice for internal searchability. Add links and/or buttons in obvious places to guide your visitors through your site. Consider how your Web site visitors will search for information. How would you search if you knew what you were looking for? How might you use your site if you didn't know what was available? Think about what you've experienced when you've visited particular Web sites. What made certain sites easy for you to use? Which sites left you feeling frustrated, and why?

It's difficult to predict exactly who will visit your site, but it's a safe bet that if visitors don't find what they need in the first minute, they will hop off your site and onto another. Add an internal site search feature so visitors can quickly find what they are looking for.

If you plan to offer a newsletter, updated content, or e-commerce, add a member registration form and/or a link to your shopping cart. You should also include a feedback form. Consider how you want people to interact with you. If you offer graphic design services, for example, you may want to include a FTP (File Transfer Protocol) program for uploading and downloading files. Or you may need password-protected extranet access for each of your clients.

CAPTURING INFORMATION

People love free stuff. Asking visitors to register to receive a free white paper, e-book, article, music download, or product demo will help you capture e-mail addresses and other contact information. Entice visitors to provide feedback on relevant issues.

SURVEYING CUSTOMERS

Online surveys will provide information on customer concerns, needs, preferences, and staff encounters. They also shed light on how you are perceived in the market. Well-constructed surveys can serve as a market barometer. Done right, your Web site can

become part of your overall information management system. By capturing contact information and demographic data with surveys, you will gather knowledge that can help you make informed business decisions going forward.

ENCOURAGING BOOKMARKING

Remind visitors to bookmark your site to keep them coming back.

TRACKING RESULTS

There are free tools that can help you analyze visitor behavior on your Web site, from the number of visitors in a day, week, or month to the number of hits per page, the number of unique visitors, and more. Tracking visitors and results after e-campaigns and social media blasts can help you evaluate the impact of your efforts and investment. It can also show you where and when to invest more effort and guide your ongoing Web strategy.

Valuing the Customer Experience

The job of every Web guru is to engage customers with a company through its Web site. Respect a visitor's time by making information easy to find. Most visitors search business sites for specific information and not for entertainment. However, edutainment, which provides important information in entertaining ways, can capture attention when it delivers value, humor, and relief from stress and/or matches the preferred learning modalities of visitors.

Easy-to-find telephone contact information, live help, and/or instant chat programs enhance the consumers' experiences. Prominently placed feedback forms let visitors know you care what they think. Member portals that welcome customers by name and track history for them not only provide an electronic ego massage but also reflect on your own company's service ethic. Feed all information you gain through feedback forms to your leadership teams and managers for consideration during departmental meetings about product development, marketing, sales, finance, training, and customer service.

Optimizing Your Web Site

Search engine optimization (SEO) is the art of designing your Web site and refining your codes to increase the likelihood that your site will be displayed higher in the search results page when keywords are typed into a search engine box. Web sites that are listed at the top of search engine returns receive more views than sites further down the list. Search engines use automated software programs to crawl the Net, detect and gather information on Web pages, and return that information to the search engine database, where it is analyzed. Because search engines are regularly reprogrammed, there is no single magic bullet that will work with every search engine every time. But a long-term strategy based on a keen understanding of your customer profiles is essential. Check Web site analytics, available through your Web programmer or site host, to understand how people are using your site. Doing so can provide insight for ongoing decisions.

Be sure to regularly review, analyze, and interpret back-end data. Follow that by a revision of sales and marketing strategies based on what you learn from Web analytics (e.g., hits, views, pages, visitors, peak usage periods, purchasing conversions, and usage patterns). You will then enhance return on investment.

ORGANIC (UNPAID) SEARCH

The most cost-effective search strategy is to prep your site so it generates desired organic search results. Optimizing a site so it is found through keyword searches, links, and free directories saves advertising dollars, although it will cost you time and/or money to prepare the right copy and use Web site optimization tools. When search engine crawlers decide that content and site architecture is valid, they will index and rank those sites in the search engine database. Those Web sites that best match the search engine logic will appear at the top of search engine results lists when users type in keywords or phrases used consistently on those sites.

Search engines also detect page titles, subject lines, words, and phrases. They do not detect words that are contained in photo images (i.e., jpegs or gifs), unless those images are tagged with data the search engines can read. While keywords must appear in content, information must also be coded so that search engines can recognize and evaluate it. Metatags help search engines distinguish information such as text, photos, and tables. Essentially, these tags are data about data, which is the basis for computer programming. Search engines recognize several programming languages, such as such as XML (Extensible Markup Language), which provides coding rules that enable technical manipulation to enhance syntax and searchability, and HTML (HyperText Markup Language), which also provides structure for headings, paragraphs, text, lists, links, quotes, and typefaces. HTML also enables search engines to recognize embedded images and options.

Some search engines only catalog part of your document. Others catalog every word. You can maximize your Web site exposure by placing keywords in the title frames of your Web site and in the top paragraph of your content whenever possible. It also helps to repeat keywords, as practical, throughout your Web site. The best keywords and phrases to tag on your site will be those that are highly relevant to the subject and content of each Web page on your site.

PAID SEARCH OPTIONS

Paid search is another search engine marketing (SEM) option. Pay-per-click (PPC) advertising on major sites such as Bing (which bills itself as a decision engine), Yahoo!, MSN, Microsoft, and Google allows you to prominently display an ad link to your Web

site alongside organic search return lists. This outbound marketing strategy pushes your message to prospects. The downside of PPC is that you pay per click, whether or not a visitor buys from you. Being at the top of a PPC ad list means you will get more clicks. The key is to get clicks from people who are qualified prospects. Ask your ad consultant for guidance on placement statistics, costs, budget, and return on investment.

PAID KEYWORDS

Search engines offer free tools that help you pick the right keywords for your organic and paid searches. Prices for words vary, with high-volume, core-industry terms costing more. While you pay more for them, that may do a better job of routing your customers to you. Key phrases with longer word strings (i.e., long tails) may cost less because they get fewer hits. Nevertheless, they can deliver not only the curiosity seeker but also the more serious buyer. When setting up SEO or paid search criteria, consider what problems buyers are trying to solve. Use that knowledge to create and embed search terms that will drive your sales, and manage your search engine efforts.

PayPerPost

While most PPC programs focus on driving traffic to Web sites or blogs, some bloggers will write entries and post on blogs for you for a PayPerPost (PPP) fee, working to drive traffic to your site.

LANDING PAGES

Whether running a campaign by direct mail, e-mail, SEO, or paid searches, you'll want to guide prospects to the right information by tagging individual campaigns with a specific landing page Web address (i.e., an URL, or Uniform Resource Locator). Doing so will help you track where results come from. For best results, landing pages should direct users to the exact content they searched for, not a generic home page. For example, if someone is searching for information on botox treatments, linking them to a page on your site about collagen injections won't help you close that botox sale. There is no guarantee that visitors will seek out more information on their own. If you want visitors to know more about your other products, add those products to the same page with the keyword or phrase your visitor used.

Build a better landing page by helping people find exactly what they are looking for. Your landing page may benefit from clear subcategories (e.g., children, teen, adult; men, women, children; client, agency, advertiser; and industry, segment, target. Providing relevant headings in your product catalog, rather than a catchall stock-keeping unit (SKU) for more generic categories such as shoes, jewelry, and furniture), can help buyers locate and choose the exact products they want for the purposes they need.

SQUEEZE PAGES

Many Internet marketers turn their landing pages into focused squeeze pages. To close the sale, squeeze pages narrow your message down to one major point. They focus information on the product for sale, and they link visitors directly to the buying system. When visitors click on the link, they receive a thank-you note, buying instructions, and/or a direct link to the shopping cart. Buying what's offered is the only option on a squeeze page. You can set links to squeeze pages in your e-blasts, individual e-mails, or other pages on your Web site. You can also publish links to your squeeze page in a blog, or you can publish the squeeze page address in a print ad.

TRACKING

Use the data you get from results of SEO and PPC efforts, and landing pages to fine-tune and adjust your digital marketing campaigns. Test copy with different vertical and target markets, and study variance in your sales conversion rates. As you learn what works and what doesn't, you can adjust your campaign for better sales results.

Leveling the Playing Field

The Internet is the world's most democratic, consumer-driven, and prolific advertising medium. It offers even small companies and individuals big bang for their investments in Web sites, blogs, and social media. Often, for little more expenditure than the time spent doing the task, you can influence attitudes and outcomes.

While online networking tools give the average person unprecedented power, the explosion in social media also gives marketers and professionals more work. But by making time for that, you can reap big dividends. You can create a blog in just a few minutes using free Web-based software (e.g., check out www.blogger.com, http://wordpress.com, and www.hubspot.com). You can tweet a message, post your own press release, or blast an e-mail or YouTube campaign. With social media, you can reach more people, much faster than in days when news was channeled mostly through publicists to journalists.

Demystifying Social Media

Before the Internet, marketers had to travel to trade shows, book hotels for seminars, and allocate big dollars for various multichannel advertising campaigns. The results were hard to measure. Today's marketers have audiences at the ready, across the world, 24 hours a day, 7 days a week (24/7)—thanks to social media. Now, results are easier to track.

WHAT TO DO WITH SOCIAL MEDIA

Join the conversation. If you don't say anything, people will assume you have nothing to say. Use social media platforms to do these things:

- Educate and inform
- Share links to news articles and interesting blog posts
- Comment on current news
- Share product news
- Offer advice
- Ask advice
- Pass along a great story
- Tell what you do
- Issue a challenge
- Connect your colleagues
- Monitor what people are saying about you, others, and products
- Provide a testimonial
- Get a testimonial
- Respond to problems
- Get in on the conversation

In a social context, conversations of all varieties abound on the Web. On the business side, product news can be shared in an Internet instant. Here are some popular sites:

- **Facebook.** This social networking site connects people with friends and business colleagues.
- **LinkedIn.** This networking site is used mostly by professionals.
- **Twitter.** This blog site allows micropost updates (140 characters, maximum) through which people can follow the activities and posts of others, or be followed in real time.

What's great about these sites is they connect you with people who have given you permission to share your news. Those people choose to become your Facebook friend, connect on LinkedIn, or follow you on Twitter because they want to. That makes them part of your target audience. They have chosen to care. Think of social media as your cocktail party in cyberspace.

Here are some more popular sites:

- **YouTube.** On this video platform you can post videos for free or watch thousands of videos published for personal, social, and business benefit.

- **Digg.** This combination social media and ranking site is where people post content and also evaluate it. Posts that draw rave reviews work their way up the engine to the first page. Digg also advertises meetings and events.

GETTING STARTED WITH SOCIAL MEDIA

Search for topics of interest to you and find out who is blogging about what. If you turn up lots of results, you've probably found an interested, engaged market for your products or services. If you can't locate a blog, it may be a sign that there is little market interest or a need to educate and inform people, as is the case with emerging technology. The key is helping people uncover what they don't know.

Once you register on a blog or social media site, ease yourself into the melee by observing the conversation for a while. When you have a handle on the flow and personalities, try asking a question or answering one. As you respond to queries on blogs and e-networks, you will build your social media personality. The skinny is that social Web sites are like small communities. Follow the same relationship building rules that you would in a face-to-face networking forum. Be authentic. Don't sell. Educate instead, in a helpful way, as you respond to queries and people will begin to take notice of your name and advice in your online forum. Take time to listen to the online conversation and member styles before responding. Whether writing your own blog or responding to someone else's, restrain yourself from promoting. Focus your efforts on building trust. As you do, don't be surprised if you get an e-mail or call from someone who has been following your posts online.

Building Online Communities

If you haven't already joined an online community, get on the Internet and start building your presence this week. Online networking forums operate as membership sites. Once you sign up, you can create a profile with your name, business description, job description, Web site, and contact information. Then you can set permissions to share that profile with members of that membership site and/or protect your profile from public viewing. These online networking sites allow you to maintain a list of contacts, meet new contacts, and share your contacts with others.

Don't know how to find the person you need? No worries. Networking sites include a search tool. Just enter a category, such as "lawyer," or type in the name of the person you are seeking and the search engine will provide you with a list of possibilities from which to choose. You then can send a message to the person or people with whom you want to connect, or you can ask them to join your contacts list. Facebook calls these contacts "friends."

When networking online, reach out to others with invitations to join your network. Ask colleagues and clients to recommend you to others in member forums. As you do so, you will build your online presence.

Using Blogs in Your Marketing Strategy

Blogging is among the newest marketing sports and an effective way to move up your site in search engine rankings. Blogs offer a 24/7 contact opportunity, and have equalized the public relations playing field by giving even the least likely contender an opportunity to play journalist. By creating your own blog, where you can post your news, share thoughts and opinions, and invite others to opine, you can connect with untold numbers of Web visitors at no charge. And you will have the potential to brand yourself in yet another forum.

At http://blogsearch.google.com, you can search for blogs by your topic of interest. Technorati (http://technorati.com) is another search engine that tracks and ranks blogs, by category. This site publishes original content (e.g., blog reviews, breaking news, trend pieces, keyword-tagged articles, and opinion-focused posts) if your article is timely, news focused, interesting, and well written. Blogging on Technorati can help you build expert status and promote your brand, as all articles accepted appear on the site's RSS and Twitter feeds and Google News.

Wondering when and where you should blog? Blog when you have news, want to share thoughts and information, or seek to sway the opinions of others. You can start your own blog or type your thoughts into an open blog someone else has set up on a relevant topic. Decide on the purpose of your blog, and honor it by giving readers a reason to come back.

Starting a blog is easy. You can set up your own blog for free. But to make sure it works for you, optimize the impact of your communications with appropriate keywords, phrases, and metatags and alt tags. *Alt tags* provide text in the background of a photo or space area which enables a search engine to read and interpret a description of the image or area. Visit http://wordpress.com, or http://moveabletype.com, and you can be up and running with your own blog in under an hour.

Post news and comments on your blog and other blogs that target your target audience. Your blog can position you as an expert in your field, or it can position your firm as an expert resource. Post only information that adds value to your brand. As you focus on adding value for others and becoming a trusted resource, you will develop a following that adds value for you.

GETTING NOTICED

It's not enough to be on the Web. People need to know you're there and seek you out as a resource. Do this to boost your blog's ratings:

- Update content frequently.
- Write on topics that your target market is likely to search for.
- Leave your blog address when you post on other blogs.

- Set up a link exchange with other bloggers who are writing on your topic.
- Use your most important keyword(s) in your blog name.
- Tag your keywords and images for search engine recognition.

PROCEED WITH CAUTION

Blogs, and all Web content, can be viewed by anyone. Use caution when communicating. As a business blogger, be prudent in your approach to controversial topics, such as politics, religion, and sex. A prospect or client may not agree with your opinions, which could cost you business.

LINKING STRATEGIES

Because inbound links carry more SEO weight with some search engines than outbound links do, offer to set up reciprocal links with bloggers and Web sites that are a good fit for your message. Getting good links from authoritative sources can enhance your overall searchability and thereby your Internet presence.

BUSINESS AND CORPORATE BLOGS

The fastest way to annoy potential customers is to overmarket to them. Do not use business blogs to hawk products and advertise for sales. Instead of superselling, use your corporate blog to inform and educate customers, address client concerns and issues, share important information, and respond to feedback.

Although blogs present great opportunities for companies, they also pose risk. Develop and communicate a policy that explains your company's blogging rules to employees. Doing so will help avert legal and professional problems, such as dissemination of trade secrets, private financials, and other information that could result in organizational disruption or crisis. Lastly, take a clue from attorneys and health-care providers. They always add a disclaimer and/or limitation of liability to Web sites and blogs. Err on the side of caution.

Twitter

Twitter is an interactive relationship-building microblog in which brief updates are called "Tweets," and are issued and may be read in real time. Twittering offers access to potential customers, affiliates, and contacts who send and receive quick, short business or personal updates that can be forwarded to create a viral buzz. Before registering for Twitter (or setting up any blog), decide whether you will be representing yourself or your business; then develop your online personality accordingly.

Getting your company's name out on Twitter will increase your brand presence. Here are some uses for Twitter (and other blogs):

- Inform colleagues of happenings, events, and helpful information of interest to them
- Update customers on your company events, news, and promotions
- Provide product and service updates
- Promote your Web content, blog posts, podcasts, and videocasts
- Share news and observations in real time, as events unfold

GETTING STARTED ON TWITTER

To get your own account, go to http://twitter.com and enter a user name and password. Choose a name (i.e., a "handle") that will represent you well and make it easy for people to recognize you. Random, obscure, or metaphoric handles, and names with numbers will blur your branding. Upload your photo, and begin providing snapshot updates on what's important to you. Use Twitter to share tips, insights, and special offers; ask for information; offer advice; and engage potential customers.

BUILDING A TWITTER FOLLOWING

Start following others and there's a good likelihood they will follow you, too. You can find people to follow by using the Twitter search tool. Search the topics you are most interested in. See who is tweeting on them, and become a follower of the top 10 in each category. Before you know it, they will check to see who you are and follow you, too. The more followers you gain, the quicker you will build your Twitter presence. As with every marketing endeavor, it's important to evaluate whether your efforts are hitting the mark. If not, you'll need to consider why, determine how you can tweak your tweeting for stronger success, or decide whether or not to put your efforts elsewhere. Type your company name or relevant keywords into the Twitter search box and you will see what people are saying (or not saying) about your company and brand. Respond accordingly. Twitter is crawled by search engines, with ranking factors that include your number of followers as well as your behind-the-scene tags. Visit http://twitter.grader.com to check your ranking in the Twittersphere.

TWITTER SEARCHES

Twitter also offers geographic coding so you can see where tweets come from, which is a helpful feature when market segments are being considered. In January 2010, Twitter rolled out a Local Trends feature, which reveals what people are talking about at state and city levels.

USING TWITTER FOR MARKETING RESEARCH

To quickly hone in on market opinions, precede your search with :) and :(signs, and Twitter will return posts with positive or negative attitudes about your search topic. To track a topic, use a hashtag, (# sign), followed by your search term, and it will code your search and make your post easier for others to find.

The media you use to market your company should fit with your overall strategy, based on your purpose, personality, and target markets. If your target market is technophobic, you don't need to focus much effort on Twittering. Likewise if you target the teen market, LinkedIn's professional reach won't have much impact.

New Products

As new Internet technology devices to text marketing and digital advertising hit the market, consumers wrestling with download time and sellers are challenged to make sure their information downloads across multiple browsers in the way it is intended to look. When building Web-based messages, test them in multiple formats, on multiple browsers and PC and Mac platforms, so you will know how people are viewing your brand messages.

Making the Most of Your Time

It's easy to get sucked into the vortex (aka, the Web). Ever expanding, it is the ultimate black hole. The Internet is just one of many marketing tools at your disposal. Because your time is an important resource, treat your Internet marketing effort as you would any other marketing task. Set limits on your time, just as you do with your marketing budget.

Finally, as you participate in multiple online forums, you may be challenged to keep track of it all. Rather than update multiple social sites individually, you can save time with an aggregation tool. Aggregation programs allow you to collect updates from several social networking sites at once. After registering and customizing a dashboard, you can target the updates you want, or you can post updates yourself. Resources such as Flock.com (http://flock.com) and Steamy.com (http://steamy.com) focus on outbound messaging. They will automatically feed the information you post to your contacts via the social media sites you use. Alternatively, your friends can subscribe to your own feed at http://friendfeed.com. Send them a link and they will be able to see all of your posts to multiple sites in one location. To learn more about continually evolving Internet-marketing resources, post your questions on your own social marketing sites, conduct Internet searches, read technology magazines, ask friends, or consult your technology provider.

Quiz

1. Posting messages on blogs and social media sites, choosing the right keywords, and setting up cross-links are:

   (a) Search engine optimization strategies

   (b) Strategies for attracting traffic to your Web site

   (c) Part of every market segmentation effort

   (d) Background information for Web site analytics

2. Creating a customer profile:

   (a) Is a strategy for segmenting your market

   (b) Improves your customer service attitude

   (c) Clarifies the characteristics of your target market

   (d) Gives you a basis for tracking

3. The Technorati.com Web site (http://technorati.com):

   (a) Tracks and ranks blogs

   (b) Tracks and ranks search engines

   (c) Ranks other Web sites

   (d) Provides technical information for Web analytics

4. Offering relevant content, using a site map, and making sure that links open windows within your Web site are ways to:

   (a) Make your site sticky

   (b) Boost your search engine ranking

   (c) Increase your conversion rate

   (d) All of the above

   (e) Only choices (a) and (b)

5. By creating a list of criteria, you can:

   (a) Identify your perfect customer

   (b) Build a better customer profile

   (c) Learn how to analyze your Web site

   (d) Get closer to your conversion target

   (e) Only choices (a) and (b)

6. RSS feeds allow you to:

   (a) Provide content developed by someone else

   (b) Save time and money in content preparation

   (c) Keep your Web content fresh

   (d) All of the above

7. To move customers forward in the Internet sales process:

   (a) Include a call to action

   (b) Create a storyboard

   (c) Insert metatags into your copy

   (d) All of the above

8. Social aggregation tools make it possible to:

   (a) Create a thorough view of your target market

   (b) Integrate a blog and a Web site

   (c) Manage multiple social media updates from one place

   (d) All of the above

9. Use your corporate blog to:

   (a) Inform and educate customers

   (b) Address client concerns and issues

   (c) Share important information and feedback

   (d) All of the above

   (e) Only choices (a) and (c)

10. To reduce risk with business blogs and Web sites:

    (a) Issue a policy that explains your company's blogging rules to employees

    (b) Limit your postings

    (c) Add a disclaimer and/or limitation of liability to Web sites and blogs.

    (d) All of the above

CHAPTER 11

Networking and Referral Marketing

Networking is the process of building business connections through social interaction in personal and/or online forums. Networking forums enable you to use your interpersonal skills to build rapport and relationships. Networking can increase awareness of your brand while helping you meet people with whom you can exchange contact information, build relationships, and/or do business. In this chapter, we will focus on how to use networking to support your strategies for business, relationships, and referral building. With strong networking skills in your business toolbox, you can accelerate your business branding, referrals, and sales growth.

If you network at all, you may have been approached at some point by a slick, smiling dude who quickly pressed a card into your hand, bragged about his product, tried to sell it to you, and also urged you to give up the name of a prospective customer. At that point, you probably edged backward and looked for someone to whom you could pass off that goofball. For your own benefit, resolve never to provide an introduction for anyone who doesn't understand the etiquette of rapport building.

Networking provides connections to prospects, customers, vendors, colleagues, and other business resources, if you do it right. First, you must establish relationship credibility. With personal referrals and testimonials as the valued stock in trade, networks and businesses grow through personal introductions. These introductions increase comfort among individuals who are meeting for the first time, help put a prospect's mind at ease, and pave the way toward sales.

Word-of-Mouth Communication

Networking is powered by word of mouth. Word-of-mouth communication once was a well-kept marketing secret, but it has become a marketing platform in its own right. Most people prefer to do business with people they know, like, and trust. When they don't know the right person for a job, they often ask a friend, relative, or business colleague for a referral. Therein lies the power of word-of-mouth advertising. As you develop a reliable product or a reputation for serving people well, you will enjoy the benefit of increased referrals and testimonials.

How to Network

Over the past quarter century, face-to-face networking groups have sprung up in business communities across the globe. For years, networking happened serendipitously as people met through groups and later over the telephone when people followed up on initial contacts. Today, it happens strategically. In recent years, networking opportunities have exploded across the Internet. Web-based networking tools serve as a springboard to new relationships. This new vehicle makes it possible for people to connect and stay abreast of who's who. It helps networkers share business questions, concerns, needs, and industry news, as well as personal and/or business information, without the need to leave the office. Via the Internet, networkers connect with more people than ever before—potentially millions of others—making geography irrelevant.

Networking is an art governed by formal and informal rules. Knowing the rules will empower you to become an excellent networker. The paragraphs that follow explain what you need to know to become an expert networker.

PLAN FOR REFERRALS, NOT LEADS

When connecting in person or on the Web, most people network to get leads. Savvy people network to get referrals. According to Dr. Ivan Misner, founder and CEO of BNI, the world's largest business networking organization, there's a big difference between a lead and a referral. Leads are easier to find than referrals, but they are less useful. You can get leads by asking business associates for names of prospective customers, reading ads, culling through a phone book, reviewing the business cards in your pocket, putting out an online query, or picking up business cards from a shelf in a diner. Leads are simply names of people you can call to inquire about their readiness for your products or services. You need to follow up every lead with a cold call. In other words, you have no prior relationship with or connection to the person whose name you turn up, nor do you know if that person is qualified to do business with you.

A referral is a big step up from a lead because it speeds relationship building. A referral is made when you receive the name of a prospective buyer from someone who knows what you do and has spoken with that prospect about you. Your networking contact (the referral giver) has confirmed the prospect's interest in your product or service, thus prequalifying, and obtaining permission for you to connect. The beauty of a referral is that the person to whom you have been referred is expecting your call. When you deliver a referral to a colleague while networking, you are sharing the gold. As you give referrals to others, you also increase the likelihood of receiving referrals yourself. As Ivan Misner says with his BNI motto, "givers gain." Once you receive a referral, you will be on the fast track to closing a sale.

PLAN YOUR NETWORKING STRATEGY

Before you enter a networking group, make sure that your networking strategy also makes sense in terms of your overall business needs. Think about whom you already know that can provide an introduction to the right people, companies, or groups. When networking online, reach out to others with invitations to join your network. Ask colleagues and clients to recommend you to others in member forums. As you do, you will build your networking presence. Learn enough about your business and industry to serve as a resource for others. Answering questions in online networking forums can help you establish your presence as a business expert.

KNOW YOUR PURPOSE

Before attending a networking function or linking up online, determine your marketing intention. Decide what you want to get out of a particular meeting or online interaction. Ask yourself these questions:

- Whom do I want to meet? In what industries? For what purpose?
- What kind of referral will I ask for?
- How can I be very specific in asking for the kind of referral I want?
- Whom do I want to help while I am out networking?
- How can I help other people to meet their own networking goals?

Some people network simply to meet others and raise awareness of themselves and their personal or business brands. But good salespeople network to generate qualified referrals—people with the potential to become good customers. The best networkers take time to generate reliable referrals for other people. The more qualified referrals you make for others, the faster you will strengthen your own relationships and earn the trust of other people in your networking group. When you prove yourself committed to people in your group and produce qualified referrals for them, you will be rewarded with referrals from others.

PREPARE IN ADVANCE

Learn something about the networking group or forum you are about to join. Ask friends and colleagues about it, or research it online. Google the names of people you expect to attend a particular networking event, and learn something about them. Read the news, and gather information on current events and new businesses in your region before heading out to a networking meeting or networking online. Learn about issues of interest to people in your networking groups. That information will give you something relevant to talk about, and that will help strengthen your relationships. Later in this chapter, you'll find tips on starting networking conversations.

Before heading to a face-to-face group for the first time, practice your personal introduction and elevator speech in advance (we show you how below). Find out the dress code, in advance, too. Some groups require business attire. Others are casual. Some may be formal. Dress appropriately, and make sure your clothes are pressed and clean. Once you've arrived, study the room layout. Then, enter the room with confidence and good posture. Smile and make eye contact with others as you move through the room.

BE APPROACHABLE

To stand out and be recognized, it helps to wear something unique when networking. An unusual piece of jewelry or a brightly colored tie or lapel pin will provide an opportunity for people to strike up a conversation with you when they don't know what else to say. While shy people may have trouble asking your name or inquiring directly about what you do, they often will have no problem saying, "I love that necklace!" or "Oh, you are wearing a Red Cross pin! Does that mean you a board member, or did you win a Red Cross award?"

While networking, take care to monitor your own body language. Uncross your arms, and make a conscious effort to appear friendly and approachable. A bright-eyed, interested demeanor works wonders when it comes to encouraging strangers (or acquaintances) to engage in a conversation with you.

If you are wondering what to do with your hands, here's a tip for you. It's okay to keep one hand in your pocket, but not both. Always keep one hand available for gesturing or a handshake. Subtle cues in your body language can tell a lot about you. Be aware of the signals you are sending when you network. And take note of the communication bread crumbs left by others.

FOCUS ON RELATIONSHIPS BEFORE SALES

Networking is more than the practice of handing out business cards. To be successful, you must build relationships. To do that, you must understand what the other person needs and what it will take to build a win-win outcome. Ask questions to learn what other people need and how you can help. (Remember, the goal of networking is to get and *give* referrals.)

PLAN YOUR CONVERSATION STRATEGY

Once you conquer your fear of making a mistake, you'll actually enjoy networking. Prepare yourself by having a conversation plan. Planning and practice makes perfect.

LISTEN WELL

Instead of launching into a monologue about yourself and your products, take time to ask questions of the people you meet. Let them talk more about themselves than you do about yourself. Listening will provide valuable clues to step up your overall conversation. It also will help you learn what you need to put your own value proposition in the right context. As you learn about others, you will become a valued resource yourself, full of information that can be helpful to people in your community. People will soon think you are a great conversationalist, mostly because you listened well and said very little. Before you know it, you will have heard a piece of information that will help you provide someone with a referral or will benefit your own business. When you listen well and start giving referrals, you will have mastered the art of networking.

Starting the Networking Conversation

Not everyone is a born networker. Many people don't know what or how much to say about themselves at a networking function. Some are uncomfortable with entering new groups. Others are shy about learning online technologies. Some people don't know how to start a conversation with a stranger. And nobody wants to make a mistake. Fear of mistakes can hold you back from networking effectively. Learning how to manage networking conversations will prepare you for successful outcomes. Two approaches to networking conversations follow: the business conversation (which focuses on articulating your elevator speech), and the online conversation.

THE BUSINESS CONVERSATION

Seasoned networkers make the most of their networking time by homing in on business needs. Many networking groups will offer you the opportunity to present a short introduction of yourself and your business. Known as an "elevator speech" (because it should take no longer than the span of time it takes to explain what you do while riding in an elevator), this short introduction usually runs from 30 to 60 seconds. You can benefit by developing short and longer versions. Depending on the size of the group and the meeting format, you may you get an opportunity to speak for two or three minutes. You also can post your elevator speeches on your Web site or excerpt details for your online profile.

The Elevator Speech

The goal of an elevator speech is to present yourself and your value proposition. In other words, it is your chance to quickly and concisely explain how you help others. After hearing your name and company, people need to know why they should care about what you do. When constructing an elevator speech, think about how you want to be viewed by others (your personal brand) as well as what is unique about how you help people. What do you want to be known for? What problems do you solve? What value do you bring? Focus on solutions and benefits, rather than features. For example, instead of saying, "I provide marketing services," you might say, "I help people connect with new customers by showing them the most current and most effective ways to promote their business over the Internet."

Once you've worked out your elevator speech content, rehearse it frequently. Test it on friends and colleagues until it flows comfortably for you. Then test it at networking functions, and see what kind of response you get. As you get to know people in the group, ask for feedback about your elevator speech. Listen to the follow-up questions they ask you. That will give you a clue to what may be missing in your speech. It also might demonstrate that you have succeeded in engaging them in a thoughtful conversation and a request for more information. That is your goal.

If you are shy about public speaking, join a Toastmasters group in your area. Or hire a coach to help you learn how to network effectively. Many executive coaches provide insight as well as networking introductions. In addition, many networking groups, such as BNI and chambers of commerce, offer ongoing networking education classes for members.

ONLINE CONVERSATIONS

Hundreds of social marketing forums, such as LinkedIn, Facebook, Plaxo, Twitter, and Flickr, make it possible to share contacts and information, from photos to news, via RSS feeds, blogs, and business tools, all online. While most introductions happen interactively, online networking programs search for commonalities among individuals and their profiles and relay automatic messages suggesting the names of people with whom you might want to connect. To maximize your Web-based networking, start by setting up your own profiles on social networking sites. (See Chapter 10 to learn more about building your own online community.) Remember that word-of-mouth advertising does not discriminate between good and bad. Never say anything in an online forum that you would not be proud to have repeated.

Networking Etiquette

Artful networkers know how to build rapport and put other people at ease. Joining strategies—which help demonstrate that you understand and relate with the experience and sentiment of another—can help establish rapport. Such strategies include repeating in your own words what someone else is saying and reflecting your understanding back to them. That helps validate your connection to them. As you restate or "backtrack" people's statements to them, you make them feel like they are being heard. Also, by carefully observing the people you speak with, and matching your gestures and speech pace to theirs, you can set them at ease. Maintaining reasonable eye contact is another way to make people comfortable. Let your eyes move naturally, as you would in a conversation with a friend or colleague.

ENDING A NETWORKING CONVERSATION

Not everyone you meet will be a good contact for you. Be gracious, regardless of your initial judgment about the business potential involved. The more you learn about people, the more opportunities you may uncover. If you sense that it would be worthwhile to have a follow-up conversation, ask if it would be all right to contact that person after the meeting. If so, ask how that person would prefer to communicate: by phone, e-mail, or in person? Then follow up according to your agreement. Also ask whether you can connect with their online network.

As with any social situation, it's extremely important to be polite. Even if you believe you have no interest in further conversation, don't just run off. When you've run the course of a conversation, and you know it is time to move on, look for someone else in the room to whom you can introduce your acquaintance. It will make the transition less awkward. Then you can move on while leaving that individual in another's capable hands.

PASSING BUSINESS CARDS

Business cards are important because they contain your contact information. Many people don't give passing a business card much thought. But presentation of business cards in the Japanese culture is akin to art, much like a ritual, and taken quite seriously. Japanese businesspeople will present their cards with two hands, and often with a slight bow. When receiving a card presented that way, accept it with your own two hands, give it a long look, turn it over, comment, and express appreciation for the card. Presenting your card in the same way will help you build rapport. Ask questions about your colleague's company, but avoid personal questions. Also note that many Japanese business professionals prefer not to shake hands. Should you receive a gift from a Japanese businessperson, honor him or her by opening it when presented. Unlike Americans, who often believe a gift should be held and opened in private, the Japanese expect you to open the gift in their presence. Again, offer appreciation. Be polite, smile, and avoid criticizing others, especially your competition. These are good rules to follow when doing business in any cultural setting.

When you know you will be networking or conducting other business with individuals from different cultures, do some homework in advance to make sure you understand cultural variations and expectations. (See Chapter 8 for more information on people, business, and culture.)

Common Networking Mistakes

It may be tempting to look for a better contact when you are speaking with someone in a networking meeting, but make a habit of protecting the dignity of every person with whom you speak. Rather than scanning the room to find someone more interesting to talk with, keep people engaged with questions and ask them whom else in the room they would like to meet. Then walk them over, and make an introduction when you can. If you don't know the right person, offer to help them find the right person, before gracefully excusing yourself. Then, remember to come back or call to close that introduction loop, whenever possible.

Before another person will entrust you with the names of his or her own valued contacts, you will have to earn their respect, and trust. You can build credibility more quickly by helping other people meet their own networking needs—even while you are scouting out people who can help you keep business humming. When other people recognize and come to believe you have their best interest at heart, you will gain their trust. You also can build trust and credibility by following up as you promise to do, providing reliable information, making helpful introductions, and providing astute and relevant information.

Where to Network

Networking groups vary, based on interest and locale. Physical meetings take place in a multitude of settings (e.g., libraries, churches, golf courses, and diners) and forms (e.g., office parties, executive breakfast gatherings, women's groups, and professional organizations). Networking groups may start out with an intimate foursome and grow to include hundreds of people. Some networking groups are free, but most groups charge a fee to join. Costs can range from $5 a visit to several hundred dollars per year or even thousands of dollars in initiation fees. Some networking groups are more exclusive than inclusive, particularly those designed only for high-level decision makers and CEOs. In other groups, you must have a sponsor and will be vetted before you are allowed to join.

Whatever group you network with, the key is to surround yourself with a diverse group of committed, professional people. Real networking power is not only in the number of people in the group but also in the number of qualified buyers those people know. It's been estimated that everyone in business knows at least 200 people; so networking with one person can actually open you to 200 possible prospects. Multiply that by the 200 or so people you may know, and you'll see the potential for growing contacts through networking.

Networking Outcomes

Networking presents outstanding opportunities for developing strategic alliances, partnerships, channel partners, joint ventures, and affiliate marketing programs. Search out and build relationships with people and companies who share your market. Extend your sphere of influence. For example, a marketing professional would do well to meet printers, people who specialize in graphic and digital arts, and others who can refer business to your company. The marketer of a law firm would benefit from alliances with lawyers from practices who concentrate in different areas, as well as other business executives connected with their areas of legal specialization (e.g., hospital representatives for health-care attorneys, product manufacturers for patent lawyers, home-care agencies for eldercare lawyers, and accounting firms). By connecting with people who are already connected to your target market, you can tap into your colleagues' circles of influence and through them meet a client base that matches your own target market. Likewise, you may be able to provide introductions of value to those business associates. Accountants would establish referral relationships with payroll companies, insurance and risk management firms, lawyers, and representatives from other professional service companies that target the same market.

CHOOSING FROM THOUSANDS OF NETWORKS AND CONTACTS

A look through the business calendar of your local newspaper will provide an instant view of business networks in your region, along with information about where and when they meet. A search of the Internet also will turn up relevant groups, from formal professional and trade associations to casual meet-up groups and online forums. Ask your colleagues and clients where they network, and try out those meetings. If one of your clients participates, it is likely that you'll find other potential clients there as well.

You can simplify your choices by prequalifying a prospective group. First clarify your reasons for networking. Look for a group that's a good match for your needs, in terms of culture, location, and membership. When you locate a group you plan to visit or check out online, attend a few meetings and look for clues to the organizational culture. Visit that group more than once to get a good sense of whether it will be productive to invest your time and resources. Before getting too involved, make sure the group is one that you respect. Read the group's mission statement. If it doesn't have one, perhaps you would prefer a group with more focus and organization.

Finally, remember that networking is a commitment of time, not only during a meeting, but also after the meeting. To gain referrals, you'll need to put in some legwork generating referrals for others. This effort must be made on your own business or personal time. Between the cost of time, membership fees, meals (when networking takes place over lunch or dinner), meetings with group members, and prospects in between membership gatherings, your networking effort represents a substantial investment. When calculated out, the cost of attending weekly networking groups can run a small business between $2,000 and $10,000 a year. If networking is part of your marketing plan, be sure to research costs and allocate a budget line.

Quiz

1. A lead is as valuable as a referral.

   (a) True

   (b) False

2. The difference between a lead and a referral is:

   (a) Referrals are introductions to someone who is expecting your call.

   (b) Referrals are made at networking meetings while leads are made online.

   (c) Leads are qualified prospects.

   (d) Referrals always turn into a sale.

3. Effective networking happens when people:

   (a) Plan for referrals, not leads

   (b) Know your purpose

   (c) Prepare in advance

   (d) Listen well

   (e) All of the above

   (f) Only choices (b) and (c)

4. An elevator speech:

   (a) Is a short introduction that communicates business value

   (b) Is Web language for "small talk"

   (c) Should be limited to traveling

   (d) Is never more than 30 seconds

5. The purpose of business networking is to:

   (a) Close sales

   (b) Enjoy cocktail party conversation

   (c) Build relationships that lead to referrals

   (d) Qualify prospects

6. Common networking mistakes include:

   (a) Not paying attention to the person with whom you are speaking

   (b) Asking for referrals before you build a relationship

   (c) Passing out business cards

   (d) Not shaking hands

(e) Offering help too soon

(f) Only choices (a) and (b)

(g) Only choices (a), (b), and (d)

7. A great way to network is to surround yourself with:

(a) People who can give you leads

(b) A diverse group of committed individuals

(c) People with money to buy services

(d) Social marketers

(e) Business service providers

8. You can find networking groups:

(a) In business calendars

(b) Online

(c) By asking colleagues

(d) Observing where clients network

(e) All of the above

9. A statement that will help people remember you is called a:

(a) Reminder

(b) Personal statement

(c) Tagline

(d) Brand position

(e) Tip

10. A good networking conversation:

(a) Helps qualify prospects

(b) Puts people at ease

(c) Requires follow-up

(d) All of the above

PART FOUR

Practical Strategies for Marketing Campaigns

CHAPTER 12

Planning a Marketing Campaign

In previous chapters, we focused on how to apply integrated marketing and branding principles, and incorporate into your business endeavor the 7 Ps of marketing (product, position, plan, people, placement, price, and promotion). As you've come to understand, marketing is not a single action. It is as much a process of qualifying your products for the market as qualifying the market for your products. Everything you do in market planning, from product research to competitor analysis, prepares you to eventually implement a marketing campaign. A *marketing campaign* is a series of structured activities designed to increase brand exposure, stimulate product demand, develop leads, and connect you with customers. This chapter focuses on how to roll out a marketing campaign with attention to detail-driven implementation.

Like politicians on the campaign trail, marketers employ tools—direct mail and e-mail campaigns, house-to-house canvassing, retail surveys, Web sites, social marketing, and promotional giveaways—to capture attention and sway consumer opinion. As with a political campaign, besting the competition is the name of the game. And, as every candidate knows, marketers have only so long to do it before their effort is judged a success or failure. While voters head for the polls, customers vote with their pocketbooks. They make their opinion heard on social Web sites, where they rate products, opine on blogs, and spread word-of-mouth messages in social networking forums. As you plan a marketing campaign, your goal will be to develop positive encounters with prospects and customers in measurable ways.

Defining Objectives

Marketing campaigns come in all scopes and sizes, for a wide array of reasons. Marketing campaigns can help you do these things:

- Introduce a brand or product
- Increase product penetration
- Restore faith after a product or media crisis
- Foster public awareness about a social issue or concern
- Educate consumers about product features, safety, and innovation
- Respond to a competitive threat

For your marketing campaign to achieve your desired outcomes, you first need to decide the purpose of your campaign and how you will reach each intended audience. Then you can move on to determining whether you need customized messages for each segment of your marketing list. The answers will guide you to develop, organize, implement, and manage the marketing campaign process.

Managing the Campaign

Every marketing campaign has three main goals:

1. Serving high-level strategic company objectives
2. Attracting leads and surfacing qualified prospects
3. Choosing the right tactics to make your campaign a success

By nature, marketing campaigns are multifaceted and require strong project management skills. As a campaign manager, you must keep track of multiple elements, such as the campaign timeline, contacts database, copy and creative art, placement venues, your call to action, and campaign results. If you don't have a large in-house staff, you also may need to manage third-party relationships with graphic designers, audiovisual consultants, Internet marketers, a mail-order house, and promotional vendors. With so much happening at once, you will need a system for monitoring the process and tracking results.

ESTABLISHING DELIVERABLES

A campaign spreadsheet will help you determine what activities should take place simultaneously, and which must happen in sequence. I recommend grouping items on your spreadsheet by functional categories, such as advertising, publications, and Internet marketing. Take a look at the sample campaign management spreadsheet in Figure 12.1. It not only lists functional categories but also tracks progress by due date, people, status,

Deliverable	Person Responsible	Due Date	Status	Red Flags	Budget	Impact
ADVERTISING						
Copy writing						
Creative design						
Print placements						
Commercial shoot						
Television placements						
Radio spot						
Radio placements						
PUBLICATIONS						
Business cards						
Letterhead						
Doorknob hangers						
Pocket folder						
Product brochure						
Sell sheet						
Coupons						
Sales training manual						
Product user guide						
Photography/illustrations						
Community report						
Event materials						
Partner materials						
INTERNET MARKETING						
Web site design						
Product pages						
Landing pages						
Autoresponders						
Joint ventures/affiliates						
Blog update						
Social media outreach						
Search engine marketing						
SPECIAL EVENTS						
Date selection						
Venue selection						
Entertainment						
Promotional ordering						
Advertising						
Announcements/invitations						
Mail house coordination						
Partner/sponsor outreach						
Honoree selection (if this is a charitable event)						
Cosponsor participation						
Direct mail letters						
CHANNEL DEVELOPMENT						
Lead management						
Retail outreach						
Wholesale planning						
Joint ventures						
Affiliate marketing						
Private labeling						
DATABASE MANAGEMENT						
Data capture						
Data entry						
Data mining (analysis)						
Data cleaning and updating						
Data transfer/integration						
PUBLIC RELATIONS						
Press kit/press releases						
Reporter queries						
Team biographies						
Annual report						
Social responsibility						
Viral campaign						

Figure 12.1   Campaign management spreadsheet.

and budget. On your spreadsheet, you can include as many task categories as you need. You also can use the spreadsheet as a guide for your campaign meeting agenda. If you plan to set up an e-commerce program, for example, you will need to address your catalog components, shopping cart platform, merchant services, order tracking, and search engine optimization strategy. So, you would add those items to your spreadsheet under the Internet Marketing section. During your meeting, the team member responsible for Internet marketing can brief you with a status update. Assign a project manager or other team member to update the spreadsheet and distribute it ahead of your meetings.

Choosing Your Marketing Channels

Channels connect companies with customers. Each functional area of your marketing team serves as a channel in itself. Your channels may include advertising, direct mail, e-mail, Internet marketing and Web presence, search engine marketing, public relations, and community relations, print collateral (literature), publicity (including texting campaigns), special events, and trade show marketing. Other channels, such as retailers, wholesalers, and strategic partners were discussed in Chapter 6. Choose the promotional channels that best fit your campaign goals and budget.

Opportunities

Focus on the opportunities you see for differentiating yourself in your market. Scan the news and look for trends and concerns. Conduct a SWOT analysis (described in Chapter 3) and identify the best ways to shape your value proposition in response. Consider the needs and opportunities presented by current and potential channel partners. Whether you are marketing B2C (business to consumer) or B2B (business to business), you need to determine your best-play strategies in terms of messaging and medium. When selling B2B products and services, it's a safe bet that you will shape your value proposition around motivators such as the need for profit, time saving, productivity increases, and employee morale. With consumer marketing, you more than likely will home in on major product benefits and how they fill special needs in your customers' lives. Whatever you sell, focus on creating the perception of value in the minds of your target audience(s). As you do, you will determine which type of promotion makes the most sense:

- Coupons, discounts, rebates, and programs offering more for less
- Locations offering easier access to your products and services
- Convenience through expanded hours, Web site payment options, and speedy delivery
- Loyalty builders, such as special invitations and promotions to preferred customers

- Urgency drivers, offering time-limited special promotions
- Fear busters, providing satisfaction guarantees and/or warranty programs

The goal of many promotions is to eliminate fear and remorse about buying. Toyota took this tack in 2010, following the discovery of safety concerns in Toyota vehicles. The company responded to massive media coverage and consumer concern by advertising a new warranty and service program. While Toyota saw this as an opportunity, time will tell whether this approach has been strong enough to counter serious consumer concern. Once you have matched your promotion to your perceived opportunity, you must decide the scope of your effort and scale your promotional plan accordingly. When you are confident that you have chosen your strategy wisely, you will be ready to tackle copy writing and creative art.

Web Presence

There are many ways to share your message, and the fastest-growing vehicle is the Internet. Through search engine optimization, you can transform your Web site into an Internet business driver, and your company blog can become a relationship builder. With a combination of Web site banner ads, links, and search engine marketing, you can to drive traffic to your Web site, and through your Web site to your sales funnel. With an integrated Internet marketing campaign, you can reach into various target markets cost effectively using:

- E-sales campaigns
- E-newsletters
- Submissions to e-zines
- Social media transactions; in addition to participating in popular social media networks, you can create your own online community, at sites like www.ning.com, which allows you to build an entirely new networking site to which you can invite your own customers and prospects

EXPERTISE

Using your Web site as a sales channel, you may find a hidden marketing opportunity in the specialized knowledge that your company already owns. Consider transforming your content into its own sales platform. Authors, technology firms, business leaders, trainers, Realtors, and other entrepreneurs market their proprietary content in the form of podcasts, sell sheets, blogs, articles, and manuals. On one hand, you can create an easily maintained online revenue stream. Or you can use those materials as giveaways to build customer interest and loyalty. Since the demand for paid public speakers has ebbed in recent years, many experts have turned to "information marketing," the process of packaging and selling their content instead of their speaking services. They create elaborate Web-based campaigns that pull people into a marketing funnel and draw them through a series of product offers. To build their e-marketing database, they structure joint ventures with other experts to cross-promote their marketing lists, or they engage affiliate marketers to channel prospects their way.

RELATIONSHIP MARKETING

Once you bring prospects into the fold, you have a unique opportunity to provide them with value-added (free or paid) products and services. As prospects read your online promotions and newsletters, they become more familiar with you. That is the start of your relationship. Over time, they may look forward to your e-letters and eventually decide to test drive a service or two. If you feed customers valuable content, they will appreciate it and come back for more. That's why you see so many e-promotions priced at a ridiculously low $1.99 or $7.99 or $79.99, for seemingly high-value content. Marketers use fear-free price points to start the cycle. Once in the system, the interested consumer is contacted again over time and introduced to higher-priced items. The current thinking is that a good portion of those clients (more than 20 percent) will later engage at a more profitable product level.

The 2 x 2 x 2 Strategy

Developing loyal customers is part of relationship marketing. To build loyalty, bankers, for example, use a $2 \times 2 \times 2$ formula. They make personal calls to new customers two days, two weeks, and two months after they first open an account. A banking team repeatedly calls to ask whether the customers are happy with the service and/or need further assistance. Later in the year, customers are contacted again with ongoing product offers. The goal is to get seven products sold to every customer: checking account, savings account, direct deposit services, check card, credit card, automatic bill paying, and online banking. Online banking and automatic billing offers are critical to customer retention in the banking industry. Studies show that when customers use multiple products and invest their time with you, as they do when setting up an online banking account, they are less motivated to disengage. As long as the bank continues to provide excellent service, it will have customers for life. While most banks use the aggressive $2 \times 2 \times 2$ model, other companies employ $4 \times 4 \times 4$ or $6 \times 6 \times 6$ models, depending on business needs and product flow.

To capitalize on your relationships when campaign planning, think about who knows and understands the value of your brand, products, and services. Incorporate those individuals in your campaign planning, whenever possible. Transform staff, customers, friends, and family into purveyors of your brand. Get their testimonials. Involve your resellers and affiliates in spreading your promotion, using incentive programs where necessary. Also, think about who needs your services most. It's not always possible to be all things to all people and this approach can dilute your brand if you're not providing excellence across all product and/or services. Sometimes niche markets will be your best campaign play. It's possible that you will find your most loyal customers and brand ambassadors in a smaller market segment.

The most reliable way to build relationships that enhance marketing promotion is through consistent messaging and reliable service. Draw on your positioning strengths, networking relationships, and the halo gained by affiliations with popular strategic partners, affiliates, and resellers who already have a following in your target market. By tying your brand to theirs, you can absorb some of the shine from their halos and build sales bridges through their relationships.

Unshakeable Value

A steadfast goal in every marketing campaign is to help customers understand the utility— and unshakeable value—of products and services. Your campaign should communicate your value proposition to one or more markets in ways that help people understand what problems you help them solve, where you add value, and what differentiates you from your competitors.

When planning a campaign, consider whether your current value proposition responds to the needs of your audience and/or how it might need to change. Keep an eye on the market and what your competitors are doing so you will be sure to develop a highly relevant campaign.

Publicity and Promotional Advertising

Use your team to shape the right messages and choose the right vehicles. Advertising is costly, especially if you are trying to reach multiple markets. You may include print, electronic advertising, giveaways, trade show display booths, and/or light boxes in subways or concert venues. As with any investment, you must assess your ad campaign's projected return on investment. Then match your options to your budget. Remember that a strong public relations effort (i.e., unpaid advertising) can achieve a broad reach as a complement to or replacement for paid advertising promotions.

Rolling Out Your Campaign

Depending on your needs, market scope, and budget, planning your campaign rollout can be determined in a single meeting or require a series of team meetings to discuss and coordinate all aspects of successful implementation. Promotional strategy and implementation

planning typically begin after your business objectives have been laid out, market placements determined, and the marketing team charged with developing appropriate copy and creative. A best-practice planning team includes representatives from various marketing disciplines:

- Copy and creative services
- Event planning
- Direct mail and database management
- Telemarketing
- Digital marketing
- Public, community relations
- Project management
- Video/audio production
- Internal communications and publications

Campaign Creativity

Getting started with your campaign plan goes beyond humdrum planning. It is your chance to fire up creativity. Engage your team or your favorite muse in brainstorming sessions to talk, visualize, and act out scenarios in line with your marketing goals. Think of brainstorming as a faucet for pouring out as many ideas as possible. List every idea suggested before evaluating any of them. Don't criticize ideas as they come. Just add them to your list and keep the creative juices flowing. Then, you can explore as many ideas as possible from as many perspectives as possible. Play what-if games in a no-holds-barred atmosphere (well, almost no holds). Toss ideas up, down, and sideways. Then choose the best of the best ideas to implement. Figure 12.2 serves as a reminder to think about how many ways you can present an idea to shift it from ho-hum to compelling. By shifting your perspective and attitude, you can unlock possibilities and generate new ideas.

Once you've got your inspiration, you'll need to establish a rollout process for creative development; refinement of ideas and campaign messages; picking the medium or media; coordinating with your sales, operations, and customer service departments; assigning a project team, tasks, and responsibilities; preparing for launch day; implementing the campaign (in stages, as needed); forecasting; and tracking results.

Figure 12.3 presents the strategy used by a consulting firm[1] to cultivate market awareness and clients for an entrepreneurial training program. The diagram details the work flow from identification of marketing vehicles (on the top line), such as e-blasts, videos, and purchased e-mail lists. After the vehicles have been chosen, the campaign focuses on

---

[1] Provided courtesy of Diane Kramer, Ph.D., founder of the Extraordinary Self programs, and www.ExtraordinarySelf.com.

SHIFTING A HO-HUM ATTITUDE

HO-HUM

HO-HUM

HO-HUM

HO-HUM

HO-HUM

HO-HUM

HO-HUM

HO-HUM

SHIFTING A HO-HUM ATTITUDE

© BOLD Marketing Solutions, Inc.

Figure 12.2   Shifting a ho-hum attitude.

capturing more customer data by encouraging e-mail recipients to try free products and program previews. Recipients are asked to register their e-mail address before downloads are made available. Once that data are captured, prospects are moved through the funnel with additional outreach e-mails and special offers, and directed to campaign-specific landing pages. Landing pages lead to squeeze pages, where clients encounter a strong sales close and a link to the shopping cart to facilitate and capture the sale. The squeeze page is the last page in the cycle. After clients select products to try or purchase, they later are moved through ongoing client engagement with future offers according to preset schedules facilitated by autoresponder technology. You can find autoresponders at sites such as www. constantcontact.com, www.aweber.com, and www.1shoppingcart.com.

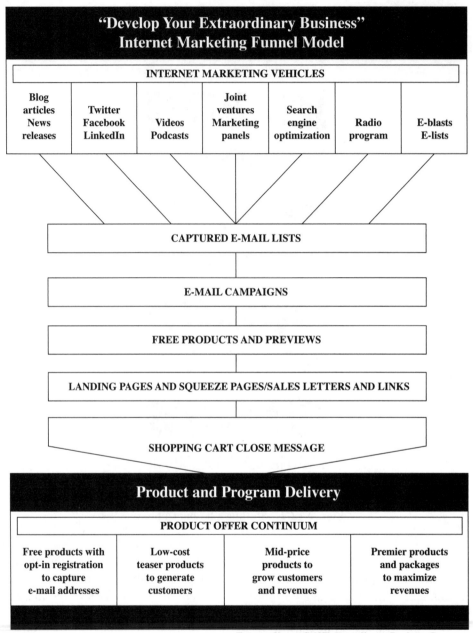

Figure 12.3 "Developing Your Extraordinary Business" Internet Marketing Funnel Model.

Measuring Campaign Results

Decide how you are going to measure your progress, and determine whether your campaign is working. Set marketing goals and measurement criteria, such as dollars spent, dollars earned, customers reached, number of target markets entered, or other desired outcomes. Then identify the promotional strategy that will best meet your needs and budget.

You'll want to know which elements of your campaign have worked best in which locales. For example, you'll need a way to tag elements of your campaign so that you will know which responses resulted from which media placement and/or aspect of your campaign. You can solve that problem by publishing different phone numbers in different media, including unique codes for each placement, or directing people to different landing pages on your Web site based on different promotions.

PREDICTING AND EVALUATING RETURN ON INVESTMENT

Successful marketing campaigns are based on numbers. Every marketing campaign must ultimately serve the overall sales strategy and business need. Campaign development presents a best-practice opportunity to collaborate with your sales and finance teams. Set up a meeting with your sales group to identify the projected or actual sales conversion rate for each product or service. In other words, find out how many prospects you must bring to the table in order to close a sale. Every industry and company has a different number. When you know what you have to accomplish in financial terms, you will be able to determine how many calls, contacts, and leads your marketing campaign will need to generate in order to uncover qualified customers and deliver reasonable return on investment. This process will help you develop a realistic budget. Tying your marketing effort to measurable sales outcomes is a step that marketing departments miss when concentrating on copy and creative services alone.

Companies often look at marketing as a cost center. By tying and converting marketing promotions directly to sales impact, you can turn a marketing cost center into a profit center. Knowing the sales facts will help you calculate the number of ad impressions (e.g., print and electronic advertising views, clicks and/or visits to your Web site, viewers and visitors to your trade booth) needed for your marketing campaign to be judged to be a success. Knowing the conversion rates, and the impact of marketing's contribution to sales, will help you understand your department's role in profit generation. If your projects are multifaceted and complex, or if you are unsure about how to project return on investment, speak with someone in your finance department or ask your accountant for advice.

You now know the steps to building a promotion and to calculating potential return on investment. (There is more information related to profit calculation in Chapter 19 on budgeting.) But you still might be wondering about return on your promotions investment, particularly when operating in a challenging fiscal environment. According to a 1981–1982 study of 600 businesses, conducted by McGraw-Hill, companies that maintained their advertising budget during that recessionary period averaged higher sales, with gains of more than twice that of the companies that cut back on spending. Even though many companies dove back in to advertise when the economy got better, those that advertised during the recession and gained marketing traction, retained stronger market share when the market improved. When you do advertise, make the most of it by building in a trackable call to action. In that way, your advertising will do double duty as a lead-generation system. By tracking and evaluating responses, you will help your sales team convert the prospects generated through your marketing effort into customers that keep your business humming.

Finally, remember that your marketing flow impacts brand value and management across internal and external channels. Every element in some way feeds another and must be monitored and tracked for value. Figure 12.4 presents a high-level process flow that demonstrates how key functional areas interconnect. Every action is interdependent and impacts another aspect of brand marketing.

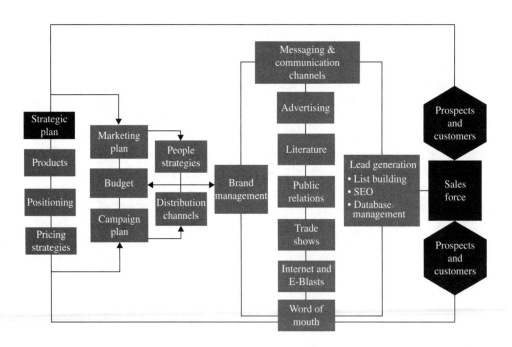

Figure 12.4 Marketing process flow.

Quiz

1. A best-practice opportunity to collaborate with your sales and finance teams is to:

   (a) Set up a meeting with sales to learn the projected or actual sales conversion rate

   (b) Contact the sales manager the day before your campaign will roll out

   (c) Speak with your finance officer after the campaign to discuss return on investment

   (d) All of the above

2. Knowing your sales conversion rate will help you:

   (a) Bridge the gap between marketing and sales

   (b) Determine how much of your marketing budget to allocate to a project

   (c) Find out how many prospects you must bring to the table in order to close a sale

   (d) All of the above

3. Marketing campaign managers need a system for:

   (a) Creating urgency in customers' minds

   (b) Meeting with corporate executives

   (c) Monitoring the process and tracking results

   (d) All of the above

4. Restoring faith after a product or media crisis, and responding to competitive threats are:

   (a) Ways to connect with your target market

   (b) Reasons for conducting a marketing campaign

   (c) Essential to marketing campaign success

   (d) None of the above

5. A main goal of every marketing campaign is to:

   (a) Serve high-level strategic company objectives

   (b) Create a joint venture

   (c) Implement an autoresponder program

   (d) Use the right tactics

   (e) Only choices (a) and (c)

   (f) Only choices (a) and (d)

6. When developing your campaign plan, you must:

   (a) Engage your CEO in the process

   (b) Rely on assumptions that worked in the past

(c) Challenge existing marketing assumptions

(d) Include an annual report

7. A campaign management spreadsheet:

    (a) Enables you to track campaign progress

    (b) Helps communicate and reinforce accountabilities

    (c) Provides a guide for meeting agendas

    (d) Should group items by categories such as advertising, public relations, and Internet marketing

    (e) All of the above

8. Which of the following are reasons for a promotion?

    (a) Coupons, discount or rebate

    (b) Time-limited offer

    (c) Opening of a new location

    (d) It's been several months since the last promotion

    (e) Your new product or service is not ready for hard launch, but your competitor is running a promotion now

    (f) Only choices (a), (b), and (c)

9. Effective campaign management encompasses:

    (a) Tracking timelines, a contact database, copy and creative, placement venues, and calls to action

    (b) Management of third-party contractors

    (c) Specific measurements of return on investment

    (d) Communication with internal and external audiences

    (e) All of the above

10. The $2 \times 2 \times 2$ and $4 \times 4 \times 4$ formulas are:

    (a) Product dimensions that help buyers double or quadruple their investments

    (b) Integral to every automated response program

    (c) Time-driven contact points for ongoing customer service

    (d) Only choices (a) and (c)

CHAPTER 13

Advertising and Media Planning

Advertising is a sales tool that enables you to get in front of a massive number of prospects in one fell swoop, with a message that informs, influences and/or persuades prospects to want your brand. Put together a multimodal campaign that mixes various media and you can extend your reach into multiple markets, niches, and locales. As you do, you will set the stage for your sales team to call on prospects or reinforce your brand with existing customers. First, you need to learn what advertising and media buying are all about.

Advertising is a dual-platform marketing tool. On one level, it is an exercise in copywriting and creative message development. But great copy and creative art must physically connect with customers before they can do their work. So, advertising's other platform addresses message dissemination—getting the word out. That's where media planning comes in. Media outlets include television, radio, Internet, newspapers, magazines, fliers, newsletters, blogs, Web sites, e-mail, cell phones, and an assortment of out-of-home public venues where you can find everything from digital televisions with rotating screens in restaurants and malls, to printed promotional literature and displays, business card racks on diner walls, and roadside billboards.

Media planning may sound mysterious, but it really is a simple cause-and-effect process of learning what you need to know so you can work out the most productive way to achieve your goals. Media planning helps you purchase the right advertising space to connect with your intended audience, in accordance with your budget and other resources. Your media plan must start with research to identify the media—or media mix—that will reach your target market(s). Once you know where to advertise, you also must plan when to advertise, how often, and what you can afford. No single medium will reach every audience. Even a mass medium (e.g., television, radio, newspapers, magazines, or the Internet) will only reach the audience that actually views, listens to, or reads it *on the days and times* you place your ad. By setting tight criteria for the individuals you want to reach, and investigating their reading, watching, and listening habits, you can home in (as a radar homing device does) more quickly and efficiently on your target market. Even though you would then reach out to a smaller audience, you would have a stronger, more relevant message for them, and a more effective media buy. For example, rather than going for broke with a single ad in a big newspaper or a daytime broadcast buy that reaches a massive audience, you could be more effective with smaller, more frequent ads in a magazine that targets the specific type of consumer or smaller niche market you want to reach. Or you might choose less expensive nighttime broadcasts on shows that attract fewer people but reach the right people for your products. That would be people who are interested and predisposed to buying what you sell.

Especially in a budget-conscious environment, you'll need to justify your choice of media and recommended buys. Today's media-rich world offers plentiful vehicles for getting your message out. To choose the best medium for your message, first, find out where the people in your target market hang out, where they go for information, whom they trust, and what they read, listen to, and watch. Learning where your customers and prospects hang out and go for information will help you figure out where to spend your advertising dollars.

Media planning itself is a strategic process. The goal is to tie your decisions to overall business objectives, market positioning, and market reach. Refer back to your company's own strategic plan and/or marketing plan to make sure that your selections make sense in terms of overall organizational objectives. For example, if you are advertising a high-end, premium product, you should advertise where the people capable of buying your product go for information. *The Wall Street Journal* or *The New York Times* may cost more than your budget allows. Advertising in major papers can cost well above $30,000 for one full-page ad and may expose you to close to one million daily readers. By comparison, advertising in a regional weekly business newspaper or monthly magazine may cost under $2,000 per page, and the shelf life of those publications (weekly or monthly editions) will be longer and probably will have longer pass-around value. So, if you target your advertising spend tightly enough by choosing the right page, sections, coverage areas (i.e., circulation), and industry publications, or explore discount opportunities and adjust your ad frequency, you can create a media plan that will be right for you. Keep in mind that repetition of more frequent ads (even if they are smaller or shorter) will boost recall, which is a critical factor in increasing brand and product recognition and trials. Remember, too, that relevance sells stuff. Develop ad copy that lets consumers know how your products and services will impact their own lives.

The only way to know what will work is to research your choices. You can learn about available options by reading the advertising information on the Web site for your target media and then calling for more information. Don't be afraid to ask questions! Your advertising representative wants to build a relationship with you and will provide the information you need.

Knowing the basics of media planning will help you buy media on your own or understand the language and strategies of the agencies or media companies that can help you make the best media buys. When you learn a little about media options, and what they can do for you, you will be better able to reach your target audience(s) and choose a cost-effective strategy.

Make your media planning tactical, as well as strategic. Once you decide on the medium that is a good fit for your audience, choose the right action plan for reaching those customers. Again, use your marketing plan as a guide. Look at your goals, and then break them down into actionable next steps. Consider these things:

- The specific demographic(s) you are targeting
- The best time to run your campaign
- The best place(s) to run your campaign
- How many impressions you need to generate enough prospects to generate enough sales calls to generate enough sales to pay for your campaign and yield a profit
- The cost per impression that will make your effort cost effective
- How frequently you have to touch those customers to get them moving
- Your call to action (that tells prospects what to do now that they've seen or heard your ad)
- What team members or consultants (if any) you need to execute your campaign
- Your specific message
- The best copy and creative positioning

Cutting through Advertising Jargon

Not every marketer has an advertising background, particularly when the marketer comes to the job by default. Business owners and novice marketers often take on the marketing role with little training and learn as they go. The key to success in advertising, as in life, is asking questions so you can learn what you don't know. To get you started, here are some of the important advertising terms and their definitions:

- **Allocation.** The amount of money you set aside to reach a particular advertising objective or execute a specific media buy.
- **Banner.** A small graphic display advertisement that appears on a Web page and is linked to the advertiser's Web site.

- **Bounce rate.** A measure of Web traffic that indicates the percentage of site visitors who click through to a different site rather than to other pages on the initial site.

- **Break position.** The commercial time slot between programs, as opposed to during the program.

- **Circulation.** The number of copies sold or distributed (print); homes in coverage area; or viewers passing an out-of-home ad, that is, a billboard, or viewing and sharing a digital medium.

- **Classified ad.** A short ad that typically targets a single purpose or product, and is placed according to an index system in the publication. Classified ads are often used to advertise jobs, specific items for sale, adoptions, and personal requirements.

- **Column inch.** A standard measure in the formula for print buying in newspapers and magazines.

- **Consistency.** Your ability to stay on message across your media selections. Consistency is a crucial element of branding. You can achieve visual consistency by creating advertising standards for use of photos, logos, trademarks, colors, and layout formats. You can help ensure message consistency by assigning an editor or staff member to review every publication and advertisement for tracking and consistency of message content and context.

- **Conversion.** The rate at which ad viewers respond by completing a call to relevant, measurable action, such as signing up for an e-newsletter, providing information to receive a download, or purchasing a product.

- **Cooperative advertising.** A cost-sharing program in which the advertising burden is borne by multiple business entities, in some combination of brand advertisers, retailers, publishers, and channel partners.

- **Cost per click (CPC).** The amount paid when someone clicks on an ad in a pay-per-click advertising campaign. The rate for this is usually determined relative to your ranking against competitors in terms of position on a page. Advertisers may bid for preferred site position using bid price as leverage. On the Google AdWords program, the cost per click will automatically adjust, based on your bid ranking.

- **Cost per point.** The unit cost of a commercial divided by the rating of the program slot where it appears.

- **Cost per thousand.** The cost per 1,000 individuals or homes reached by an advertisement, which indicates efficiency of the medium.

- **Coverage area.** The geographic region capable of receiving a broadcast signal.

- **Daypart.** The specific time segment of broadcast programming, such as prime time, daytime, morning drive, or early fringe (prior to prime time) for which commercial airtime is sold.

- **Display ad.** A form of print or online advertisement that includes images in addition to text (as you would generally find in a classified ad). Display ads are typically larger than classified ads.

- **DR TV.** *D*irect *r*esponse *t*elevision advertising. To understand DRTV, think of weekend and late-night TV infomercials and home shopping channels that lure viewers to telephone a call center and place an order.

- **Exposure.** Contact with the receiver of an advertising message.

- **Flight.** The duration schedule of your advertising campaign.

- **Franchise position.** The location or placement of an ad in a top-valued position, based on editorial content, premium spot (cover, back cover, or adjacent to editorial content), or the specific geographic market involved; a top position is usually offered in exchange for a long-term contract or premium payment.

- **Frequency.** How often you run an ad in print or on television, radio, or the Internet.

- **Hiatus.** The intervening time period between ad activity in print or on the air (e.g., a commercial may be run once a week and then be on hiatus for six days).

- **HUT.** *H*omes *u*sing *t*elevision. This measure can tell you your advertising reach when planning or buying television ads.

- **Impression.** The estimated number of people who view your ad exposures. For example, if you place an ad in a newspaper with 90,000 paid subscribers, and estimates are that two people in each household read that paper, your average impressions per ad would be 180,000.

- **Insertion order (IO).** Your advertising reservation, which must be made prior to the issue date of your ad. The IO typically specifies the start and end of the ad flight, ad size, color, description, special instructions, contact information, rate, and signed confirmation.

- **Landing page.** The Web site page a visitor is directed to after clicking on a link. The landing page typically offers more detailed information on products and services than the original page that contained the link to it. Landing pages themselves frequently include links to a more specific squeeze page (defined below).

- **Leaderboard.** A type of Web site banner advertisement that usually spans the width of the Web page and appears at the top of a Web page.

Table 13.1 Measurement Conventions

Medium	Measure
Online advertising	Clicks and click-throughs to sales pages
Web sites	Hits or unique visits over a specific time period or on a specific page
Television	Rating points and clearance (percentage of homes reached)
Radio	Coverage area, including population
Blog radio	Registered members and hits on site
Newspapers	Paid subscribers or distribution
Magazines	Paid subscribers or distribution
Trade shows	Attendees and leads generated
Direct response TV (DRTV)	Calls and purchases
Out-of-home media (posters, billboards, bus walls, airport walls, convention centers, stores, blimps, theaters, etc.)	Showings

- **Medium.** The broad category of advertising that you may choose, such as newspaper, magazine, television, radio, Internet, or in-store display. When discussing the medium, you might choose a more specific *vehicle,* such as a pay-per-click ad or a specific magazine, newspaper, or radio station or show.

- **Measurements.** How advertising exposure and reach are assessed. While all advertising promotions eventually are measured in results gained when a quantifiable program is put in place (calls received, and ultimately sales made,), each medium has its own measurement conventions (see Table 13.1).

- **PPC.** The *pay-per-c*lick fee structure used with Internet advertising. The advertiser is charged each time a visitor clicks on an ad. When purchasing PPC advertising, you can set a daily or monthly budget maximum that, when reached, will remove your ad for the rest of that budget period. This helps control costs and avoid budget surprises. You also can set PPC parameters to govern how often your ad is shown in a day (continually until used up, or revolving on a specific schedule over time.) In addition, you can bid for position of your online PPC ad.

- **Point of purchase (POP).** Displays, such as end caps and/or cashiers' racks designed to capture attention. They serve as ticklers that target the impulse buyer; they remind customers of your products before they leave the store.

- **Public service announcement (PSA).** An informative, educational advertising broadcast or article prepared and distributed on behalf of public interest as a service to the community. Most media will run a PSA free of charge as part

---

CAUTION

Paid Internet ads usually reside to the right of natural search engine results. Top placement isn't always better. Ads at the top get more clicks than ads placed lower on the page. When those clicks are from curious Web surfers rather than your target audience, they influence cost-effectiveness. You can pay less money for a position farther down and increase the chance that your ad will be clicked on by someone who was interested enough in products and purchasing to scan the list longer, rather than click automatically on the first item available.

---

of its news or community service commitment, as space allows. PSAs are usually submitted by not-for-profit organizations, helping them to protect their advertising spend, by gaining free brand exposure. Many advertising agencies will produce public service announcements at no cost (*pro bono*) or for a discounted fee.

- **Rate card.** The pricing document (often available online) that provides the cost of advertising in the vehicle, along with special instructions, such as issue and placement options, graphic arts specifications, and deadlines.

- **Reach.** The number of individuals or households that get a publication, receive broadcasts, have television sets, or click on a Web site. When you know a vehicle's demographic reach, you can calculate impressions earned. Or, you can ask a sales representative to provide you with approximate reach statistics for specific demographics.

- **Run of press.** The option of placing an ad anywhere in the paper, at the publisher's discretion, as opposed to paying for a particular spot (e.g., right page, cover, classified section).

- **Squeeze page.** A squeeze page is the last page that prospects are directed to in the Internet sales cycle during e-marketing. It is designed to close the sale or get the customer to take a specific action, such as subscribe, download, or purchase. A squeeze page rarely contains links to anything other than the shopping cart or a registration form.

Key Elements of an Advertising Campaign

What about the advertising campaign itself? There are several reasons for running an ad campaign. One of the main objectives of advertising and promotion is to establish what is called "mind share," or share of mind. Building mind share is an integral part of market positioning. This refers to the amount of attention someone pays to your brand and products as measured by the amount of time spent thinking about it, in comparison to other brands. Mind share also can refer to the development of consumer awareness about a specific product or brand and the consumers' level of predisposition to buying it.

To focus your advertising effort, start by defining your strategic goals. You may want to build brand awareness, activate interest in products, solicit a particular response (that is, a call that will generate a qualified prospect for follow-up, or encourage a direct sale.) What outcomes do you want to gain from your campaign?

- Strengthen brand awareness
- Increase mind share
- Activate awareness
- Prepare the market for a company transition or new business unit
- Introduce a new product or service
- Increase understanding of a product feature
- Differentiate yourself from your competition
- Sell a product or service
- Move overstocked inventory
- Address a crisis
- Appreciate your customers
- Support a strategic business need
- Other? What do you want to do?

Now that you know what you want to accomplish, how can you get there? Plan, check, and track. Forget the spaghetti test, in which you simply toss an idea (like a strand of spaghetti) at the wall and hope it sticks. Don't be tempted by the impulse to shoot some hastily written copy at a sales rep who stops by your shop to solicit your ad for a publication; without a plan, your impression won't stick.

Once you have determined your purpose and your audience, you need to construct a message and a call to action (CTA). Whether writing copy yourself and designing your own ad, or using a freelance designer or agency, make sure that your ad tells consumers what you need them to do: make a call, buy a product, refer a friend, ask for information, visit a Web site, and so on.

No plan would be complete without a budget. Ad pricing is influenced by reach or coverage, frequency, longevity of your ad flight, premium or run-of-press placement, color, timeslot, daypart, proximity to desirable content, and cachet of the particular media. When determining your budget allocation, you must factor in your goals and determine what is possible to achieve with your budget.

You may need to tweak your campaign over time. Depending on your results, you may want to change the vehicle, the artwork, the price points, and the access routes. To avoid overallocating money before you know how an ad element will work for you, start slowly and test-drive the campaign. Try a limited run in a representative market. Test a short-term exposure or a smaller print run, and check your results (e.g., calls, visits, sales, or cost per lead or sale). This step will help you conserve capital while allowing you to fine-tune your advertising, and/or direct response marketing campaigns.

Evaluation is a pressing requirement that must be considered in the planning stage of every advertising effort. Determine in advance what you hope to accomplish, how you will measure it, and who will take charge of the evaluation process. The data you collect will help you decide the best next steps for your ongoing advertising and marketing efforts.

Advertising and the Marketing Mix

Earlier in this book you learned about the marketing mix. With advertising, you get a chance to really dig into all aspects of the mix and exploit your own strengths. Consider advertising your mini–case study in utilizing the advertising mix. The *advertising mix* is the combination of media that you choose and use to disseminate your message. Table 13.2 describes various elements of the advertising mix. You can start a template for your own ad campaign by strategically integrating various components of the marketing mix (see Table 13.3) into your advertising choices.

Table 13.2   The Advertising Mix

Print Media	Broadcast	Internet	Out of Home
• Display ads • Classified ads • Door hangers • Driveway circulars • Coupon mailings • Direct mail cards • Fliers • Niche magazines and publications • DR TV • Public Service announcements	• Television spots • Radio spots • Spots on syndicated shows • Cable TV • Public Service announcements • Blog radio	• Interactive media • Search engine listings • Directory ads • Blog ads • Blog forums • E-mail campaigns • Public Service announcements • Online stores, such as E-Bay, Café Press, and Amazon • Web sites	• Dumpster signage • Billboards • Human bodies • Bulletin boards • Card racks in stores • Car wraps • Digital ads • Sports stadiums • Concert venues • Point of purchase displays • Store signage, racks, and endcaps • Trade shows • Seminars • T-shirts and promotional items

Table 13.3   Sample Marketing Mix Template for an Ad Campaign

Marketing Mix Element	Considerations	Your Plan
Plan	• What is the strategic goal (or goals) for your campaign? • What tactics will help you reach those goals? • How and where will you execute in what order? • What is your budget for your campaign? • How will you evaluate your progress and campaign effort? • How many new customers do you hope to gain from this advertisement? • What will that mean to you in dollars?	
Product	• Which products or services will you advertise? • What will your value proposition look and sound like? • Which benefits will you feature?	
Placement	• What market(s) will you target? • Which channel partners will help you? • What media will you use?	
Position	• What position are you claiming in your market(s)? • With whom are you competing in this advertising environment and market? • How will you differentiate yourself? • What message will define you and support your desired market position?	
People	• Which people and/or groups do you want to reach? • What image(s) belong(s) in your ads? • Which people and partners can help you execute your plan effectively? • Whom else can help you promote your message? • How will you use social media channels?	
Price	• What choices will create a cost-effective return on your investment? • How much profit can you earn? • How much of your budget will you need to allocate to return a profit on the ad?	
Promotion	• What medium or media will you use? • Which vehicle(s) will you use? • What is your call to action? • Will you provide a special offer? If so, which offers will make the most sense?	

Advertising Online

Digital technologies have leveled the playing field by enabling even low-funded fledgling businesses to build an online presence. Traditional media outlets have migrated toward Internet platforms as well. Everyone is on the Web now with Internet advertising deals. Choose from *The New York Times* and *The Wall Street Journal*, CNN, MSN, FOX, local and regional newspapers, radio stations, magazines, search engine sites, blogs, and entrepreneurial Web sites where you can match your advertisements with relevant content. Whether choosing online or print advertising vehicles, place your ads in media that contain content that your target audience seeks.

Direct Response Marketing

Direct response programs may include television infomercials (DRTV), direct mail, and/or coupon programs. Whatever your vehicle, the goal of a direct marketing program is to motivate an immediate response with a clear call to action. Remember, it is not enough to reach viewers. You need to reach those viewers with the interest, need, and means to buy your product. So, you must research how the people in your market use television media, then create a plan that will make good use of the daypart demographics and viewers or listeners per household.

Direct response marketing, particularly with television shopping programs, can be an expensive proposition to get off the ground. To return a profit, your advertisement must motivate and compel viewers to act immediately and buy right away. When planning for DRTV, you need a stockpile of inventory that can be shipped soon after orders are processed. You must set up a telephone call center (you can contract with one) to manage calls, a customer service section, and possibly a help desk to respond to follow-up queries and customer support requirements. You also need a media plan that jives with call center operations and ensures that your sales staff will be accessible during peak viewer periods and that your team is trained to respond as needed.

When planning, it is wise to start with targeted broadcasts in narrow advertising parts that will help you judge performance of a time slot and coverage area. It's important to have a contingency plan as part of your overall plan to address potential issues that could undermine your marketing efforts. For instance, if your calls outpace your inventory, will you have resources available to fill unanticipated orders? Alternatively, if your orders fall short, will you be able to continue paying warehousing fees, or will you have to run a fire sale? By planning ahead, you can avoid losing the big dollars you must spend on airtime.

Online Advertising

When using traditional ads, you can closely control your advertising spend. Your ad costs are exactly what you contract for, no matter how many people tune in to read it, view your commercial, or hear it on radio. Whether you reach one person or one million people, you

pay a fixed cost. Online advertising is another ball game, particularly when you use the pay-per-click model. The key to getting online ad views is knowing how your prospective customer thinks and searches. Digital advertising has gone crazy with opportunities. You can place ads on Web sites, search engine pages, mobile devices, and RSS feeds. Whichever tack you take, you can control costs by setting tight criteria for your target audience. By predicting and narrowing the terms that your prospective targets are mostly likely to use when searching for information, you will develop criteria for your target markets and ad campaigns. That endeavor becomes easier when you (1) learn keyword strategies, (2) understand your audience, and (3) determine a reasonable budget that will work for you. Remember, if you start small, and test variables such as strength of keywords and keyword phrases, media choices, and page positioning, you can uncover the keys to a profitable campaign. As your campaign turns out qualified prospects who convert to paying customers, you can begin to reinvest profits into a larger campaign that will help you reach more qualified prospects that you can convert into more paying customers, more revenues, and even greater profits. So let's take those strategic steps in order.

KEYWORD MANAGEMENT

When planning the keywords you will use to guide Web visitors to your Web site or ad, you must "get inside the head of" your ideal prospect. Identify the single words and phrases that your customer is likely to use. You can figure this out by thinking about the answers, solutions, or benefits he or she is seeking, and then listing what you believe will be the most relevant search words, topics, and themes in your prospects' keyword selections. Stringing words together into relevant phrases will help you further narrow your search returns. That will help you connect with the kind of customer you are really looking to reach. During your marketing research and planning, speak with prospects and customers to ascertain how they search for information and what words they use. Also, conduct an Internet search on your competitors and learn what keywords and phrases are posted on their sites.

Because Google is a popular, easy-to-use advertising resource, here's some insight to how it works. Google (and other ad platforms) offer keyword search tools that help you select keywords and phrases. Simply type your topic, category, or Web address into the search field, and the search engine will automatically generate suggested keywords for you. Then, you can insert them in your copy, set up keyword tags in your search engine optimization program, and begin attracting visitors organically (not through paid advertising.) You also can use those same keywords in paid ad copy for your pay-per-click response marketing. The tools will sort suggested words by relevance to the words you entered and reveal how many people searched that term in a given time period.

When using pay-per-click advertising, you want only interested, qualified prospects to click on your ad. So, your goal is to set up your ads in ways that will help control who clicks on them. If you are setting up unpaid search terms, you can use *broad match* keywords, which will generate search results for similar phrases and variations. For more specific targets, *phrase match* keywords can turn up your ads (or copy) when Web surfers type that exact phrase inside quote marks into their search browser. Phrase-match keywords also can generate results when the specific phrase is part of a longer string of words. When looking for tightly targeted results, try setting up your keywords in brackets. Returned search data will generate only the *exact match* to your word specifications. With this strategy, you will get fewer hits on your ad, but the visitors who click are more likely to be interested specifically in your product or service. To avoid hits from consumers you don't want to view your ad, set up some negative keywords that will restrict your ad from appearing to searchers using those specific, nonqualified search terms.

Negative keywords are words that you can preselect so they do not direct visitors who typed those terms to your site. This will ensure that you don't route unqualified prospects to your pay-per-click ads. For example, if you are looking to sell an exclusive work of art, you don't want to pay for clicks from people looking to buy a mass-produced poster.

FINDING YOUR ONLINE AUDIENCE

Success with online advertising requires you to get in the groove with your audience. As discussed in Chapter 10, take time to list the criteria for your ideal customer. Then, try searching keywords in locations, such as blog forums, YouTube, and Twitter to see what people are talking about. That will help you assess the volume of interest in your subject. In fact, you can Twitter on your topic and build a following, as long as your tweets are helpful instead of sounding like a sales pitch. As followers of a topic get to know your tweets, they may check out your Web site or blog and find themselves predisposed to your products and services. By then, they will feel as if they have come to know you as a vendor.

ONLINE AD BUDGET

In recent years, advertisers have become more comfortable with online advertising and are allocating larger percentages of their overall ad budgets to the online sector. Your online budget should flow logically from your overall marketing plan goals. Before deciding between print and electronic media, you have to understand your target market's behavior patterns and media preferences. Doing so may require you to do some research. If you don't have money for marketing research and need more clarity, look at what your key competitors are doing. Also, watch how other businesses (i.e., indirect competitors) in your market are spending their ad dollars. Observe companies you wish to emulate, within reason, and within your capabilities. What's good for another company may not be good for you. If you are working with a small budget, ask the advertising agency staff for recommendations on how you can make the most of your resources. Attend local seminars about online advertising and use of social media. Not only will you learn what's new (as media options, strategies, and technologies are continually changing), you also will meet business owners and professionals with similar issues and questions, and you'll be able to network (another form of advertising) at the same time.

How much to spend is a personal decision, based on your business model and bottom-line returns. First determine how much new business you need to generate from your ad campaign. Then consider your overall resources, and scale your budget accordingly. Start small and test the waters. As you check results (i.e., clicks and conversions), copy and creative, keywords, page placements, frequency, vehicle, and even medium, you will gain data and evidence to guide future decision making. Then you can build on small successes to create bigger and better advertising results.

Working with a Freelance Graphic Artist or Agency

If you don't have an advertising and creative team inside your company, you can benefit by hiring a freelance graphic artist or an advertising agency. The benefits of using them can well outweigh the costs. Advertising and design professionals can help you sharpen your message and polish your delivery. And, they can usually do it in less time than it would take you to complete the same project. While there is a cost involved, professionals already have the right computer programs and tools at their disposal. They are experienced in preparing artwork to match print or digital specifications, which results in higher-level output and better quality reproduction. What's more, these professionals can work with you to design visuals and layouts that can be repurposed for sales collateral and other projects. This will result in an even greater return on your investment.

To make the most of your relationship with a graphic artist, spell out your requirements in advance. Give plenty of lead time so the designer can schedule the job to meet your needs and avoid speed-related mistakes and the need for rush charges. Also, build in lead time for proofreading. Ask for a printed (or e-mailed) price estimate in advance that explains whether payment will be project based with a predetermined fee or billed hourly and at a certain rate. Prices vary significantly, based on the artist's experience and mastery of marketing. Less-experienced graphic artists may charge as little as $20 or $30 an hour, while seasoned professionals may charge $125 to $150 per hour. Agency rates may bill in the neighborhood of $250 to $300 or more per hour, depending on the project and the individual assigned. Most artists will include up to three sets of revisions in the project rate. Before materials are released to you or your printer, payment is typically expected in full, pending your approval of the artist's proofs. Printing costs are additional, and a separate bill and approval process is generated for the printing service. The same rules apply to printing of promotions. Get a printed price estimate, as was discussed in Chapter 2.

E-mail Campaigns

If you get e-mail, you are familiar with e-newsletters, some of which come daily, weekly, or monthly, like clockwork, whether you want them to or not. But at some point, you must have said you want them and opted into the list, which is why they keep coming back. We discussed e-campaigns in Chapter 12. Here, I want to call your attention to the *strategy* of e-campaigns. Some sellers choose the very long, mini–Web site format in which they share a message, repetitiously, with oodles of testimonials and "proof" of success. These letters spell out the benefits you will get and the life you will enjoy if you respond to their calls to action. Marketing researchers say this long-letter strategy works. In other words, it gets people to do something, order something, or at least stay in the loop long enough for you to try to sell them something else. In Chapter 15, we discuss drip marketing and the importance of staying connected through ongoing product offers and education. One way to make that process easy is to use autoresponders.

AUTORESPONDERS

When you start an Internet marketing campaign, you can take advantage of a shortcut. You can set up an autoresponder series that will send out your e-mail messages according to a predetermined cycle that you only have to set up once. First, you create and load a series of messages into the e-mail autoresponder program. Next, you tell your autoresponder at what time or process intervals to mail out that message. The autoresponder series then starts on a particular day. You may schedule it to send a series of follow-up messages you set up to send out two days hence, five days hence, ten days hence, or whatever time frame you choose. Or you can set it to send another e-mail after receiving a reply from a prospect. Once you've established the criteria, your e-mail messages then will go out automatically. As a result, you will be free to focus on other marketing tasks while the technology does your advertising and marketing work for you. Most e-mail blasting software and shopping carts allow you to segment your lists so that you can send targeted autoresponder messages to particular subgroups of prospects or clients.

Getting the Most from Your Ad Dollars

Remember that profit is the reason you are in business, so let your higher purpose guide your advertising decisions. To build revenues, plan ethical ad campaigns that will drive revenues through media that are strongly connected to your target audience. Also, choose media outlets that are willing to work with you on price and placement so you can tend to your bottom line and gain maximum impact. Remember that almost everything is negotiable. Ask for the deal and position you want. You often can work out a better buy simply by asking for it. Ask for information about special promotions and ask the following:

- What else can you do for me?
- Is there a sale in the works?
- What would happen if I took a different page?
- What if I placed the same ad again?

Another option is to tell an ad vendor you need to think about your decision. Call back closer to deadline when the seller may want to close out available inventory. Even in a buyers' market, when sellers may be more willing to lower pricing, it helps to approach ad purchases with a win-win spirit. Don't make your ad exec squirm for your business. Try to work a deal that works for both of you. Building a good relationship can reap benefits in the long run.

Ask to be placed on the advertising department's mailing list in all your targeted media. Also ask for an upgrade when you purchase, such as a buy one, get one, (buy one ad, get one free, aka a "bogo" sale) or a premium page placement as a faith builder. Finally, before buying advertising, always ask about the media's demographic reach and tracking. Make sure it meets your expectations.

Internet Radio as a Resource

For people whose advertising strategy includes building their public profile as an expert, Internet radio shows are growing like wildfire. BlogTalkRadio (www.blogtalkradio.com) offers a free, intuitive, user-friendly platform for getting your message out. All you need is a phone connection and you can broadcast, live or taped, over the Internet. Your message is instantly recorded and syndicated automatically. While the service itself is free, there is an upsell available with premium services for editing podcasts and moderating and screening calls. This platform also allows users to choose Skype as a host, so you don't have to dial and pay for phone time.

Blog radio is not just a tool for small entrepreneurs. Major corporations, such as PepsiCo and Century 21, use it to broadcast messages from senior leadership to a graphically dispersed field team. Back in the day (and still today), many corporations used broadcast messages and telephonic conference systems for the same purpose. The difference is that the BlogTalkRadio Web site already had more than five million listeners at the time of this printing, and that number continues to grow.

To use BlogTalkRadio, simply go to the Web site and create your own profile, metadata, and keyword tags. You can tweet automatically from the site and share that information in real time. Alan Levy, founder and CEO of BlogTalkRadio, has shared five tips for building a radio following:

- Create good content and tag it. People will find it and increase your audience virally.
- Prepare and present a good-quality show, consistently.
- Leverage tools [such as] Facebook and Twitter to promote the show.
- Invite engaging guests onto your show.
- Blog about your show.

Once you have established a radio show, you can use it to advertise products and events, and to build relationships with colleagues and consumers across the globe. With streaming technology, hosts of radio talk shows and Internet seminars are able to connect with audiences and build a worldwide following. With an investment of time, a small-to-moderate financial investment, and a targeted strategy, you can build connections for your brand, your products, and your services with small niche audiences around the world. That is what advertising can do for you.

Advertising Ethics

A particular advertising promotion is using bodies as advertising real estate. As an ad campaign, this concept is fairly new, but the ingenious part of the campaign is the target community: the body "real estate" belongs to high school students attending the Orange County Public Schools in Orlando, Florida. Those students have agreed to lease out their faces for logo painting, and the promotion provides advertisers with access to the student body, their families, school faculty, and community members. Local businesses are pleased to have their logos worn on students' faces for contracted time periods, and students are enjoying this school-spirited type of promotion.

This interesting strategy also presents an opportunity to discuss the issue of ethics in advertising. Given that the medium is people, and minors at that, it is incumbent on school officials, the community, and advertisers to ensure that the process and advertising quality is nonexploitive. This advertising strategy helps raise funds for school programs, and gives youngsters an opportunity to participate in a socially responsible marketing program (that is, one that serves the community). At the same time, it is clear that children represent an impressionable and vulnerable audience. So, when choosing your own advertising venues, take note of your community's special needs, and ensure that you balance ad creativity with ethical standards. While advertising is designed to persuade, it is the advertiser's responsibility to decide how much pressure is too much. We discuss the topic of integrating ethics, morality, and social responsibility in Chapter 18.

All advertising should pass tests of integrity and acceptability, given by your own company, the specific media in which you are placing the ad, and society at large. Professional organizations in the advertising field provide standards and guidelines for advertising ethics (see Chapter 18). Individual media also maintain their own guidelines for acceptability, based on the specific needs and concerns of the particular media enterprise. In short, advertising guidelines typically require the following:

- **A clear indication that the copy and creative art submission is clearly separated by style and content from editorial pages.** For example, some companies run what are called "advertorials." An *advertorial* is an ad that looks like a news or feature article. Advertorials mirror the content, layout, and/or font style of the vehicle in which they run; thus, most media require them to be clearly marked as being advertisements. Some papers allow the word *advertorial* to be used in small print somewhere on the ad itself, usually at the bottom or top border of the page.

- **Credible claims.** Advertising must be believable and/or backed by evidence.

- **Conformance with industry and/or government regulatory requirements.** Some industries, such as finance and pharmaceuticals, require the use of specific taglines and disclaimers.
- **Decency.** Ads should conform to society's moral code.
- **Dignity.** Advertising should not compromise the integrity of others or take advantage of vulnerable individuals or populations.

Quiz

1. Run of press refers to the option for:
   - (a) Running an ad anywhere in the paper
   - (b) Running an ad many times in the same edition
   - (c) Running an ad based on the printer's schedule
   - (d) None of the above

2. HUT is a term used to describe:
   - (a) The location of heavy coverage utility towers that broadcast commercially
   - (b) The number of houses using television
   - (c) Homes under emergency television broadcast reach
   - (d) None of the above

3. Franchise position refers to:
   - (a) The location or placement of an ad in a top-valued position
   - (b) Placement near in-demand television or print content
   - (c) Positions that are sold at a premium price
   - (d) All of the above
   - (e) None of the above

4. An advertising campaign requires which of the following components?
   - (a) An advertising strategy and a media plan
   - (b) Budget development
   - (c) Message content
   - (d) All of the above
   - (e) None of the above

5. Evaluation measures should be established at the end of every advertising campaign. True or false?
   - (a) True
   - (b) False

6. Your ability to stay on message in a series of ads is known as:

    (a) Call to action

    (b) Consistency

    (c) Context

    (d) None of the above

7. To make the most of your marketing dollars, ask:

    (a) What else can you do for me?

    (b) Is there a sale in the works?

    (c) Suppose I take a different page?

    (d) What if I placed the same ad again?

    (e) All of the above

    (f) Only choices (b), (c), and (d)

8. Strengthening of brand awareness, increase in mind share, preparation for a market transition, introduction of a new business unit, and introduction of a new product or service are examples of:

    (a) Advertising campaign issues

    (b) Strategic advertising goals

    (c) Media planning

    (d) None of the above

9. The term "advertising impression" refers to:

    (a) The feelings and perceptions you create in the minds of target customers

    (b) The share of mind you develop in a target market

    (c) The estimated number of people who view your ad

    (d) None of the above

10. Credibility, honesty, dignity, and conformance are examples of:

    (a) Advertising copy requirements

    (b) Ethical guidelines for advertisers

    (c) Skills required of advertising team members

    (d) None of the above

CHAPTER 14

Organizing a Public Relations Effort

Public relations (PR) is the aspect of marketing promotion focused specifically on building positive relationships with the public, community groups, and the media. Public relations practitioners strive to communicate business messages, organizational messages, and policy messages in ways that build trust, positively influence opinion, and create goodwill.

The Role of Public Relations in an Organization

As a public relations practitioner, you can play an important role in helping your organization identify and manage perceptual and business risks. By reflecting on research information about consumers, policy, and issues, you can provide managers and organizational leaders with valuable insight and recommendations to help enhance your organization's image, industry standing, and position in the community.

PR professionals strive to control corporate messages, making sure that they are beneficial and consistent and help maintain continuous positive regard in the eyes of the public—consumers, vendors, alliance partners, media, and investors, among others.

They target and share messages with various groups. They work to start a positive buzz and stimulate others to keep it going.

Known for putting the best possible spin on tough news, PR agents have earned the moniker "spin doctors." Good PR professionals understand the value of building good relationships by presenting their companies' stories with honesty, integrity, and expertise. PR experts often use prior business and educational experience to concentrate in a particular market vertical, such as professional services, technology, staffing, or health care. Regardless of their background, PR agents help companies tell the right stories and communicate policies and actions in ways that gel with and/or positively influence public opinion.

In today's crowded media markets, hot news is just a click away. And, with the world operating on information overload, the PR challenge is to access the right target audience and provide it with relevant and valuable information. When developing your own PR strategy, make it a priority to understand your audience and to shape your message in a way that will generate the response you need to drive your business forward. That may be brand recognition, goodwill, a request for information, and ultimately a sale.

In the line of duty, PR practitioners factor in research on issues and trends, public opinion, and organizational responses tied to the company's strategic business and marketing goals. They create plans and budgets, and they allocate resources for disseminating that information to the public.

While paid advertising, brochures, Web sites, and organizational behavior are all employed to get specific messages out to the public, the discipline of public relations has traditionally centered on building relationships with journalists in print and broadcast media. But, PR specialists also may be called upon to develop communication strategies and special messages for internal publics such as employees and shareholders.

With the advent of the Internet and the explosion of social media platforms, it is easier than ever for companies and individuals to communicate directly with the public. Press releases targeted exclusively to journalists are increasingly being replaced with news and video releases for direct public consumption on Web sites, podcasts, blogs, and Internet radio. Other public relations vehicles include print advertising, publications, annual and community reports, special events, trade shows, conferences, newsletters, town meetings, surveys, direct mail, video productions, affiliations with special causes, community presentations, and any opportunity to create positive, value-driven relationships with constituents.

PR agents also help channel information to external publics, including the business community, trade associations, civic organizations, community members, and supply chain partners. Most public relations campaigns require multiple elements to influence or control public perception. They include:

- Knowledge of organizational goals, representatives, and contributions to society
- Identification and understanding of the target audience
- Understanding of public knowledge and perceptions relative to the topic
- A plan for communicating information
- Plan management

- Budget considerations, including allocation of campaign administration, printing, distribution and wire service, video and audio production, and other expenses such as manpower, salaries, and infrastructure costs

- A method for soliciting feedback

- A method for analyzing and evaluating results

This chapter will show you how to develop a PR campaign by helping you focus on key considerations and questions. As you answer them, you will develop your own campaign strategy.

Laying the Groundwork

You can get started by clarifying your goals, the audiences you need to reach, and your key messages. Here are some questions to ask yourself:

- What are our organization's overall message and needs?

- Is our current message right for our new, and/or evolving needs? What changes do we need to make in our message, if any?

- What are we seeking to accomplish?

- What do we need to communicate? (Be specific.)

- Who needs our message?

- Where does our audience go for information now?

- How will we get the message out?

- Are we communicating to a homogeneous group or to multiple groups?

- How are they alike? How do they differ?

- How aware are intended audience members about our product, story, or particular message now?

- What is their current level of perception? Friendly and onboard? Hostile or undereducated?

- How does our audience feel about our company and/or particular message now?

- Do they have a special problem or need?

- What is their attitude toward our company now?

- Will we target different audiences and media outlets in different ways? If so, how can we tweak our message so it remains consistent but will still resonate with each target demographic?

- Which stakeholder groups are involved?

- Should we vary our message in any way for a particular group?
- Are they educated about our message, product, or company already?
- What else do they need to know?
- How will we evaluate our efforts?

Developing Key Messages

Your message has the power to make or break public perception. How you communicate it impacts your ability to control or influence beliefs and attitudes about your organization, products, and/or services. Ensure that messages are clear, concise, and consistent when repeated and across audiences.

First, decide what story you need to tell. Then shape your message so that people know why they should care about it. Make it specific, easy to understand, and relevant to their interests. Here are some questions to consider:

- What does my audience need to know at this point?
- What might they need to know in the future? (Would you communicate different information to a new user or an acquaintance than to a user or group with whom you have a long-standing relationship? How might your message change?)
- How is this particular message different from previous messages?
- How can we "hook" a reporter or get someone to care about our story?
- What special challenges will we face in communicating our key messages?

Identifying Media Channels

When public relations practitioners—PR people—communicate company news, they must decide where and how to place that information. To learn that, they pay attention to the local, regional, national, and global media, and assess which media engages the target audience they want. They learn what kind of stories different media outlets favor, and that helps them decide whom they should target with a press release or phone call. They learn the deadlines of the publications and media outlets they hope will publish their news.

As a rule, PR agents work to cultivate "earned" media placements rather than pay for advertising. Learning where to submit your news is more than half the battle. Take time to learn what different media outlets communicate about and who writes news relating to your topic. Read the editorials, opinions, and reporters' blogs, as well as industry blogs and social marketing sites. There is a wide range of media you can use to reach your target audience. But, make sure that the people you are trying to reach actually use the media to which you reach out. In addition to submitting news to the big networks and media outlets in your area, contact and ask for press and advertising kits from the local TV and radio stations, newspapers, magazines, Web sites, blogs, shopping guides, and newsletters serving your audience. Local professional organizations and networking groups typically publish monthly or quarterly newsletters, and they are often on the lookout for member news.

MAKING YOUR MEDIA CONTACTS LIST

Once you've chosen your media outlets, you'll need to identify the right person to receive your news. Contact each outlet and ask who handles the kind of news you have to share. Most media venues have beat reporters who cover a particular type of news. Others have general editors, and many newspapers and TV stations have assignment desks, which are the first step for PR queries. Media Web sites often list reporter contacts and blog content. If you can't find the information you need on the Web, call the general contact number and ask about reporters' beats and general deadlines. Create a list of targeted media and place it in a table of information with the notes you accumulate about reporter preferences such as news interests and contact methods.

Remember that monthly newsletters often need calendar information at least six to eight weeks in advance of your events. Weekly newspapers typically require a two-week minimum advance notice for calendar items to make it into a timely edition.

To learn more about the media, and particularly the media in your region, contact organizations such as the Fair Media Council (FMC), International Association of Business Communicators (IABC), the Public Relations Society of America (PRSA), and other journalists, PR and advertising organizations in your region. Attend a few of their regular meetings and you'll meet the people—both journalists and PR practitioners—who are driving the news in your region.

CONTACTING THE MEDIA

As with any business transaction, courtesy is key. Unless you have breaking news, never call a reporter on deadline days or times. When you reach a reporter, identify yourself, your organization, and your purpose. Before calling, prepare yourself with a hook of one or two sentences that will engage the reporter's interest.

Getting the Right Fit

To get a hit in the media, learn the difference between a news story, a feature, and a calendar item. News connotes action. It means something has just happened, is happening now (breaking news), or is about to happen. News is time sensitive and deadline driven. Nondeadline stories are known as "features." Features may be trend articles, investigative reports, and human interest or enterprise stories. Announcements, such as staff appointments and awards, typically belong in a section about newsmakers or news briefs. Direct your information about educational programs, seminars, and professional meetings to targeted print and on-line calendars. A press release works well for event information or breaking news. A personal outreach to a reporter may work better if you are pitching a feature story.

Pitching Tips

Pitching your story works like every other business introduction. You have got limited time, and you have got to use every bit of it to your advantage. Figure out what will engage journalists and get the public talking about you, and you will have the hook you need to bait a journalist. A *hook* is the positioning twist that makes your story appear to be novel and compelling. Try the following strategies for standing out in a crowd.

BAITING THE HOOK

To make your hook catchy, think about what makes your story compelling. What is the real takeaway for readers? Why should they care? Hooks should be unique and provocative. They should also help the journalists visualize how they can title and/or tell your particular story. A hook is what catches the attention of a news editor, journalist, or reader and entices him or her to want to know more, especially when your story isn't exactly news. Try the following hooks on for size.

MAKE IT SHOCKING

Create a jolt by telling journalists something they didn't know *and* why it makes a difference. Shock with statistics on prevalence or lack of prevalence, and what that statistic means to real people. You can do this in person or via a press release.

CASE STUDY: Press Release Approach
Employing Shock Value

Training for Change, Inc., a training and consulting group, prepared to issue a press release on Tobacco Intervention Practices (TIPs). The lead stated, "A new DVD tutorial featuring a ground-breaking tobacco cessation program for behavioral health providers is now available. The two-part tutorial offers a readiness assessment, staff development, cultural development, and organized change strategies."

Deeper in the release, it explained that "over 70% of mental health patients smoke cigarettes, and 90% of people with schizophrenia smoke. On average, those individuals live 25 years less than the general population due to cardiac and respiratory illnesses."

It also stated that the video "Smoke Alarm," which was developed by Training for Change in collaboration with the nonprofit Clubhouse of Suffolk, recently won an award from NYAPRS NYC [New York Association of Psychiatric Rehabilitation Services, New York City] Mental Health Film Festival and was presented as a featured film at the NAMI-NYS [National Alliance on Mental Illness–New York State] 2009 Annual Conference.

While the program and awards evince outstanding credentials, credentials are far less compelling than a quick, dramatic statistic. After a PR consultation, the company decided to lead off with the shocking statistics. The numbers quickly told what was happening and the 25-year impact on lifespan clarified why that was important. The press release was picked up and published in numerous locales.

HIGHLIGHT A TREND

Observe what's happening around your business or social community. Then decide how your business, product, service, special knowledge, or story fits in to that trend. Share your take on it. What do you see happening? Is your own company on trend with environmental concerns, charitable gifts, social responsibility, fashion, or the latest technology? Are more people staying home because of the weather, or the influenza virus, or a fear of violence in your city? If so, how has that impacted you and the companies around you? If not, why not? How does your perspective fit in with that of others?

BREAK IN WITH BREAKING NEWS

Knowing the news is critical to making the news. Follow breaking stories and figure out the hook that will deal you into a story. For example, if a hurricane is about to hit, and you manufacture hurricane shutters or electric generators, you have a good reason to call the press. Offer tips on hurricane preparedness or how to decide on the right shutters or generators for you. Follow TV and Internet news feeds and capitalize on opportunities to comment on subjects in your bailiwick.

CUT THROUGH THE CLUTTER

Call a newspaper and ask for the assignment desk. Tell the editor you want to comment on a breaking story. If there's a disease outbreak, and you are a health-care professional, ask for the health editor or medical writer. If you're a statistician and you think numbers are doctored, say you've got an opinion to share. If you are an environmental scientist, and there's been an oil spill, reach for your media contacts list and start dialing.

If you don't get a call back from a journalist, you still can build your own buzz. Issue your own news release on your Web site or blog. Get your Webmaster to tag and optimize your keywords so people will find you when they query the topic. Write about your perspective

on other blogs. If you've got a lot to say, consider starting your own blog radio show. Or send a newsletter, e-blast announcement, or post information on social media forums.

RAISE A CONTROVERSY

Journalists love writing about controversy, especially about issues where the stakes are high, emotions are involved, and opinions differ. Pose a question about your issue of concern, and offer an answer. Ask the journalist's opinion. Get him or her talking and you just may hit the sweet spot.

OFFER A SURVEY

With online technology, surveys are simpler than ever and inexpensive to conduct. Survey people on your Web site or your blog. Check out www.surveymonkey.com or other survey sites you can use to put out a question of interest. Gather the data, and share the results. Results are news.

INCLUDE A REAL-LIFE ANECDOTE

Illustrate a special concern, incident, or trend in a way that tugs an emotional reaction. Think about how your product or service impacts people, and tell that story. Talk about the challenges people face in working out problems or they joy they find in the solution. Personalize your pitch by identifying people with the experience to comment on your topic before you call the reporters, so you will be prepared to give them reliable sources.

OFFER AN ANTIDOTE

Do you have the one solution that beats all others? Does it help the sleepless to rest easy, the consultant to track hours on the job, the deadbeat dad to pay up child support, the jobless to find work, the frustrated to communicate better, the injured athlete to clinch a title, the unattractive to feel beautiful? Does it relieve the overworked? Repel water? Or keep your unwanted relatives from visiting for too long? Offer up your antidote to a common problem.

SHARE A TESTIMONIAL

Evidence is your own antidote to marketing fluff. Case studies and client testimonials referenced in a press release capture interest. A third-party reference is more powerful than you tooting your own horn.

COUNT 'EM UP

How many ways can you flip a pancake? How many networking tips can you give? How many ways can you lose a pound a day? Numbers capture attention and can help a reporter organize the thrust of a story. Try a baker's dozen. Or lucky sevens. Just make the numbers work for you. How about mentioning these things:

- The top three ways to get what you want from your teenager
- The top five things every business needs for success
- Seven office decorating secrets that maximize productivity
- Ten things you can learn from an executive coach

Work with what you know. Make a list, and offer it up.

ADD A REASON FOR THE SEASON

Some stories play better than others at certain times of the year. Winter, spring, summer, and fall all offer different news opportunities. Boat captains and bait-and-tackle shops can reel in stories at the start of fishing season. Health-care practitioners can issue seasonal safety tips.

DECLARE A DATE

Pick a date and declare a special observance. With 12 months in a year, and 365 days cycling regularly, you've got countless opportunities to tie in with existing observances or to create your own.

ISSUE A CHALLENGE

Think about the challenge you can offer to your target audience. Or take my challenge: put this tips guide to work by calling 10 journalists in the next month and get your name into print.

LEAD BY EXAMPLE

Make your story come alive with neat examples of the story you want to tell. Evidence rocks with reporters.

PLAY ON WORDS

Tap into a reporter's playful spirit with spirited hooks and/or puns. Try these: turn your business into a vacation; learn about the hard return on soft skills; how to do more with less; or how to sip champagne when you have beer pockets.

OFFER A DEMONSTRATION

Watch for opportunities to showcase your business, products, or services by demonstrating the results process. What does your business change for others? How can you make that

story visual? Offer a public demonstration. This is a great strategy for a TV pitch. Tell the editors how and why watching a particular demonstration will change someone's life.

WALK A MILE IN YOUR SHOES

Set aside a day where journalists can team up with someone in your company and mirror their work. When I was a print journalist, this PR strategy proved effective. I took up a hospital PR director's offer for me to walk a mile in a nurse's shoes, and I ended up writing a full-page story on the hospital's AIDS unit.

Before pitching your story, remember to research media personalities. Decide which journalists or talk show hosts would be the right fit for your story, and show how they can become involved with your story, products, or service and entertain or involve their viewers or listeners. Also plan ahead so you will have more than one hook on your line. If a journalist rejects your first idea, don't hang up. Jump in with another approach. The first one may not have communicated the real value; the next pitch might.

Establishing Media Relations

- **Make a list of local media and editors' fax numbers.** Have them on hand when you need them. Don't send e-mail to people whom you don't know, unless they publish their e-mail address with a request for story ideas.

- **Be short.** Short sentences and no more than one-page releases are best. Remember, you are not writing the article; your goal is to get the reporter to call you so you can build a relationship.

- **Be specific and honest.** Do not exaggerate. Extreme claims will make reporters wary.

- **Make it easy for the reporter to use your information.** Ask yourself, what is in it for the reader? Remember that the journalist often has to sell the editor on why this news item belongs in the paper. The bottom line is, if you can show relevance to the readership, you will have a better chance of getting your news published—for free!

Creating Your Press Kit

A *press kit* is a folder of information, or an electronic selection of files, known as an electronic press kit (EPK) that you can send to your media contacts after you have made a connection and someone has asked for information. Here's what press kit items should include:

- A background on your company
- At least one press release

- A professional business portrait and/or a high-quality photo of you in your business setting

- A list of previous press hits

- A selection of articles in which you have been quoted or featured. Highlight your name if you are one of several people quoted.

- Also prepare an EPK that you can e-mail to contacts, as needed. Place all elements of your press kit on your Web site in a "media room," where journalists can find and download the background information they need. If using a PDF (Portable Document Format), make sure it is editable so that journalists can easily copy and paste for their stories. You will make it easier for them to share your story and minimize errors at the same time.

Writing Your Press Release

Press releases are communications written to inform the media about news and events. They may convey information about an industry happening, company event, business accomplishment, new concept, product launch, or individual.

Press releases should rarely exceed one page, double-spaced. The purpose of having a press release is to invite a press query. It is not an article. It is a teaser that should inspire a reporter's interest and prompt a call for more information. Follow the KISS principle: Keep It Short and Simple. Pay attention to tense, using past tense for hard news and present tense for human interest and feature style reports.

With five basic sections, press releases should be typewritten, spell-checked, and formatted to meet journalistic standards and expectations. Stick with standard 12-point font (or 14-point font for titles, if space allows) such as Times, Times New Roman, Arial, or Helvetica.

THE HEADER

The heading should include the name of the contact person, telephone number, and e-mail address. An organizational logo is fine to add, but don't be surprised if it is not used in print. It is not the journalists' job to advertise your company, but it is *your* job to build brand recognition. Never use your press release to sell a product or service. Sales literature belongs in the advertising section. Use your press release to inform and educate.

Above the title to the left indicate whether the story is ready to roll, with the words "For Immediate Release" in boldface or "Embargoed until [your specified date]" if the media should hold the release, as in the case of an exclusive story, an upcoming product release, or a special announcement. An embargo (a hold directive noted on a press release) is used to give reporters time to prepare their stories in exchange for agreement not to publish before the issuing organization has approved the information for public consumption.

Reporters are generally obliged to follow the embargo criteria, such as approved release date (typically worded, "embargoed until . . .") in order to protect trust and ensure the flow of ongoing information. The embargo term also may be used internally during the organizational review cycle. Whenever possible, **do not send out anything you don't want printed.**

THE TITLE

Keep your title short, limiting it to no more than six or seven words that fit on one line, whenever possible. Use boldface for the title.

THE INTRODUCTION

Start your press release with the most important information in the first one to three sentences. Use a compelling hook or lead that focuses attention on what is happening. Press releases are for quick reads and should contain only the who, what, when, where, why, and how. As mentioned, they are designed to create interest, not to serve as a lengthy news article.

THE BODY

Provide the evidence, a quote from the company president and/or other relevant experts, along with their title(s) and affiliation(s). This is where you expand on the who, what, when, why, and where. Remember that the journalist's job is to determine relevance, so focus on benefits, rather than features and capabilities. Getting to the value will make that task easier. Easy is attractive when journalists are pressed for time.

THE CLOSING CALL TO ACTION

End your press release with a call to action, such as: contact us for more information, or register early by calling a phone number or visiting a Web site.

While the contact information on the banner of your page is for the media's use, you may have a different phone number or e-mail address to be used by the public when they respond.

THE BOILERPLATE

Written in eight-point or nine-point text and inserted into the page footer is a short paragraph describing the company that issues the release.

CAUTION

Include an action photo whenever possible with your press release. In-the-trenches action photos convey more meaning than a headshot or a grip-and-grin picture of dignitaries shaking hands or lined up for a group mug shot.

Timing Your Release

If there is a major earthquake, war outbreak, election, or political scandal, your own news release might sink to the bottom of the editor's desk and remain covered up until it is too late to be covered in the media. Releasing news early in the week is usually better than the end of the week, when papers may be thinner or the lure of weekends may call more loudly than work. When making your media list, find out when stories are typically assigned, and send your news out accordingly.

SENDING IT OUT

You can send a press release by fax or e-mail, post it on a Web site, or use a press release service, such as PRNewswire (www.prnewswire.com). Most journalists today prefer to receive press releases by e-mail, while some media outlets enable you to upload a press release via their Web site. Whether you are using a press release or an e-blast to promote your business, make the e-mail subject line as catchy as possible. Don't call reporters to ask if they have received the unsolicited press release you sent. But if you have spoken with a reporter who has requested information, you can go ahead and follow up with an e-mail message or phone call to confirm receipt, if needed.

Building Relationships with Journalists

The best way to begin a relationship is to show interest in what interests the other person. Before calling about a story, research potential reporters. Read their blogs and articles so you will develop a frame of reference for your discussion. Approach them in a friendly, informative way, with respect for their time. Be positive and receptive to their feedback. Reporters spend most of their time asking questions. You can toss out a few of your own as you build rapport. Take notes on what you learn, so you can refer back to an event in a follow-up conversation (e.g., "How did you enjoy that play you went to?" or, "Did your daughter enjoy her birthday party?").

When you call a newspaper and someone answers, it helps to ask for help. Most people like to help. If you don't know whom to ask for, explain what you are calling about and ask if he or she can put you in touch with the right person. After you've gotten a journalist on the line, ascertain that he or she has time to speak with you (e.g., "Hello, this is Donna Anselmo. I'm calling to propose a story about the topic of courageous conversation. Do you have a moment to speak now?"). If so, get right to the point. Then, use your conversation and listening skills to build rapport.

Talking with Reporters

The bottom line when speaking with reporters is to be honest. Most reporters have excellent insights and a second sense about when someone is avoiding an answer or

shifting the discussion in another direction. Before calling a reporter take time to prepare the following:

- A list of what messages you want the reporter to come away with (use bullet points)
- A list of probable questions the journalist will ask and your bullet-point responses
- A selection of company materials that are relevant to your conversation positioned near the phone, so you don't have to go looking for them and will be able to respond more fluidly and confidently

If you have never spoken with a reporter, you may want to consider media training. This instruction can range from speaking with a PR professional before meeting with a journalist to being videotaped in a mock interview session (which is especially helpful for TV interview training). You may also arrange to have a public relations professional on site when you do an interview. Over the years, I have sat with CEOs while they have had a reporter on the phone, so I could cue the CEO as needed with information or slide over a note with a key point during the interview.

If a reporter contacts you, and during your conversation you realize that your company or story isn't the right fit at the moment, see if you can help the reporter find the right connection. Offer the name of someone you know is a reliable expert and might be willing to comment. The reporter may remember you as a helpful resource and call on you in the future when the right opportunity comes up.

Controlling the Media Interview

The goal of all publicists is to control or steer a reporter in the direction you want to go.

When you have time to prepare in advance, make a list of 3 to 10 questions you would like to answer and send them to the reporter, along with a short bio they can use to introduce you. In hosting a weekly talk show, which broadcasts live every week, I ask my guests to let me know what's most important to them. Because my BOLD*TALK* Business Radio show is a talk-show feature format more so than news, I request a list of topics or questions they would like to cover. It makes my job easier and makes them more comfortable during the interview. When sending your information by e-mail (the communication tool preferred by most journalists), ask when might be a good time to follow up. Follow-up is key to success. Also ask for a recording of your broadcast or a PDF of a printed article. You might have to pay a small fee for it, but you can then use the material on your Web site to build your own personae as an expert.

Developing a PR One Sheet

One tool for talking with reporters is a "one sheet"—a single sheet of printed information that tells your story succinctly and lets the media know what is most compelling about you. To create a one sheet, think in short sound bytes. Sections should include the following:

- **The grabber.** This is a brief description of what distinguishes you or sets you, your company, or your product apart from competitors. The grabber should be no more than one to three sentences that tease the reader into wanting to learn more.

- **The body.** Shape the body around your value proposition. Before drafting your value statement, think about why you do what you do or what problem you, your company, or product solve. Explain your value based on the outcome(s) you need: an interview or a call for more information on your product or service. Include three to six sentences about benefits you bring and impact you deliver.

- **The list.** Use bullets to list topics you can address in an interview on your subject and/or intriguing questions you can answer. You also can add the time it would take you to discuss each topic.

- **Contact information.** Tell the reader how to contact you: name, postal address, e-mail address, phone number, and Web site address. Also add your one sheet to your press kit and electronic press kit.

Press Release Checklist

When you've completed your draft, review it. Check yourself by using the following list:

- My press release is informative and not like a sales push.
- It answers who, what, when, where, and why.
- It is short: one page or less.
- I provided a quote or testimony, if needed.
- I included facts and did not exaggerate.
- I properly identified people referenced in the release.
- I proofread my document.
- My tense is consistent.
- Subjects and predicates are parallel.
- I researched intended media and targeted the release appropriately.

Building Your Relationship with a Journalist

To see that your relationship with a journalist is a good one that will provide results, see that you do the following:

1. **Understand the journalist's job.** That job is not to serve the interest of your business but to attract listeners, viewers, and readers. Journalists who do their

jobs well stay employed and write more stories, which in turn enhance the media, attract advertisers, and make ongoing publishing possible.

2. **Research that media before you call.**

3. **Understand and meet deadlines.** Never call the day before a weekly goes to press. Never call to pitch a daily at deadline hour.

4. **Always follow through.** Provide contact information and other data exactly as you promise, and deliver it on time, as promised.

5. **Be a stickler for sending accurate and complete information.**

6. **Be brief.** Time and media space translates to money. Remember that reporters have limited time.

7. **Be professional, prepared, neat, and on time for interviews.** Even if your interview is by phone, dress and wear shoes. The right attire can help you stay focused on business even if you are speaking from home, on a weekend, or while on vacation.

8. **Be ready to respond with intelligence and grace.** Pay attention to communication basics and common courtesy.

9. **Be realistic about the importance of events.** Plan for appropriate publicity. For example, if your news is about an upcoming event, prepare it for the calendar section. If it is a new product release, target the right section editor. If it is of major interest to the community, push it to the managing editor and/or your favorite reporter.

10. **Send a brief note of appreciation.** Show that you value the time they've spent with you and their consideration of your issue. Do not thank a reporter for running your article, but feel free to mention your appreciation for his or her effort.

11. **Appreciate your own efforts, and track results to demonstrate the effectiveness of your effort.** Depending on project goals, you can track outcomes, such as the number of press hits in particular media or on specific topics, impact on volume sold, amount of positive versus negative coverage, and/or change in consumers' product or service awareness. Tracking can be accomplished by measuring data; incorporating a specific phone number or landing page in a particular press release and counting phone calls or visits, respectively; using pre- and post-release surveys; calculating social marketing and blog mentions; and/or contracting with a media evaluation service, such as Media Hound, Vocus, or Biz360, which are companies with software that can help track results.

Table 14.1 will help you decide how to match your news to the right media outlet.

Public Relations Campaigns

Some public relations efforts are singular. For example, a company might send out a one-time press announcement about a new hire. Or a school district might issue a school closing announcement based on a weather advisory. A psychologist might offer an occasional public

Table 14.1 Matching Messages to Media Vehicles

Sample Provider	Type of Message	Traditional Vehicle	Social Media
Business coach	Announcement of an upcoming educational program and date	• Newspaper calendars • Online calendars • Networking and organizational calendars • News editor • Company Web site • E-blast	• Facebook • Facebook fan page • Blog • Reseller blogs and pages • Online calendars • Twitter
Technology company	New product launch	• Individual journalist who writes on new products or who covers your industry • Your Web site • Television or radio news editor • Wire service • E-blast	• Facebook • Facebook fan page • Blog • Webinar • Notice on LinkedIn • Mentions on Twitter
Small business enterprise	Appointment of new CFO or key division manager	• News editor • Web site	• Facebook • Blog • Word of mouth • Update on LinkedIn pages • Twitter announcement
Not-for-profit organization	Post-event announcement	• News editor with photo release • Company Web site • Company newsletter	• You Tube video • Facebook fan page • Blog • Twitter comments
Corporation	Award from national organization to individual or company	• Company Web site • Company newsletter • Regional newspaper, television, and radio editor • Wire service	• Company blog • Company fan pages • Twitter mention • Updates on LinkedIn
Small business or large corporation	Internal staff award announcement	• Employee newsletter • Hometown newspaper of awardee	• Instant messenger • Word of mouth • Blog • LinkedIn update • Twitter
Small business or large corporation	Establishment of new division	• News editor and/or individual journalist • Company Web site	• LinkedIn profile • Facebook • Blog • Twitter
Small business or large corporation or not-for-profit organization	• Community education seminar • Professional conference or trade show • Community event	• Television news assignment desk • Newspaper calendars • Online calendars • Networking and organizational calendars • News editor • Company Web site • E-blast	• Facebook • LinkedIn • Blogs • Twitter • SMS text service

talk and notify a target audience, or a company might issue a response to an adjustment in stock prices. By comparison, a public relations *campaign* is a structured effort to achieve a specific public relations goal over time and in stages. Some examples of PR campaigns follow.

SAMPLE PR CAMPAIGN 1: THE SCHOOL DISTRICT BUDGET VOTE

A school district begins planning in September to favorably influence residents who will vote on the school budget the following May. Over the course of the year, school officials structure a campaign to enhance community relations and public opinion about school programs and overall administration. The campaign includes a series of newsletters distributed by the district to the public. Award assemblies and open house nights also factor into the campaign, as do public hearings on the budget, and special budget advisory information as the vote draws near. Throughout the year, school administrators and teachers respond to daily events and crisis situations in a manner consistent with policy, procedures, and brand messages conveyed about the district throughout the year. The district coordinates with the teacher's union, which is allowed to lobby for the budget, while school district administrators are not. (They are only allowed to present the budget for voter consideration and action.) Four months before Election Day, the district invites journalists to attend board meetings, steps up personal outreach to the press with engaging story ideas, and endeavors to present an honest, fiscally responsible persona to the media and the community. By the time the vote is held, every voter has received at least one mailing about the budget vote, as well as several newsletters about student accomplishments and fiscal management of the district over the year. If the campaign worked, the budget is passed.

SAMPLE PR CAMPAIGN 2: CORPORATE MERGER OR ACQUISITION

A publicly traded technology company has had a rough year, due to litigation, court costs, and a settlement assessment. The company's client base and its overall reputation make it attractive to another company seeking to grow by acquisition. As word of an impending merger is whispered around water coolers and in the cafeteria, the PR team is called in and briefed on the financial situation as well as the status of premerger discussions. The team assesses the current internal climate and recommends a town meeting to brief employees. The team creates a PowerPoint presentation that addresses questions of concern:

- Why the merger is on the table
- Anticipated benefit to customers
- Anticipated timetable
- Impact on employee headcount
- Branding considerations, e.g., intended name of the combined entity and new logo

- Integration team members
- Transition management team
- Announcement of shareholder meeting

The PR team also develops a plan for communicating to external entities, such as clients and the media, about the merger. The team decides to create a merger-launch tagline that will inspire ongoing loyalty among employees and clients. It recommends "Service, Loyalty, Value" and prepares a media statement about the combined mission, supported by a statement about the solid reputations of each of the individual companies participating in the intended merger.

SAMPLE PR CAMPAIGN 3: PRODUCT LAUNCH

A small fragrance company is preparing to launch a new perfume. The marketing team is small, and the CEO, who is up to her elbows with the manufacturing, finance, accounting, and sales departments, usually handles press commentary. The company needs to generate awareness of and excitement about the new product. The CEO decides to retain a PR consulting firm to build a buzz by managing pre- and postlaunch communications. The consulting firm conducts a survey to assess consumer interests and awareness, works hand-in-glove with the advertising department, and plans press releases about the brand, the individuals involved, and initiates a social media campaign to build buzz about the new product launch. The firm schedules monthly meetings with the company's marketing department to gather feedback and provide recommendations for ongoing public relations opportunities.

SAMPLE PR CAMPAIGN 4: NONPROFIT ORGANIZATION'S AWARENESS INITIATIVE

A child-care organization wants to get out the word about the importance of high-quality child care in the community. It turns to a marketing firm to help shape and disseminate key messages. Believing the organization is one of the best-kept secrets in the region, it sets two basic goals for the PR campaign: (1) educate the public about child-care issues and the availability of quality child-care services in the area, and (2) lay the foundation for a public fund-raising campaign.

Here's what PR planning includes:

- Developing key talking points for three specific audiences: employers, families, and community members
- Assembling information on how child care impacts employers
- Making the message relevant to the corporate arena, families, and community members, respectively

- Identifying media outlets and local journalists interested in child and family issues, as well as topics relating to the economic impact of child-care services
- Creating a one-year timetable to host a major fund-raising event
- Setting a fund-raising goal
- Engaging the business community in fund-raising and PR strategy
- Calling media contacts throughout the year (as news events allow) and sending press releases to raise awareness of organizational issues and events
- Arranging a meeting with the regional paper's editorial board to educate members about the issue
- Arranging for cable television to prepare and televise free public service announcements about the organization and upcoming events
- Naming the event
- Choosing the honorees who will be recognized at a fund-raising dinner
- Developing a logo and graphic theme for invitations and announcements
- Planning and executing a fund-raising kick-off luncheon on the premises of a world business leader headquartered in the region
- Creating an awards program and related messaging to support the fund-raising initiative
- Procuring members of the business community to serve as honorees
- Developing memos with talking points and contribution solicitation letters for honorees to use when communicating (note the word-of-mouth marketing strategy)
- Creating an advertising plan to support the event
- Procuring free and half-price ads in regional papers and magazines
- Sending out PSAs (public service announcements) that air on the radio
- Earning articles in various newspapers, magazines, and newsletters
- Advertising the event in the organization's newsletter

Table 14.2 details a sample task list with status reports that helped keep this sample project on track.

Communicating in a Crisis

Nobody likes surprises. But they happen all the time. Damage control requires expert advance planning, at-the-ready internal and external communications programs, and a finger kept on the pulse of public opinion. Strategic analytical skills, the ability to evaluate contingencies, and predict potential outcomes are necessary. Sharpening those skills and processes before you need them will pay dividends.

Table 14.2 Sample PR Plan with a Project Timeline of Eight Weeks

Milestone	Date Due	Status	Needs / Red Flags
Finish press release.	Done	Draft is completed.	Approval is needed.
Establish media contacts for above.	Done	Contacts made with *Networking* magazine *Long Island Business News* *Huntington Observer* *Northport Observer* *Newsday* Posting on Web site	
Develop a one sheet about organization with key questions the press would find of interest	Done	It has been submitted for approval.	We need feedback on coaching topic.
Develop a press kit, both regular and electronic versions.	June 30	We created the one sheet format.	We need a photo to complete it.
Review and provide a report on Web site text.	July 15	Process is already under way in the marketing department. We will solicit input from other colleagues as well.	Time allocated for this project may conflict with time needed for trade show planning.
Gather a list of competitors for Web site reviews and to get on their e-mail lists for trend analysis.	July 30	Searching for list of local competitors. I need you to provide input; also I will check a published book of lists.	
Follow up with a reporter after the article that ran in the *New York Post*.	Done	We connected via e-mail and planned for a future article.	
Prepare pitches based on follow-up to the distributed interest survey and worksheet.	Ongoing	We have been pitching story ideas to television, radio, print, and online media. We have one reporter interested in the relationships concept for a magazine article.	
Prepare a corporate outreach case study.	Needed by mid-July	We need to develop a design prototype that will serve as a case study graphic in the training manual.	Decide which client to profile.
Prepare a cover letter for a corporate outreach promotion of case study.	Depending on when the case study information is complete		First we need to know which case study the CEO prefers to use.

First, work on building a trustworthy organizational image. Companies who exercise due diligence in developing and living up to their standards of excellence are more likely to garner public sympathy during a crisis situation. Also, honor the basis for your relationships with reporters. Share only honest, noteworthy news and provide them with information that helps them do their job well. Doing these things in advance will go a long way in the effort to maintain high positive regard for the organization in times of challenge or crisis.

EXAMPLES OF A CRISIS

Crises emerge when actual facts and public opinion conflict with the brand promise. For example:

- A CEO of a large company is criticized for spending money to fly to Washington in a private jet when the goal has been to testify about the organization's financial difficulties and ask Congress for a bailout.

- International banking organizations are reviled for paying bonuses to executives shortly after receiving federal funds designed to provide business relief.

- A doctor is dismissed after administrators learn from the media that he had served time in jail and had been implicated in poisonings of patients and colleagues.

- A vice president of human resources is sued by a female employee for sexual harassment.

- A school district is ranked at the bottom of the state report on academic achievement.

- A charity is accused of excessive administrative costs.

Each of the preceding scenarios could have been avoided if executives had watched for warning signs of a problem and regularly took the pulse of employees and public opinion. The good news is each experience is a learning opportunity and provides a chance to do the right things right going forward.

As a PR spokesperson, your goal is to communicate your perspective, as well as essential information *before* stakeholders and public opinion mongers reach uninformed conclusions. By observing organizational culture and events with an eagle's eye, you will be ready to spot a crisis in the making and employ damage control strategies in advance.

Best Practices in Crisis Management

The following are some best practices that will help your organization sidestep and/or better manage a crisis, regardless of the circumstances.

PLAN FOR THE UNEXPECTED

Recognize that a problem is only one mistake away. By encouraging your organization to adhere to quality standards, maintain open dialogues, and establish a learning culture, you will set the stage for success and lower the chance of failure.

CHOOSE THE COMMUNICATIONS TEAM

Advance planning is important. Choose the key team members who should be involved in developing crisis management messaging. Decide who will communicate with internal and external publics during a crisis. Authorize a single spokesperson or a small group of individuals to release information in a strategic way when a problem occurs. The goal is to present a unified, organized front to employees, the public, and the media that tells your story your way. Involve the team in discussions, and surface all issues and potential solutions.

GATHER THE FACTS

When a mishap occurs—and, whenever possible, *before* one happens—focus on ferreting out the facts, potential outcomes, and potential solutions right away.

CLARIFY YOUR OBJECTIVES

Decide what you need to communicate and how you will do it. Co[...]
satisfy the needs of the organization as well as the need for public info[...]
your communication priorities and decide how to tell your story you[...]

ACKNOWLEDGE THE CHALLENGE

Acknowledge that you have encountered a challenging situation and that you a[...]
to resolve it. While it might be tempting to lay low during a crisis, it's important for company leadership to be seen. Don't hide and hope it will just go away. It won't. During a crisis, you can create an opportunity to demonstrate what leadership is about. You also can demonstrate your power to resolve a problem.

TAKE CONTROL

The one who releases the story essentially controls the story. If you see an unavoidable crisis, share the story in a forthright way before the press releases it without your participation. For example, if you are an auto parts manufacturer and you detect a product flaw before a fatality occurs, plan a press conference to inform the press of the process that led to detection and issue a product recall. If you are a hospital and a patient has died on the operating table because of an unexpected electrical outage, call reporters with whom you

have a good relationship and tell them the story before they find out from an outraged family member. Again, you may hold a press conference, explain the situation, and control the message.

If you operate in the health-care environment, the defense sector, or a security industry, you must balance regulated confidentiality issues with your desire to openly discuss an event or breach of process. While honesty and forthrightness are important when you are handling a crisis, you may be advised by legal counsel not to comment when confidentiality issues and/or litigation are involved. Note that the information herein does not constitute legal advice. Consult an attorney for direction on issues that may present legal and/or financial risk.

LEAD WITH COMMITMENT

Your currency in managing a crisis is the goodwill you already have established. By making integrity a priority and focusing your effort on doing the right thing in a challenging situation, you can reinforce your company's public persona and strengths, address the facts, and demonstrate your power and commitment to resolve a problem.

Your goal during a crisis is to maintain a balance among communication goals, ethics, and legal and regulatory requirements. Success will hinge on your ability to assess a situation and respond appropriately. Learn the facts *before* you communicate about the issue or event. Uncertainty fuels the rumor mill, so fill the void quickly with facts.

Company spokespeople must communicate with sincerity and take responsibility. Take time to inform employees before releasing bad news to the media and other external audiences. Your employees will appreciate the heads-up. And you will avoid the negative impact of employees hearing bad news about your company from a client or the media. That kind of scenario erodes trust.

COMMUNICATE CLEARLY AND CONTINUOUSLY

Prepare key message(s) at the outset. Hold frequent internal meetings to update the team, share information, and assess ongoing communication needs. Outline action steps for communicating what you know about the situation and what you learn from it along the way.

What to Do

- Assess the situation and develop an action plan.
- Identify the stakeholders. Who will be affected by this problem now? Who will be affected in the future?
- Consider outlining negative news and predictions early on so that the adaptation and healing process can begin and you can move forward.
- Decrease the potential for rumors. Be timely.
- Explain what the crisis means or could mean.

- Be honest, tactful, and mindful of perceptions, and don't sugarcoat the truth.
- Communicate quickly and frequently with all stakeholders.
- Communicate accountability and responsiveness.
- Communicate organizational stability and clear direction.
- Stay on message. Repeat yourself like a broken record, when you need to.
- Provide a guideline, script, or fact sheet to managers who must disseminate information.
- Provide a fact sheet to the media to help reduce reporting errors.
- Keep communication lines open.
- Enable a feedback loop so you can gather information, comments, and opinions and use them to manage ongoing responses.

What Not to Do

- Offer too little information, too late.
- Provide insufficient research, evaluation of a situation, and documentation of its impact.
- Try to hide the truth.
- Don't have enough trust that your audience can understand your issues and honest intentions.

Tips for Communicators

- Think in sound bytes.
- Focus on where you want to be with your message.
- Pause before answering. Take time and a breath when you need it.
- Admit what you don't know. Find out the answer. Then follow up.
- Prepare to correct loaded remarks.
- Don't become defensive or ornery. Just stick to the facts.
- Never assume the audience knows your topic. Provide all relevant information to dispel rumors.
- Present your position to multiple media outlets.
- Use formal communication channels, such as town hall meetings with employees and stakeholders, broadcasting of phone calls, department meetings, webinars, and media interviews to ensure proper communication inside and out.
- Give advance notice of opportunities to discuss the problem.

The Alternative to "No Comment"

Reporters hate hearing the words "no comment," so don't say them. First, it creates the impression that there is something to hide. Second, it gets reporters' backs up, because they want to deliver a compelling story, and those two words don't help. When you are restricted from releasing information by legal or regulatory requirements, let reporters know that you are open to providing as much information as possible but you are presently constrained from answering their specific questions. When restricted by a legal covenant or government regulation, the same thing would hold true. Prepare a sound bite that will play better than "no comment."

Most organizations are prohibited from discussing issues relating to individual personnel, contract negotiations, or pending litigation by law or policy. So, unless a reporter is a raw novice, he or she knows, even before asking the question, that you cannot comment on certain topics. That will not stop reporters from hoping you will slip up, particularly if they keep pestering you.

Always maintain a conversational tone, keep your cool, and be sincere. Remember that reporters are just doing their job, which is to gather comments and information.

So, let them know that you understand their needs, are concerned, and will do whatever you can, whenever you can. You might say, "If it becomes possible to talk more in depth about this, I will certainly let you know."

PROVIDING BACKGROUND FOR A REPORTER

Sometimes, the PR spokesperson is not the right source to release sensitive information. Some information should come directly from the CEO or another company official. If you know a reporter from experience and trust his or her integrity, you might want to help prepare that person to write an upcoming article by providing "background" for the story. When you know it is advantageous to assist the reporter, you might consider sharing background information with the stipulation that the information you provide may not be attributed to you and must be verified by another person who will agree to attribution, before it can be published. It is the reporter's job then to contact another source and ask about that information. In this way, you can help control the story by sharing relevant facts in the right perspective, and referring reporters to reliable sources.

OFF THE RECORD

Tread softly when providing background information, and remember that there is really no such thing as "off the record." There is always the chance that it will turn up in print, particularly when the publisher or editor demands the information from the reporter. Having a witness to the request that information provided as background is intended to be off the record, may dissuade a reporter from passing that information on. One PR expert I know lets the reporter know that a third party is present and listening during the (phone) discussion. By doing so, she avoids a reporter saying, "I didn't know this was off the record." Instead of going off the record, stay on your main message, and repeat it, whenever necessary.

Evaluating Public Relations Efforts

Since PR is typically maintained as a cost center rather than a revenue center, demonstrating results is imperative. Data gathered from results tracking allows managers to assess effectiveness, monitor progress, learn from mistakes, forecast results, manage expectations, and plan for needed change.

Lack of evaluation can put both your PR program and your organization at risk. Without evaluation, you will not be able to tell whether your approach and efforts have been benefiting your organization and/or your stakeholders. Use an evaluation tool to help you assess which efforts get the best results. Doing so will help in deciding where to focus your time, efforts, and resources in the next evaluation cycle. Use the Key Results Area Performance Evaluation worksheet in Table 14.3 to guide your evaluation effort.

Table 14.3   Key Result Area Performance Evaluation

Milestone	May	June	July	Aug.	Sept.	Oct.	Nov.	Dec.	Jan.	Feb.	Mar.	Apr.
Planning Results												
Strategy and organizational alignment details decided												
Quarterly plan established												
Special projects completed												
Messaging												
Targeted verticals identified												
Targeted messages developed												
Outreach Results												
Press releases sent												
News releases posted												
Media contacts												
Number of Media hits												
Number of Media/self-initiated contacts												
Number of Media callbacks												
Number of print hits												
Number of broadcast hits												
Number of online queries												
Outlet Diversity Results												
Print												
TV												
Radio												
Digital												
Word of mouth												
PSAs												
Event/trade show												
Business Results												
Clients captured												
Clients contacted												
Client queries made												
Clients engaged												
Alliance events held												
Speaking opportunities established												
Total viewer/listener impressions												

Quiz

1. A beat reporter is a reporter who:

   (a) Covers police blotters

   (b) Covers a particular topic or industry

   (c) Beats other reporters to an exclusive

   (d) None of the above

2. A package of information used to educate media contacts is called a:

   (a) Press kit

   (b) Backgrounder

   (c) Press release

   (d) Business portrait

3. The term "earned media" refers to:

   (a) Articles published in media at no cost

   (b) Stories that earn the interest of the media

   (c) Advertorials

   (d) Only choices (a) and (b)

   (e) All of the above

4. PR professionals earn media placements by:

   (a) Learning about what journalists communicate

   (b) Inquiring to find out who writes news relating to your topic

   (c) Reading editorials and opinions

   (d) Reviewing reporters' blogs

   (e) All of the above

5. A _____ is used for communicating event information and breaking news, while a _____ makes sense when pitching a feature story.

   (a) Press kit/press release

   (b) E-blast/telephone call

   (c) Press release/personal outreach

   (d) News release/press release

6. Telling a reporter, "I need to check on that," "Let me think about that," or "I will get back to you as soon as possible," is a tactic to:

   (a) Give yourself time to think of the right response

   (b) Control a story

   (c) Communicate during a crisis

   (d) All of the above

7. The term "media hook" refers to:

   (a) A way of pitching your story

   (b) The positioning twist that makes your story appear to be novel and compelling

   (c) The process of fishing for journalists online

   (d) None of the above

8. _____ articles can be about people or products and can be run almost anytime.

   (a) Feature

   (b) News

   (c) Column

   (d) Calendar

9. When you are restricted from releasing information by legal or regulatory requirements:

   (a) Let reporters know that you are open to providing as much information as possible, but that you are presently constrained from answering their specific question

   (b) State that you have no comment

   (c) Ignore reporter queries

   (d) All of the above

10. Background is information:

   (a) That you tell a reporter to create noise and deflect from negative news

   (b) Shared with the stipulation that it may not be attributed to you and must be verified by another person who will agree to attribution, before it can be published

   (c) Biographical information contained in a PR kit

   (d) None of the above

CHAPTER 15

Loyalty Strategies for Customer Retention

In many ways, marketing is an outbound process, focused on pushing products, services, and brand messages from companies to consumers. Together with newspaper and magazine advertising, television commercials, radio spots, printed literature, and direct mail, companies flood their markets with product messages. But the goal of every loyalty marketer is to engage customers in lifelong relationships by drawing them to the brand mentally, physically, and emotionally, with value-added promotions. This chapter focuses on creating value over the long haul through a series of inbound marketing strategies designed to build ongoing relationships with customers. It will teach you how to attract leads as well as prospects and long-term customers.

When discussing quality management and ethics, we often talk about doing the right things right. The same principle applies to loyalty marketing. It's not enough to do just anything. You must consciously choose the right thing to do. That means working with purpose, acting strategically, and selecting activities that tie directly to the results that are needed. First, you need to plan how you will connect with customers who have learned to tune you out. But, before launching a loyalty marketing program, or any other marketing campaign, you need to know and address these two things:

- The reason(s) your customers initially entered into a relationship with you
- The best ongoing activities to add mutual value down the line

Those answers will help you build stronger customer relationships and a value-driven loyalty marketing program. Satisfied customers will help you generate repeat business, testimonials, and referrals.

Ten Steps to Strong Relationships

There are many things in business you cannot control. But, luckily, you have the power to influence your customer relationships. With creativity, resources, and ongoing customer touch points, you can develop a high-impact loyalty program that delivers ongoing value to customers. In turn, your company will benefit when your customers reward you with ongoing business. You'll also need patience and the perseverance, because loyalty building starts with the first encounter and deepens over time—when you do the right things right. A few simple steps will help you build relationships that breed loyalty. Here are 10 helpful relationship-building tips:

STEP 1: FOSTER A BUSINESS CULTURE THAT MEETS THE NEEDS OF BOTH CUSTOMERS AND COMPANY

Focus on quality and integrity. Stand up for the words behind your mission. Align every daily action with your company goals, and make every message count. Schedule meetings as needed to review processes, procedures, and client satisfaction. Determine together what needs to improve. If you are in transactional business focused on commodity sales, carry only products that you and your customer can rely on. Set standards for your business transactions, and train your team in the golden rule: treat others as you would like to be treated.

STEP 2: SET A GOAL TO TRANSFORM GOOD CLIENTS INTO GREAT CLIENTS

Clarify whom you want to attract and retain as clients. Carefully choose your target audience, and make sure it is a good match for your products, services, and company culture. As you get to know members of that audience and their preferences, you will be better able to offer products and services that delight them and keep them coming back.

STEP 3: DELIVER PRODUCTS THAT MEET OR EXCEED CUSTOMER EXPECTATIONS

You can delight customers with responsive customer service. Once you decide what you sell, your job is to stand behind your products and services by delivering value across your service chain.

STEP 4: RESPECT CUSTOMERS' CONCERNS

Always make sure that your customers feel that they are heard. When questions, problems, or concerns are raised, show customers that their perspectives and opinions count. Honor their concerns by listening in an unbiased, objective way. Acknowledge their feelings, seek a shared goal in resolving the problem, and work toward a win-win outcome.

STEP 5: RESPECT CUSTOMER TIME

Respect customer time, demonstrating professional courtesy. Be on time for appointments. Approach business in a polite, friendly way, but focus on the business at hand rather than eating up time with personal conversation. (See Chapter 16 for more information on communication style.) Resolve problems quickly. Follow up as promised, within the expected time frame.

STEP 6: BE ACCOUNTABLE

Take responsibility for solving problems when they arise or for finding the person with the authority and ability to resolve the concern. Triage problems, and know your escalation process. Problems typically result from a missed step in a process (e.g., quality review, manufacturing, or customer service) or a faulty process. When you are confronted with a problem, use that situation as an opportunity to repair the process. By focusing on the process when something goes wrong, you will defuse personal antagonism, and derail the "he-said, she-said" syndrome, as well as blame games. Problems also can arise from mismatched expectations, which are part of the communication process. Reviewing the process often will help you determine the origin of the mismatch. Focus on how you can enhance go-forward communication while also resolving the issue at hand. Accountability is a form of respect.

When it comes to service, it's essential to set the bar high. Once you do, you will be held to the same high level of accountability in every encounter. Building and maintaining loyal customers means no snoozing on the job. You cannot become complacent. You must earn your customers' trust and loyalty every day. If you want to catch your customer smiling again, you must perform superbly at every encounter. You must approach every customer interaction (and transaction) with the same level of enthusiasm, efficiency, and quality focus that you demonstrated on day one.

STEP 7: STRIVE FOR OPEN, WIN-WIN COMMUNICATIONS THAT ARE FAIR TO BOTH PARTIES

The customer-is-always-right approach does not always work. Sometimes customers' expectations are unreasonable, or they do not make sense in terms of what they really need to solve their stated problem. Frank conversations will help eliminate a hidden agenda and provide a comfortable context within which to ask questions. You don't want to base

your actions on assumptions. Ask the customer what he or she expects in terms of a resolution. Then, share your company's perspective and strive to develop a mutually agreed-upon solution.

STEP 8: BE CLEAR ABOUT EXPECTATIONS

Prepare your customer when projects or circumstances may change. Provide clear and honest communication, starting with your product packaging and running down the line.

STEP 9: SET RELATIONSHIP BOUNDARIES

Clarify roles and responsibilities. Let your customers know what you need from them in order to serve them effectively. Make sure your staff understands their role in satisfying customers. Provide customers with written documentation of processes and product guarantees. Provide your team with written job descriptions and customer service manuals.

STEP 10: PLAN THE RIGHT PROMOTIONS

Loyalty marketing often includes promotions, such as reward programs, gamelike punch cards, coupons, and free or value-added services (as discussed in Chapter 9).

Building Lifetime Value

Once you've built the foundation for your relationships, you can turn your attention to nurturing them.

FOCUS ON QUALITY, NOT QUANTITY

In years past, door-to-door salesmen made repeated house calls. Historically, loyalty marketers have offered ongoing promotions and stayed in touch via direct mail. In recent years, e-mail campaigns have entered the field. So, whether you are using personal calls, direct mail, a Web site, or e-mail to stay in touch with your customers, make sure to reach out only when you have something new, different, or valuable to say. Avoid the temptation to stay in touch only to keep your name in front of customers. Unlike brand image communications, which are designed to continually cultivate awareness, a loyalty campaign is designed to add ongoing value.

FOCUS YOUR EFFORTS ON YOUR BEST CUSTOMERS

To stay profitable, every company must maximize resources. Use your database as a repository for customer intelligence. Because e-mail campaigns are permission based, use them to market to people who have opted in and thereby agreed to listen. It's a great place to start.

Also identify (using e-mail lists and/or other lists) which customers provide you with your most profitable business. Then allocate your resources and concentrate your effort on reaching out to them effectively. To decide what will work, try applying a SWOT Analysis to the loyalty process (see Chapter 3). Look at the opportunities you have to grow business within or across products, services, and divisions with each of your existing customer groups. Also look at your company's strengths and weaknesses in addressing them. Consider how you can turn a weakness into a strength, or whether a particular weakness (such as budget, staffing, or knowledge shortcoming) requires you to put your effort elsewhere until you can correct it. Finally, look at what is happening around you. Are your competitors doing a better job of connecting with customers and garnering more repeat business? Have they been poaching your customers? If so, analyze why, and map out a combat plan.

Drip Marketing

Drip marketing is a strategy for staying top of mind with clients by connecting with them regularly. Like a slow-water irrigation system that keeps soil moist for plant growth without flooding the field, drip marketing maintains a continual positive flow of value-driven information to clients. Think *drip*, *drip*, *drip*, and make that your personal marketing mantra. Drip marketing methods may include campaigns via e-mail, postcard, letter, and personal outreach that keep your name, products, and services in front of customers so they will remember you when they need what you offer. Drip marketing is a particularly good strategy if you have a long sales cycle, a complex product offering, or both. You want to be sure that when your prospects are ready to buy (or buy again), they will think of you first. Some companies make the mistake of assuming that providing an occasional promotional item (e.g., a pen, calendar, or notepad) is a sufficient reminder. Not so. The right premium, one that has lasting value, is a good start. However, your competitors are probably providing the same trinkets. You need to stand out. Drip marketing will help. Here's how you can make your drip marketing campaign highly successful:

- **Pay attention during sales calls, discussions in your shop, and/or meetings.** Ask probing questions and listen to customers' broad concerns. Make customers feel special and remembered by sending a news article on a topic of interest to them, or an industry or news alert on a hot business topic. My banker forwards economic updates to me periodically. It makes me feel remembered. More important, the information she sends helps me do my job better. Through ongoing education, I can become a better resource for my own clients. As a result, my banker has become my trusted advisor. And, I won't be easily tempted by a special offer from an untried bank. I'll keep my money in the bank that butters my bread. That's the desired outcome of loyalty marketing.

- **When you identify a hot spot for customers or learn something of special interest, write your own article and post it on your Web site or blog.** Send a link to your suspects, prospects, and customers.

- **Start a company blog and invite your customers to comment.** When they do, follow up with a thank-you to let them know you noticed.

- **Give a referral to your customers.** Business should not be a one-way street. Use your own customer base as your list of preferred vendors, whenever possible. Remember, the givers gain philosophy, which holds that people who give referrals also get referrals, and is mentioned in Chapter 11.

- **Send an e-newsletter, monthly or quarterly, depending on what's in it and what makes sense for your business/industry.** Again, don't send it just to send it. Your content must have value for your prospect. A value assessment is part of doing the right things right.

- **Before sending an e-newsletter, think about your recipients and qualify where they are in your process.** Will the same content work for everyone? Probably not. When developing nurture strategies, make sure to segment your mailing lists into suspects (people who have never bought from you and may or may not be qualified buyers), prospects (people who have clicked on your links, called for more information, or met with you to discuss your products and services), and customers (people whose buying patterns you can evaluate and who may need additional services now or down the line.) Once you've segmented your list, you can write relevant copy for each group and develop targeted offers. Segmenting your market is an important tactic for bolstering your response rate—providing you follow the rules of value-based selling.

In Chapter 7, we defined value as perceived quality divided by cost. To differentiate yourself from myriad competitors, you need to be the best value in town, whether that value is derived by price or the strength of product dimensions. Value selling is a three-step process. First, you must understand what drives your customer. Next, you must show customers how your product or service helps them solve their own problems with business, lifestyle, or personal life. Finally, you must demonstrate the difference between you and your competitors. When you prove that your products and services offer the best solution for the money, you will be rewarded with stronger customer ties and increased revenues. As you master your value proposition, you will translate your efforts into sales, enhance overall brand value, capture more market share, and set the stage for long-term relationships.

NURTURE STRATEGIES

Drip marketing isn't just about promoting sales. You can use it to nurture relationships, too. If your business model allows (e.g., if you have enough people on your team), customize your outreach as much as possible. Send items of specific interest to particular customers in your pipeline. Sending free offers, holiday greetings, birthday cards, and news clippings are excellent ways for letting customers know you care. Every touchpoint is an opportunity to exceed expectations. Another way to delight clients is to stop by their offices with a small gift occasionally. My banker drops off boxes of cookies and jugs of coffee at client offices.

> **CAUTION**
>
> It takes more effort (and money) to win new customers than to retain them. Make it your goal to fill your pipeline with new prospects while continuing to serve existing clients in the ways they have come to expect.

Loyalty Marketing Strategies

The goal of every loyalty marketing program is to generate repeat business. Once you have developed a reputation for excellence and positive emotional currency with your customers, you can reinforce your appeal through positive interactions with them and delivering added value along the way.

SHOWING THE LOVE

Show your customers how much they mean to you in tangible ways, and on an ongoing basis, not just once a year on Customer Appreciation Day. As with personal relationships, customers like to know they matter and that your acknowledgment is sincere. Here are some great ways to "show the love" to your customers.

1. **Thank them when they give you business.** When they are in your store, thank customers for their visit or purchase. Call them when you learn that they've placed an order. Write and mail them a note—handwritten, whenever possible. The etiquette rules we learned in grade school still apply.

2. **Give customers a virtual hug.** It may not be possible to physically hug your customers, but it is possible to get to know them. Whenever you can, learn and use their names. Show interest in their lives. Ask about their jobs, family, interests, hobbies, and challenges. That means you need to engage them in conversation when you see them. If your only interaction with your customers is via the Web or e-mail, offer a member area on your Web site. When they log in, greet them with a screen that acknowledges them by name.

3. **Track customers' buying behavior.** Learn what, when, and why customers purchase. Look for their product affinity and you'll get a sense of what they value. Learning your customers' preferences will help you build your business. Use a database whenever possible to keep track of customers. Offer them a bar-coded card you can swipe when they make a purchase; that way, you can track individual customer transactions in your own system. Creating a sort function in your database will also help you keep track of product popularity and provide data-driven insight for your buying and marketing decisions.

4. **Send customers a greeting card.** Remember their birthdays and anniversaries. Use forms or a book on your counter to collect dates of birthdays and anniversaries. If you're an employer, remember that you have internal customers, too. Acknowledge employee birthdays and anniversaries. Remember also strategic allies, channel partners, and business colleagues. SendOutCards (www.sendoutcards.com) makes sending cards easy by allowing you to upload your database and track client birthdays, anniversaries, or other significant markers via computer. This automated system not only enables you to customize cards, but reminds you when to send cards and handles the physical mailing for you. My SendOutCards representative, Ray Bodee, of Melbourne, Florida, sends me cards regularly, which surprise and delight me each time. By taking time to visit my Facebook page, and copying a photo of my family, he was able to make me a customized card that ensures I will always remember him and his service. You can stay in good touch by making note of how long customers have been using your product or service. Also, be aware of your customers' business timeline so you can acknowledge significant business anniversaries, such as 10, 20, or 30 years in business.

5. **Let customers know that they matter.** If you haven't seen them in a while, reach out with a postcard, by phone, or via e-mail. Send them a survey to find out why they haven't been shopping lately, and offer them a perk for filling it out.

6. **Offer customers a special deal.** Perhaps you can provide an extra service with a purchase, present a discounted fee for early-bird purchasing, a coupon for a future discount, as well as advance notice of a sale. Companies, such as JCPenney, Macy's, and Indian River Furniture, regularly send catalogs with special offers to customers on their preferred customer mailing list. Such offers include the opportunity to preshop a sale before it is open to the public or the chance to qualify for a special purchase. American Express advertises advance ticket purchases for in-demand concerts. Anyone who holds a Platinum American Express card gets an early crack at those tickets.

7. **Listen to customers.** When a question, problem, or concern is raised, show customers that their perspectives and opinions count. Then, show or tell them how you are using that information to deliver a more valuable product or service. In that way, you will let them know their feedback is valued.

8. **Be accessible.** When you learn there's a need, whether you find out through marketing research or a customer complaint, make it known that you want to resolve the issue. Of course, not every customer call is about a problem. Customers like to know that they can communicate with you about positive experiences as well. Even very large companies have found that accessibility differentiates them in their industry and markets.

9. **Respond quickly.** Even when you cannot resolve a customer's issue then and there, you must acknowledge receipt of questions or complaints as quickly as

possible. If you can't address an issue immediately, call to let them know you have received their query and will address it soon. Whenever possible, specify your timeframe for resolving a problem. Then recontact the customer as soon as you can answer the question or resolve the issue.

10. **Honor your promise.** Make sure your offers tie in with your business mission and center on customer service. Deliver on time. Guarantee your products and services. Live up to the expectations you set.

11. **Give them a gift.** Customer reward programs can take many forms, from a small gift or premium to a coupon for a free service. Rebates on purchases are another approach used often by telecommunications organizations and computer companies. Other companies offer free shipping once a specific purchase amount has been reached. Airlines and credit card companies cultivate loyalty by enabling customers to earn "miles" to use for airfare, hotel, and other amenities.

Still other companies offer a free trial, sometimes called a "test drive." This is a particularly good strategy when new products are introduced. The beauty of a test drive is that it provides a fear-free opportunity for customers while also establishing the basis for a sale.

Last but not least, give customers a gift they care about. Everybody loves presents when they are given sincerely and reflect the needs and desires of the recipient more than the giver.

Long-term profitability and loyalty will be earned based on your integrity and the value of your product, not via promotion alone.

Response Marketing

Also known as "direct marketing," response marketing is a technique for making a sale by generating a response right in the moment. Direct marketing strategies are characterized by their strong calls to action. Direct marketing may be conducted by the following means:

- Direct mail
- Person to person
- Telephone
- Web sites
- E-mail
- Television
- Radio
- Any method of marketing that attempts to make a sale right then and there

Infomercials are a popular response marketing strategy that promote an immediate "Call Now" response from viewers or listeners. Shopping channels, such as QVC and HSN, require marketers to carry high-inventory loads to ensure timely product delivery.

When planning a direct response campaign, you need a plan to address callers. If you don't have an inside call center, you can contract with a response marketing firm that does. To succeed with response marketing, you will need a media plan that reaches your target audience, a well-trained call center team, billing and payment protocols, inventory, warehousing, quality control, and a shipping and fulfillment plan.

Direct Mail and E-mail Success Strategies

Direct mail is one of the most frequently used and expensive methods for raising operating capital. So, it is crucial for you to know why you are planning a direct mail promotion. Most direct mail promotions generate a 2 to 5 percent response rate. Rates vary, depending on the accuracy and relevance of the mailing list. However, even when you don't make a sale, you may consider the branding impact of continually having your name in front of customers. Study results vary, but most show that it takes anywhere from 7 to 27 times of seeing your name in print before prospects start to pay attention.

With that in mind, you need to have strategies in place to make your direct mail and e-mail campaigns effective. Two strategies in particular will help you get the most out of your direct mail and e-mail marketing efforts:

- **Choose the right list.**
- **Make the right offer.** Make sure it is relevant and targeted to your audience's profile and needs.

Other strategies are also quite effective:

- **Be specific.** "Call for more info" is not an offer. An offer explains the tangible and/or intangible benefits a client receives when doing business with you. In this case, "Return the enclosed card to learn how you can . . ." is a more specific approach. It would also be quite effective because, after taking action, your respondent would find out the benefits.

- **Choose words carefully, and emphasize the positive whenever possible.** People do not like words that tell them what they can't do. For example, instead of saying, "Don't wait," try, "Call now." Or instead of saying, "Don't drink," say, "Drink responsibly."

- **Set a deadline, and create honest urgency.** For example, state: Return this form by [date], and you'll get best choice of merchandise, a higher-level discount, premium placement in our publication, or preferred seating at our special event. Customers will more than likely see the logic in your call to action.

- **Beware of putting customers off with hard sales tactics.** For example, avoid: "You have only 24 hours to respond." If you create urgency through benefits rather than artificial deadlines, clients are more likely to feel served than sold.

- **Make responding easy.** You can do this with a dedicated 800 number, a Web address that takes you directly to a squeeze page, or a short and simple order form or reply mechanism in an e-mail message. Provide both write-in and telephone options, and prominently position your contact information (e.g., phone and fax numbers and a Web site address).

- **Think ahead, and think smartly.** To know whether a promotion will work, test a mailing on a small, qualified zip code or list before investing a lot of time and money. Use a code to keep track of the results. Sales generated from a coded mailer or landing page promotion will serve as a handy reference for managing the quality and results of your next program.

Enhancing Your E-mail Campaigns

Every e-mail campaign should follow the basic rules of good communication. Be quick and crystal clear about the benefit you provide in every communication. Choose graphics and bullet points to help tell your story in a succinct, easy-to-read way. Structure your e-mail message in the same way as your press release. Follow the who-what-when-where-why premise. Capture attention using an intriguing subject line that indicates the benefit of the information inside. Personalize your communication as much as possible. Mention your customer's name, if your program allows.

Use your knowledge of your customer's buying history when considering which promotions to send. Then track your opt-in rates, click-through rates from page to page, and squeeze page results and you will learn more about customer preferences in your database. As you learn more, you can build customized and automated loyalty program promotions. You can also grow your list and engage your customers by adding links to your Twitter, business Facebook, and LinkedIn profiles to your e-mail campaigns.

List Building

So, where do you get a mailing list? You can rent a list from a direct mail house or online service. But your best resource will be your inside list of customers and qualified prospects. Whenever possible, start with your own database and work outward. Input names you gather from responses to forms and surveys, white papers, articles and podcast downloads, and click-throughs on Web pages and banner ads. Public speaking events and trade shows offer other great opportunities to gather names for addition to your database. As you collect business cards, enter the information into your database. If you don't have time to type contact information into a database, invest in a card scanner, which will

automatically populate the information into your database. Then, you can upload the data into your personal digital assistant (PDA), e-mail contacts list, and/or comma separated values (CSV) file. You also you can hire a virtual assistant to do it for you.

Another list-building strategy is to tap into your customers' connections. Try a promotion that asks customers to refer friends and colleagues. Offer them a treat for doing so.

You can build your list by sharing names with other consultants who have a similar audience. For example, lawyers and accountants, wellness coaches and fitness experts, as well as printers and graphic designers often share common target markets. By cobranding or sharing information through collaborative marketing endeavors, you can access the right kind of customers.

The objective in response marketing and loyalty campaigns is to create a magnetic list—one that draws prospects to you. The best way to achieve that is to identify qualified prospects and clients. Populate your lists with people whom you know have a need and/ or interest in what you are selling. Then engage those people with compelling content.

MAILING LIST CHECKLIST

Just because you buy a list doesn't mean it is accurate. You must stay as engaged with your list as you expect your customers to stay with you. Track returned mail, e-mail bounce-backs, undeliverable messages and customer responses to you. To develop the right list, you should make a few crucial decisions and ask yourself some important questions. Use this checklist:

- Decide exactly to whom material should be sent. Prospect qualification is the most important step in the direct mail process.

- Make sure the list is updated. Monitor returned mail, and clean the data by eliminating the people with faulty addresses.

- Decide which specific action we want the person to take. Include a prominent call to action.

- Review the mailer from the audience's point of view
  - Is our primary objective clear?
  - Have we stated at least one, and preferably two, benefits in our message?
  - How does the message flow? Does the packaging match the message?
  - Does the outside envelope or outside flap encourage me to open it?
  - Is the letter the first thing I see when I open the package?
  - Does our letter include all important points?
    - Readers' needs
    - Benefits and value we bring
    - Call to action

- Way to respond
- Visuals that support the copy
- Is the reply information clear?
- Is it easy to reply?
- Would I respond? Why or why not?

Revisit your lists at least once per quarter to check the list quality, based on results. It's safe to assume that at least 10 percent of addresses will go bad every year because people change e-mail providers, move to new locations, switch jobs, and change phone numbers. As a result, you more than likely will receive a number of "not deliverable" messages from the post office, as well as bounce-backs from e-mail servers. Your goal is to minimize bad addresses by continually culling your lists. Doing so will keep both e-mail costs and postage costs down.

You can keep your database fresh by collecting new information in a number of ways:

- **Using e-mail, a Web site, or telephone calls, ask prospects to update changing information.** Be aware, however, that if you migrate from one autoresponder program to another, you may not be able to automatically transfer your database. Asking customers to update their own data may increase opt-outs, because the process of opting out is quicker than filling out a new form. Whether or not that happens will depend on how engaged the customer is with you and how much he or she likes your products or services. Nevertheless, keep a place on your Web site where customers can update a password-protected profile.

- **On your Web site, require that customers, prospects, and other visitors complete a short contact form when attempting to download a free PDF, e-book, or white paper.** At the minimum, ask for a first name and title. The more information you request, the higher the likelihood that respondents will disengage. First, build trust with customers by providing value-driven information. As customers get comfortable with you and your message or choose to buy, they will provide more detailed information such as phone number and address.

- **To manage leads, get the right data.** Surveys and forms can help you qualify prospects. But prospects may input false or misleading information, and this can affect whether and how they get funneled through the sales pipeline.

- **Keep forms short to combat form fatigue and disengagement.** When marketers ask too many questions, questions that are too personal, or questions that appear to be irrelevant, respondents are likely to quit the survey and opt out of your list.

Conducting Cost-Effective Campaigns

Don't get discouraged if you don't get an immediate response. Expect that it will take time for prospects and ongoing customers to respond to your offers and queries. Embrace the process as a learning opportunity, and tweak it continually for best results. Start with a commitment that you will send only meaningful information with relevance to your consumers' life, work, and success. That will increase the likelihood of prospect engagement. The longer consumers stay engaged, the more likely they will be to purchase your products.

Today's marketers realize the benefit in focusing on target markets and tweaking the campaign along the way. They've learned that targeting and continual refinement based on results is cost effective in the long term. By analyzing the individual buying patterns of your customers, you can increase sales over time. Start by studying when customers purchase (i.e., the season, month, or day). Learn what types of products customers typically purchase. Track their response frequency, and look at how recently they purchased from you or inquired about a service. Track whether they've opened e-mails, clicked through to product offers, sent queries to you, and/or bought something. You can study what they buy and how many steps it took you to convert a prospect to a buyer.

By monitoring customer responses over time and integrating what you learn, you can improve the results of your e-mail campaign. When you see good results (e.g., visits, click-throughs, and queries) with particular clients in your pipeline, you can turn their information over to your sales team. As you monitor customer behavior, you can further segment your lists based on company priorities as well as customer buying patterns. Then, you can channel individuals into the right automated e-mail campaigns and stay in touch with them.

> **CAUTION**
>
> List building is about quality not quantity. You can have thousands of names on a list, but the only names that matter are those that belong to people who have a connection to you and what you are selling.

Reducing Liability

The Federal Trade Commission (FTC) sets the rules for all commercial messaging. The CAN-SPAM Act, a law that sets the rules for commercial e-mail, establishes requirements for commercial messages, gives recipients the right to have you stop e-mailing them, and spells out tough penalties for violations.

The CAN-SPAM Act applies to all commercial messages transmitted electronically. For the purpose of advertising or promotion of a commercial product or service, the law also covers individual business-to-business e-mail. The law is easy to follow. Here are the requirements, as stated on the Federal Trade Commission Web site (www.ftc.gov):

1. **Don't use false or misleading header information.** Your "From," "To," "Reply-To," and routing information—including the originating domain name and e-mail address— must be accurate and identify the person or business who initiated the message.

2. **Don't use deceptive subject lines.** The subject line must accurately reflect the content of the message.

3. **Identify the message as an ad.** The law gives you a lot of leeway in how to do this, but you must disclose clearly and conspicuously that your message is an advertisement.

4. **Tell recipients where you're located.** Your message must include your valid physical postal address. This can be your current street address, a post office box you've registered with the U.S. Postal Service, or a private mailbox you've registered with a commercial mail receiving agency established under Postal Service regulations.

5. **Tell recipients how to opt out of receiving future e-mail from you.** Your message must include a clear and conspicuous explanation of how the recipient can opt out of getting e-mail from you in the future. Craft the notice in a way that's easy for an ordinary person to recognize, read, and understand. Creative use of type size, color, and location can improve clarity. Give a return e-mail address or another easy Internet-based way to allow people to communicate their choice to you. You may create a menu to allow a recipient to opt out of certain types of messages, but you must include the option to stop all commercial messages from you. Make sure your spam filter doesn't block these opt-out requests.

6. **Honor opt-out requests promptly.** Any opt-out mechanism you offer must be able to process opt-out requests for at least 30 days after you send your message. You must honor a recipient's opt-out request within 10 business days. You can't charge a fee, require the recipient to give you any personally identifying information beyond an e-mail address, or make the recipient take any step other than sending a reply e-mail or visiting a single page on an Internet Web site as a condition for honoring an opt-out request. Once people have told you they don't want to receive more messages from you, you can't sell or transfer their e-mail addresses, even in the form of a mailing list. The only exception is that you may transfer the addresses to a company you've hired to help you comply with the CAN-SPAM Act.

7. **Monitor what others are doing on your behalf.** The law makes clear that even if you hire another company to handle your e-mail marketing, you can't contract away your legal responsibility to comply with the law. Both the company whose product is promoted in the message and the company that actually sends the message may be held legally responsible.

Commercial mass e-mail service providers, such as AWeber (www.aweber.com), 1ShoppingCart (www.1shoppingcart.com), and Constant Contact (www.constantcontact.com), help maintain the opt-in/opt-out lists. These commercial programs can help ensure that your mail gets where it's going and that you comply with legal regulations.

Monitor Your Brand

Today's technology (and its expanding, interconnected reach in the future) enables people to air their buying grievances with the entire Internet-connected world. People share their experiences, both good and bad, through online postings at retailers, by commenting on various blogs, and by starting their own blogs to rave or rant. Where previously they only influenced those with whom they had a direct relationship, customers now have the power to influence those they don't even know. Make it your goal to give your customers something to rave about and minimize their opportunity to engage in negative talk. Stay attuned to trends in the market and perceptions about your brand. Doing so will enhance the value of your lists and your overall loyalty marketing effort.

Quiz

1. Drip marketing is:
   - (a) A marketing system for plant growers
   - (b) A way of touching base with clients once in a while
   - (c) A loyalty marketing strategy for staying top of mind with clients by connecting with them regularly
   - (d) None of the above

2. Companies benefit from loyalty marketing when:
   - (a) Customers reward them with ongoing business
   - (b) They can create a cost-effective plan
   - (c) They use a good marketing list
   - (d) All of the above
   - (e) None of the above

3. Before launching a loyalty marketing program or any other marketing campaign, you need to know and address _____ and _____.
   - (a) Your best prospects/the price of campaigns
   - (b) Why your customers entered into a relationship with you to begin with/which are the best ongoing activities to add mutual value down the line
   - (c) A target market/an e-mail list
   - (d) Direct mail concerns/the CAN-SPAM Act

4. To build lifetime value in client relationships you should:
   - (a) Focus on quantity of relationships
   - (b) Focus on frequency of mailings
   - (c) Focus on enhancing relationships with your best customers

(d) All of the above

(e) Only choices (a) and (c)

5. Which of the following is not a loyalty marketing tactic:

(a) Setting relationship boundaries

(b) Setting expectations

(c) Respecting customers' time

(d) Planning the right promotions

(e) Ignoring customer complaints

6. A SWOT Analysis will not provide guidance for structuring a loyalty marketing campaign. True or false?

(a) True

(b) False

7. Which of the following strategies will not help you build a credible mailing list?

(a) Going through existing customer lists

(b) Tracking e-mail openings and click-throughs on e-campaigns

(c) A pay-per-click banner ad

(d) Tracking nondeliverable mail and bounce-backs of direct mail list returns

(e) None of the above

8. The CAN-SPAM Act applies only to bulk e-mail. True or false?

(a) True

(b) False

9. As you master your value proposition, you will:

(a) Translate your efforts into sales

(b) Enhance overall brand value

(c) Set the stage for long-term relationships

(d) All of the above

(e) None of the above

10. You can keep your database fresh by:

(a) Collecting new names and information

(b) Asking prospects to update changing information

(c) Weeding out people who don't open e-mail or click-through pages

(d) Asking other companies to share their lists with you

(e) All of the above

(f) None of the above

PART FIVE

Targeting Sustainable Marketing Success

CHAPTER 16

Managing a Marketing Team

Based on values, beliefs, and practice, behaviors develop into patterns—styles of operating. Management behaviors follow suit. They are influenced by prior management interactions, workplace expectations, and company culture. Each manager brings a distinct style to the office, from a disinterested, laissez-faire approach to appropriately involved, permissive, team-oriented, or highly authoritative and controlling methods. With training, mentoring, or ongoing coaching, managers can develop styles that complement the needs and work of their team. Or they can operate in a clueless vacuum leaving employees to run the ship on their own.

Effective management is strategically aligned with goals of the campaign, department, and organization. As a manager, it's your job to set the tone, expectations, and subculture for your department. This presents an opportunity that goes beyond any single action, day, week, or month in the life of your business. It gives you the chance to positively impact your company for the long haul. Assessing your own management style will help you determine and build on your strengths, overcome weaknesses, and lead your team in achievement of marketing objectives.

Management Style Factors Influencing Success

While entire books are devoted to management theory and styles, this chapter provides pertinent highlights to help you uncover and utilize influencing skills and business strategies that maximize marketing productivity. For centuries, autocratic leaders and managers controlled worker outcomes through a rigid hold on company and industry knowledge. Only those with access to the right business intelligence could excel. Managers supplied employees with only as much information, training, and education as was needed to execute a specific task. Their behavior fostered a controlled, hierarchical, top-down enterprise. The Internet's expansive information flow has made management more transparent in recent years. As information has become more accessible, many organizations also have become more democratic and participatory.

As a marketer, you should be committed to maximizing communication flow and business results. How you view your own management role affects not only your performance but also the performance of your entire team. As you read through this chapter, think about where you fit on the management continuum and what you can do differently to enhance performance of your marketing team.

Awareness of your management style is a first step to influencing your own behavior. You can consciously choose and develop a style that serves the highest needs of your group. Choose your desired style based on your goals as well as the abilities and behavior of your team. If that management style doesn't come naturally, identify and develop the skills you need. An adaptive management style is based on the ability to shift skill sets as needed, and can help you get the most out your team. Figure 16.1 shows how management

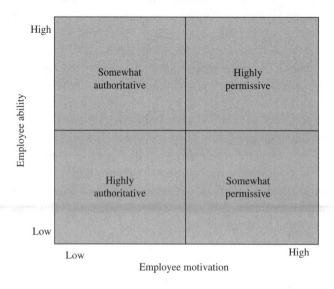

Figure 16.1   Adaptive management style by employee ability and motivation.

actions range from authoritative to permissive based on the ability and motivation levels of employees. As employees develop higher-level skills, managers can begin delegating responsibility and helping teams build competencies. The result will be individuals with the necessary skills to manage tasks and projects independently in the context of a team.

When managers trust the abilities of their team, as evidenced by the degree to which they are willing to delegate responsibilities and give up control, group dynamics shift. Trust is tied to beliefs about motives as well as comfort with risk. Building trust with your team requires vesting yourself in the success of the people with whom you work. Intradepartmental trust will grow when your team members know that you have their best interest at heart.

Managers are responsible for choosing and/or developing team members so that each individual reaches the skill level needed to perform daily work. If a team member lacks skill but is motivated to learn, you will need to take a somewhat, authoritative approach, which includes setting expectations and consequences. You also can provide training for him or her, and guide and encourage that member. As team members build higher competence, you can allow them more leeway in project management, adopting a more permissive style. In the case of a team member with low skills and low motivation, a manager must decide whether that individual is teachable and can develop a team-centered work ethic. When values and skills don't match the requirements of the job, managers need to be willing to have a conversation that helps the employee get on the right page; if the conversation is effective, needed change will happen. If not, the employee will more than likely face termination.

Figure 16.2 summarizes, in four quadrants, the competencies and styles of peak performers. To be a highly effective manager, you must develop these competencies in yourself. You also need to assess and develop these core abilities in your team to ensure really strong performance and team integration. The most important quadrant is emotional maturity and intelligence because it forms the basis for the other competencies. Individuals who learn to maintain their own inner resilience—no matter what kind of external failure feedback they receive (e.g., impact of poor market conditions, lower revenues in their company, or interpersonal challenges)—become highly effective team leaders and performers. Without inner resilience, people are easily stopped, discouraged, slowed down, stressed, and/or engaged in distressing interpersonal conflict. Whether you are leading or participating on a team, developing the competencies to influence other team members in a win-win spirit is crucial for success. Key competencies include maintaining rapport, understanding other people's point of view, and being able to negotiate differences.

Managers with extraordinarily strategic and decision-making capabilities demonstrate the ability to think long term, from multiple perspectives simultaneously. This enables them to plan effectively, budget appropriately, and focus on innovative solutions. The fault of many teams is their inability to plan into the future and take into account changing market conditions.

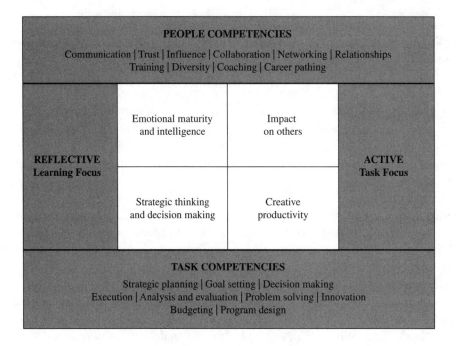

Figure 16.2 Extraordinary self peak performance model.

Managers with high-level creative productivity are able to adapt easily to changing circumstances and create innovative solutions that fit changing environments. Individuals who master these competencies don't get stuck in the solutions of the past. As Albert Einstein said, "You can never solve a problem on the level on which it was created." As you consider your own management style, take stock of your own perceptions, thoughts, feelings, and goals.

Developing a Mission-Centered Team

Follow these steps to develop a truly mission-centered team. Ellen Cooperperson, founder of Corporate Performance Consultants in Hauppauge, New York, and coach to Fortune 500 executives, among others, provides leadership in the art of team building. The following tactics mirror her approach:

1. **Set the vision and course.** Define your direction, and explain why and how it fits with your company's mission. When people embrace the mission, they know where to place their focus. Empower them to make decisions that align with the mission and are consistent with organizational values. This will help

people anchor their work effort to the company's purpose. Without that anchor, employees have a tendency to muddle through tasks without understanding their relationship to overall success. Purpose builds energy, and energy fuels a productive culture.

2. **Assign and expect accountability.** Without accountability, projects fall through the cracks, time is wasted by duplication of effort, and people may blame others when projects aren't completed on time. Without accountability, a company won't be able to respond effectively to reports or change as needed. Without accountability, a company operates in reactive mode, and managers find themselves continually putting out fires or immersed in crises. With accountability, managers and employees "know who's on first." They make sure that if team members find that they cannot fulfill or have not yet fulfilled a promise, they still own it. For example, if you can't meet a deadline, just say so. Don't wait for someone to catch you being late. Teach your team to step up and acknowledge when the ball belongs to them. Lead the pack by example. Expecting accountability and responsibility in the context of a team will drive an ownership culture. An ownership culture will drive productivity and strong business performance.

3. **Communicate.** High-performing teams communicate well. By comparison, dysfunctional teams exhibit lack of trust, disagreement, and an environment in which meetings go on too long or too often with no set agenda and results. Dysfunctional also experience fear and/or unwillingness to engage in healthy conflict. When people are unwilling to engage in courageous conversations—discussions that must be had despite discomfort—they have no real commitment to moving forward the mission and vision. Without commitment, there is no accountability. Lack of accountability results in inner tension, blaming, opinion mongering, and reduced productivity rather than the habit of working toward joint solutions. By comparison, healthy communication encourages people to bring their thoughts to the table.

   Fostering healthy organizational communication means recognizing that people communicate in different ways. A culture that encourages employees toward clarity enables team members to mirror and paraphrase what others say, which helps enhance and validate comprehension. It also gives people an opportunity to be heard. When people feel heard, they feel appreciated, and that satisfaction shows in their work. By comparison, disgruntled employees can shift and tarnish culture by communicating their anger to colleagues and clients alike. As a manager, you can transform a blame-it culture into a solve-it culture using win-win communication to reinforce preferred internal culture. You can integrate feedback, good and bad, from employees, suppliers, customers, and strategic partners to increase your team's understanding of your company culture and performance issues. Attention to feedback will fuel your team's competitiveness. Every marketing team needs competitive skills to meet internal and external marketing goals.

Your goal as a manager must be to fuel a sustainable departmental environment in support of a sustainable business enterprise.

4. **Focus on quality.** High-performing, mission-centered cultures do not tolerate mediocrity, because mediocrity does not feed the mission. A quality focus keeps the brand promise front and center. Customer complaints, high rejection rates during sales calls, increasing returns, and lack of repeat sales all are quality issues. Some organizations focus quality concerns on products. Others focus on service. Companies that focus on work-life quality are able to balance employee needs with company requirements, for a positive employee-centered culture.

Within your team, focus on managing delivery of quality work products, from marketing research to marketing campaigns and collateral through program evaluation.

5. **Build morale.** Employees who work for paychecks without a real sense of commitment often breed cynicism, pessimism, and complaints. When employees don't feel challenged or engaged at work, organizational pride erodes. Employee-centered teams fuel brand identification and engage with the mission. Satisfied employees serve as brand catalysts, mirroring cultural expectations internally, and reinforcing company beliefs and promises beyond the walls. Employee-centric cultures with clearly defined expectations, accountabilities, communications, and quality standards breed mission-centric processes and higher productivity.

UNDERSTANDING COMMUNICATION STYLES

Communication styles affect everything from the success of a marketing presentation to team buy-in and customer response. Communication styles reflect personal perceptions, attitudes, and beliefs. Understanding communication styles gives you a chance to shift perspective in the moment, step into another's shoes, and see the world through someone else's lens, so you can decide how to communicate effectively.

Peak performing managers develop the ability to shift communication styles frequently, to accommodate the styles of those with whom they interact. Our neural wiring influences how we communicate, as do our thoughts, perceptions, and beliefs. Human resources professionals use various diagnostic tools to assess communication styles. The DISC assessment, developed by William Moulton Marston, describes four behavior styles (**d**irect communicators, **i**nfluencers, **s**teadfast supporters, and **c**autious and conscientious communicators), each with its own approach to communication. You can acquire the full assessment, to take online or on paper, by contacting a human resources consulting firm or searching for resources online. You also might want to invest in a training program to practice and further develop your team's communication skills. In the meantime, here is a brief synopsis:

- **Direct communicators.** They are highly competitive, results oriented, and demanding. They typically speak more often and listen less often. They are quick decision makers, and are impatient for the bottom line when communicating. When speaking to *D*-style communicators, it helps to be brief, keep to the point, and don't take their abrupt style personally. Their demeanor is not a reflection on you. Their style mostly reflects their personal perception of the world, not their perception of you in particular.

- **Influencers.** Typically, these communicators are very verbal. They tend to be congenial, persuasive, and optimistic. Strongly relationship oriented, the *I*-style communicator is highly diplomatic. The *I*-style communicators share information freely. With more regard for preserving the relationship than insisting on performance, they may be less concerned with tasks than with people's impressions.

- **Steadfast supporters.** *S*-style communicators are good listeners, who pay attention to the needs of others and are organized and reliable. Unlike *D*-style communicators and *I*-style communicators, *S*-style communicators often prefer to work alone, tend to be quieter, shy, and may be more easily intimidated. Followers rather than leaders, they respond better to less formal, low-key requests than to demands.

- **Cautious and conscientious.** *C*-style communicators concentrate heavily on details and are highly analytical, contemplative, and fact driven. Less creative than others, they focus on details, with a need to cross every *t* and dot every *i* before moving forward or closing out a project.

Each style has benefits and drawbacks. The key is learning to observe the styles of others on your team, understand what makes them tick, and respond accordingly. For example, when *C*-style communicators and *D*-style communicators interact, a communication mismatch is likely. The *D* personality may lose patience for the minutiae so important to the *C* type, and the *C* type may feel unappreciated and unheard.

EVIDENCE OF A MISMATCH IN COMMUNICATION STYLES

When the following things are happening in your organization, you most likely have a mismatch in communication styles. You need to take steps to rectify the situation.

- Work does not meet expectations.
- Deadlines are missed.
- Managers are easily irritated.

- Team members feel frustrated and confused.
- People focus on the wrong tasks.
- Managers continually have to restate their priorities.
- Team members do not feel valued.
- Managers repeat themselves, ad infinitum.
- People gossip and, behind the scenes, blame others.
- Conversations stop when the manager walks by.

REDUCING COMMUNICATION CONFLICT AND ENHANCING COMMUNICATION

Managers who understand the impact of communication style can reduce conflict and positively influence workflow, productivity, and relationships. Helping your team identify personality and communication indicators is a best practice for managing internal communication and developing high-performing teams.

Watching visual cues also enhances communication. Studies show that visual cues, including body language, account for more than half of information transmitted, while vocal cues (e.g., tone, intonation, and enthusiasm) account for another 40 percent. The small remainder is reserved for actual verbal content. When a person's body language and words are inconsistent, people often believe body language over spoken words, because people are wired to perceive emotions before language. If you are speaking to someone who responds with a smile but talks in clipped words and tone, do you get the sense that something else is going on?

When the telephone is the primary communications medium, vocal and verbal components become more important. That is why customer service departments train their employees to keep a mirror by the telephone to remind them to smile when speaking with customers. A voice sounds more enthusiastic, accessible, approachable, and friendly when a person smiles. Try this yourself the next time you call a customer or coworker, and see the difference in how your message is received.

WIN-WIN COMMUNICATION

A win-win communication is one in which both parties get their needs met simultaneously, says psychologist Diane Kramer. Win-win communications become possible when both parties make an effort to communicate and understand each other's perspective. When a difference of opinion or differing needs emerge, listen carefully to the other side. Take time to restate what you are hearing. Doing so will help you get a physical sense of the other person's perspective. It will also give you a chance to confirm your understanding and validate your understanding of the other party's concerns.

Then, look for the joint meaning in the situation. What is it that you are trying to accomplish together in support of your business? If you can first agree on the overall mission and/or project goal, coming to agreement on a strategy for getting there will be easier. Sometimes, it is not possible for everyone to get his or her way. Some compromises will not meet the requirements of the project or mission. As a manager, you need to determine and balance needs. By focusing on project needs, expectations, mutual respect, and the accountability of both parties to the communications and project process, you will be better able to devise a solution that serves the overarching purpose.

Assembling a Capable Marketing Team

Every marketing enterprise must manage demands across a variety of disciplines. So, a marketing team requires individuals with the complementary skill sets and background to address multifaceted work. Developing a team rich in breadth and depth enables you to adapt marketing strategies and activities as needed and builds a foundation for cross-training and collaboration.

Aside from the obvious writing skills and oral communication skills required, individuals should also have excellent project management and problem-solving skills, be capable of providing fresh insight, and understand the role of marketing in the ultimate strategic success of your business. In other words, you do not want strictly a marketing *technician*, you want a marketing *professional*.

Small professional service firms, such as accounting and law firms, may have a single marketing professional to manage all aspects of communication and special events. Larger firms and Fortune 500 companies have multiperson teams to execute on a continuous stream of marketing projects. Whatever your team's size, you need to provide coverage for the following disciplines:

- Advertising and media placement
- Copy writing
- Graphic design
- Marketing via digital media, the Internet, and e-mail
- Special events
- Research and database management
- Proposal development
- Public relations
- Telemarketing

The Marketing Team's Relationship to Others

In the first half of this book, we talked about the principles of integrated marketing, branding, positioning, placement, promotions, and connecting with your prospects and customers based on cultural factors. These objectives cannot be achieved inside a disconnected marketing silo. Every department or function within a company is part of the customer service system. Everyone's job counts, whether or not he or she personally interacts with customers every day. It is essential that all functional areas understand the marketing mission and goals, what aspects of their jobs relate to marketing, and what an optimal interaction and collaboration with marketing needs to look like to achieve successful marketing outcomes. As the marketing manager, you need to do the following:

- Clarify project goals, as well as how specific work is vital to achieving the mission.
- Identify stakeholders in other departments and disciplines.
- Establish clear process guidelines, (e.g., the marketing department writes copy and prepares creative materials; the purchasing department gathers pricing for printing).
- Communicate deadlines.
- Plan cross-team communication strategies.
- Follow up communication with project status reports.

It also is important that functional areas other than marketing understand how marketing can provide valuable information to product development, business development, account management/sales, and even contracting functions. For example, brainstorming sessions with the marketing research team and creative marketing team can provide missing data that help product development teams develop more client-centric products and services. The marketing department can help identify psychographic elements that will influence sales, by looking at customer needs rather the product itself.

MOTIVATING TEAMS

To motivate your team, you first must understand what drives ongoing excellent performance. Some people are motivated by monetary reward (e.g., a commission, bonus, and/or annual raise). Others are motivated by acknowledgment and recognition from their managers. Sometimes this can be as simple as saying, "Thank you" or, "You did a great job on that project." Many employees appreciate assignment of projects with greater responsibility and visibility. Still others are motivated when recognition is public (e.g., awards and acknowledgments are presented in front of peers).

As the marketing manager, you also must identify ways to motivate at the team level. If your marketing department is large enough, you can develop team-based recognition and reward programs. For example, the group that comes up with the best idea or approach to a marketing project or customer solution can be presented with a bonus.

INSPIRING CREATIVITY

Creativity flows when people feel safe, secure, and unburdened. When setting expectations, also communicate priorities and train your team in time management. Work to develop a team with competencies as described in the Extraordinary Self Peak Performance model (see Figure 16.2), and you will inspire creativity and success. Engage your team in committing to respectful communication so your team members will feel freer to express themselves, as well as validated. Also, make it safe to have crucial conversations—defined by Kerry Patterson, Joseph Grenny, Ron McMillan, and Al Switzler in *Crucial Conversations: Tools for Talking When Stakes Are High* (McGraw-Hill, 2002)—as conversations had when opinions vary, stakes are high, and emotions run strong. The result will be an organization committed to integrity, shared goals, and collaboration.

COMMUNICATING AS A TEAM

Just as your marketing materials must have one consistent voice, your marketing team communications must meet the same test. As the marketing executive and team leader, it is up to you to set the tone and approach for communications with the team's internal and external audiences. Everyone on the marketing team should use the same language and mirror the same messages when communicating outside the team. If you have project-specific mini-teams, each team should have a designated project leader who is responsible for communicating back to you (the marketing manager) on planning, progress, and issues.

INDIVIDUAL RESPONSIBILITY IN THE CONTEXT OF A TEAM

Your biggest challenges in leading a team are (1) balancing acknowledgment of individual contributions to the team with team contributions and (2) holding people accountable at the individual and team levels. The best way to be successful in these endeavors is to clearly set the expectations at the outset, spelled out in very specific terms. Also, at a minimum, these questions need to be answered:

- What needs to be done? By when?
- Who needs to take responsibility as the lead on each key task?
- Who is/are the stakeholder(s) for each key task?
- Who is responsible for contributing to the deliverable?
- What is the priority of each key task or activity?

Openly acknowledge accountabilities by individuals and the team when objectives are met, so that you reinforce the behaviors you want. To make this work, your performance management program and employee evaluation approach must reflect the types and levels of accountabilities you set.

TEAM MEETINGS

Team meetings help you stay on track, engender accountability, and provide a forum for exchange of ideas and knowledge. To make the most of team meeting time, follow these simple tips:

- Set up a schedule of team meetings that will take place on the same day and time every week. Use Microsoft Outlook or another tool that enables you to automatically send out the invitations and insert them into each team member's calendar.

- Create an agenda, and distribute it ahead of the meeting.

- Distribute documents for review ahead of the meeting, and ask people to submit questions ahead of time, if possible. Use the meeting time only for discussion, questions, and setting objectives and deadlines for projects and key tasks. Do not use meeting time to review the documents, as this activity is wasteful and not respectful of everyone's time.

- If your marketing team is geographically dispersed, use conference calls (there are free conference services, such as www.freeconference.com), Webinars, Google's document sharing application or other collaborative work tools, and technology that provides an interactive experience long distance.

- Set time slots for each agenda item. Stick to the time frame, unless there's an overriding reason to continue discussion about one item (e.g., it is a high priority).

- Set, communicate, and reinforce ground rules for behavior of meeting participants, including respecting others' perspectives and not interrupting others when they are speaking.

- Designate a team member to record the minutes of each meeting. Review the draft minutes, and distribute them to team members later that same day, if at all possible. Doing so keeps the discussion fresh in people's minds.

- Include in meeting minutes, at a minimum, the names of attendees and nonattendees, the time convened and time closed, a summary of decision points, a "Next Steps" section that specifies who will do what and by when (for accountability), and the date and time (and call-in number, if appropriate) for the next team meeting.

- Schedule additional meetings as needed for tight-deadline projects and if problems are being experienced.

- Use e-mail for updates to the team, as needed, in between scheduled meetings. Or use collaborative, real-time document tracking tools, such as the document sharing feature that a Google account offers.

Troubleshooting

Even the best of plans can go awry. The key is to remain calm and flexible and to concentrate on the process. The point is not only to address the problem at hand but also to prevent it from recurring. Set a goal to focus on the project goal, fix the problem, and move on. After you have resolved the immediate problem, make time to revisit it. Consider expectations and, with your team, map out a solution.

Whether your department is humming along or fraught with problems, providing just-in-time feedback as well as ongoing feedback, to individuals and team members, is essential. Before delivering it, set your goal. Conduct individual feedback meetings in private, out of earshot from other employees. Give your employee (or contractor) a chance to respond and suggest a solution. Start by acknowledging, in a nonaccusatory way, what you have observed. To avert defensiveness, focus on the problem, not the person. In other words, don't make it personal. You might say, "I noticed that your project is late," or "I see that I haven't yet gotten your report." Then pause and wait. Let your colleague fill in the blank. Maintaining silence may be difficult, but it compels the other person to acknowledge and become accountable. Whatever the response, stay focused on the goal. Ask, "So how would you like to fix this?" or "What can you do next?" Then keep the focus on moving the project forward by working with your colleague to set a date by which time the problem will be rectified. Then set another date for a review of the process. End the conversation by asking your colleague to restate what you can expect to happen going forward. Get clarity about the solution, working in a respectful way, toward a common goal. Be sure to revisit the solution in the stated time to stay on target.

Executing Special Projects

Sometimes special projects—requests from the CEO, breaking news stories, a sudden need for a trade show booth, or a change in the market—may take precedence, require immediate attention, and make it necessary for you to shift priorities. Take time to address where your special project fits with ongoing workflow. Also, communicate with all team members who are involved and/or affected by changing requirements and

potentially shifting deadlines. The best way to manage high-stakes projects is to focus on communicating goals, expectations, and responsibilities. Take time to identify any red flags, such as dependencies on other project contributors, and make a plan for keeping all concerned in the loop through status reports and clear communication of needs, purpose, and deadlines. Special projects often require the use of outside contractors. The following sections provide a guide to outsourcing.

MANAGING OUTSIDE CONTRACTORS

The effective and efficient use of outside contractors requires clear communication and written documentation of expectations about project goals and objectives, specific definition of the deliverables, and how, when, where, and to whom the project must be delivered. If your contractor will be using another company to help execute the project, you also need to address the issue of subcontracting. Err on the side of overcommunicating, and include in your contract that all subcontractors must meet the same qualifications and performance objectives as the primary contractor. It is important to raise this issue upfront, as you may only want one company to perform the work.

BIDDING OUT WORK

A best practice in preparing bids is to start the discussion early, giving you enough time to decide what is needed and to ascertain the best responsible bidder. Most companies seek the lowest-priced responsible bidder. Your goal is to choose the contractor who can help you make your project shine, in your required time frame, and at a price you can afford. By preparing project specifications in advance you will be able to ascertain in a short time whether a particular contractor can deliver what you need. Establishing bid specifications is similar to the process of prospect qualifications. Set criteria for the desired consulting arrangement. Detail your specific performance indicators and metrics, and identify any nonperformance penalties (e.g., fines or contract termination). Also describe how you will monitor performance. When both parties have the same understanding, there is less chance of noncompliance and greater chance of achieving expected outcomes.

Many companies use a proposal process: they issue a Request for Proposal (RFP) to set out project specifications and gather information from potential contractors. The formal response enables reviewers to assess the contractor's capability to meet specifications. When you decide to issue an RFP, include a copy of the sample contract, so that the potential contractor will know all terms and conditions ahead of time.

GETTING THE MOST FROM OUTSOURCED RELATIONSHIPS

Use your written RFP and contractor's proposal to guide ongoing discussions regarding scope of work. Vet your contractors, and start them on small jobs whenever possible. If the product or outcomes are excellent, consider them for larger jobs in the future. Once you've selected a contractor and the project is underway, monitor contractor performance in multiple ways, using feedback from other team members or customers, when feasible. Doing so will give you more information and will help eliminate or minimize bias that can happen when evaluations are provided by only one source.

MONITORING CONTRACTOR PERFORMANCE

Here are some best practices for ensuring that you are monitoring and managing your contractors:

- **Require and monitor progress updates from the contractor.** Ask for written status reports to be submitted with a frequency appropriate to the project; also, request oral updates periodically to fill you in on status (or as needed). This requirement should be in the contract. You want written reports because reliance on recollection is not easily verified, or a good business practice. Each status report should include mention of key tasks, deliverables, due dates, and status; identification of any obstacles; and a statement about what is being done to address these. Use Table 3.5, which is the "Milestone Progress Report."

- **Schedule ongoing conversations, as needed, with the key contractor contact.** Schedule time for regular updates and hold your contractor accountable for on-time reporting and delivery.

- **Review output.** Provide feedback to your contractor about the work product and necessary changes, and clarify questions.

- **Encourage feedback from your team.** They should let you know about what they have directly observed or heard from the contractor.

- **If applicable, have conversations with your customers about what they have experienced, observed, or heard from interactions with the contractor.**

GATHERING COST ESTIMATES FROM OUTSIDE SOURCES

Solicitations for pricing can be as simple as an e-mail request to as complex as a 100-plus page competitive RFP assembled by a project team. Internet-based technology also makes it possible to issue an RFP and solicit vendor pricing through an online auction, in which vendors can actually monitor the bid price ranking of other vendors and adjust their own bids in real time while the auction is running. Proactive planning and preparation of correct job specifications at the start of a project will enable you to more easily evaluate bids.

Whom you invite to bid also will make a difference in your bid results. Choose contractors you already know to be reliable. If you don't know a contractor, you might

put out a query to colleagues on LinkedIn asking them to recommend reliable providers, or you can look to members of your professional associations and area trade groups. Specify the date by which a decision will be made, and whenever feasible, acknowledge all bid recipients by letting them know you've received their bid and when they can expect a response. Responding to your request in a professional way may be time-consuming and costly for the bidders involved. Acknowledge and respect their time by providing project specifications that resemble as closely as possible the project at hand. When projects are complex, ongoing, and expensive, you might want to hold an open conference call with all bidders in advance of the due date. Then, you can respond to questions in a time-efficient way. Another option is to post your answers to bidder questions on your Web site. (You also may post your RFP on your Web site.)

Quiz

1. Communicating the organizational and/or management vision will:
   - (a) Empower colleagues to make decisions that align with the mission
   - (b) Help team members anchor their work efforts to the company's purpose
   - (c) Build energy to support productivity and culture
   - (d) All of the above
   - (e) None of the above

2. Managers who provide hands-on direction and regular project scrutiny are:
   - (a) More likely to provide positive feedback on the job
   - (b) Demonstrate the attributes of permissive managers
   - (c) Demonstrate the attributes of an authoritative manager
   - (d) None of the above

3. The DISC assessment is one tool for evaluating:
   - (a) Management style
   - (b) Communication style
   - (c) Conversation style
   - (d) Project management

4. A crucial conversation is defined as a conversation underway when:
   - (a) Opinions differ, the stakes are high, and emotions are involved
   - (b) Opinions matter, but the stakes are low

(c) Team members are in bad moods

(d) Managers perceive a need

5. Personal feedback should be provided:

   (a) With an entire team, so everyone will know the issues

   (b) In private, whenever possible

   (c) When team members are caught doing the wrong thing

   (d) All of the above

6. The most important competency quadrant for peak performance is:

   (a) Creative problem solving, because it leads to problem resolution

   (b) Strategic thinking and decision making, because it creates a foundation for planning

   (c) Emotional maturity and intelligence, because it forms the basis for the other competencies

   (d) Impact on others, because it affects team building

7. A person who speaks more than listening, may be abrupt, and focuses on the bottom line in a conversation is probably a:

   (a) Direct communicator

   (b) Influencer

   (c) Manager

   (d) Conscientious worker

8. Healthy environments that value communication encourage people to:

   (a) Bring their thoughts to the table

   (b) Embrace a "don't just say it, mean it" approach

   (c) Be more accountable

   (d) All of the above

9. The outcome of a win-win conversation is that:

   (a) Both parties get their needs met simultaneously

   (b) One side gets to win today and the other gets to win the next time

   (c) Both parties walk away feeling they have been heard

   (d) None of the above

10. To create a successful marketing outcome, a manager must:
    (a) Clarify project goals as well as how work is vital to achieving the mission
    (b) Establish clear process guidelines
    (c) Communicate deadlines
    (d) Plan cross-team strategies
    (e) All of the above
    (f) Only choices (a), (b), and (c)

CHAPTER 17

Managing Expectations

The difference between good marketing and great marketing is the result. Great marketing gets people to take action. Great marketers get great results by doing the right things right. They have learned what works and what doesn't. Proven approaches become best practices by consistently getting desired results. Setting expectations for great marketing is the purview of the marketing manager.

Tips for Best-Practice Marketing

Over the course of this book, we've discussed various aspects of the marketing process. This section provides a quick list of highlights. I've chosen 14 tips that will put best-practice marketing to work for you. Use them to get the results you need: stronger brand recognition, more calls and queries, more trials, and more sales. Set your expectations and that of your team—around developing ongoing best practice marketing and marketing messages. Here's how.

TIP 1: CREATE SHARP, VALUE-DRIVEN MESSAGES

Do your customers immediately understand why they should do business with you? If not, revisit the messages in your marketing materials and on your Web site, and focus more attention on customer benefits than on products, features, and capabilities. Remember that most people buy value first, products second. Set the expectation that every piece of marketing collateral clearly communicates brand and/or product value.

TIP 2: DEVELOP A 30-SECOND ELEVATOR PITCH

Imagine you are at a sales convention. Two prospects have just entered the elevator and asked what you do. You have less than a minute to explain what you do and why. Prepare and rehearse one to three sentences that clearly articulate the value you bring to customers. Set the expectation that every member of your marketing team can present the elevator pitch in a pinch.

TIP 3: TRAINING

Teach every member of the organization to effectively state the company's value proposition and provide responsive customer service. Expect that every team member will impart the tenets of value through every interpersonal communication and customer interaction.

TIP 4: OFFER EVIDENCE THAT SUPPORTS MARKETING CLAIMS

Use testimonials from satisfied customers in marketing materials and on the Web. Format your testimonials in text, audio, podcasts, videocasts, messages on hold, online fan pages, blogs, and other creative formats. Use documentation, such as charts, graphs, and case studies, for more complex sales. Demonstrating company competence and results formulates the perception of high value in the minds of customers and sets an expectation for ongoing value in every employee interaction.

TIP 5: ACT IN SOCIALLY RESPONSIBLE WAYS

Develop a values-based organization, and let your customers know your values. Prepare your products in ethical ways. Pay attention to consumer concern for social causes and global issues, and act responsibly in your market by demonstrating concern for quality, people, and the planet. Connect with charitable causes and you also will grow connections with their followers. Setting socially conscious expectations for your brand and your team will help promote business sustainability.

TIP 6: TUNE INTO THE PROFIT MOTIVE

Marketing is more than copywriting and creative services. Know what's happening inside your organization, and tie your promotions to organizational strategies and goals. Figure out how to meet those goals cost effectively. Companies that do not focus on profitability won't be around to solve customer problems for long. While maintaining an eye on the bottom line, lead with integrity. Companies that skimp on quality or ignore people issues also will not be profitable in the long run. Work with your team to ensure that every one understands expectations about profitability.

TIP 7: BUILD IN FEEDBACK LOOPS

Collect feedback at regular intervals from customers and prospects. Gather intelligence on your competition as well. Customer satisfaction surveys, telephone and onsite surveys, focus groups, chat rooms, and feedback pages on Web sites can all provide important information and hard data to consider when decisions are being made about products, services, markets, and promotions. Monitor and review feedback regularly, and incorporate the results to help improve perceptions, products, and quality, as needed. Set an expectation with your team and your company that feedback is integrated into the business process whenever it is relevant.

TIP 8: INCLUDE A CALL TO ACTION

Again, the value of marketing is its power to drive sales. Tell prospects what they can do to get the results they need. Encourage customers to contact you, visit you, schedule an appointment, share information with a friend, or buy now. Tell your customers what you expect them to do. Setting an expectation for the outcomes you want will guide them to do what you need most to validate your marketing effort.

TIP 9: OPERATE ACCORDING TO A PLAN

Make your plan into a living document that focuses on your goals while flexing with the market and your marketing resources. Set the expectation that every plan you design will maximize results in terms of quality delivered and return on time, capital investment, or both, as needed. Plan your marketing budget accordingly.

TIP 10: COMMUNICATE ACROSS SENSORY CHANNELS

While markets represent groups of people, they comprise individuals, who each respond and learn in different ways. Create communications that engage the senses and you will increase the speed at which consumers connect with your message.

TIP 11: USE DATA TO MAKE DECISIONS

Define the marketing segments you intend to reach. Then gather data, evaluate it, and use it accordingly. Doing so will align your business expectations with what is possible in the world.

TIP 12: CREATE A PROFILE THAT DESCRIBES EACH TARGET MARKET

Identify your ideal customer and market. Use those profiles of markets and consumers to guide your decisions on marketing media and channels. Taking time to match your media to your market will help you get the results you expect.

TIP 13: DETERMINE THE RIGHT MEDIUM FOR YOUR AUDIENCE

Are your target customers readers, television watchers, or theatergoers? Do they use the Internet, or do they listen to the radio? Once you know the characteristics of your consumers, choose the right medium for that group. Whenever possible, use a variety of marketing media (e.g., newspapers, radio, Internet, e-mail, brochures, and word of mouth) to reach the segments you need. Identify your expectations about which modes of communication will help reach your audience effectively.

TIP 14: COMMUNICATE ACROSS MULTIPLE MARKETING CHANNELS

Use marketing partners, such as resellers and strategic affiliates, to help broaden your reach into targeted market segments. Choose partners with excellent reputations who can honorably represent your products and services. Choose the partners whom you expect will represent your brand in the way you want customers to enjoy it.

Setting Expectations

Every marketing department has two types of customers: (1) internal colleagues in need of your expertise and support, and (2) external customers in need of the honesty, integrity, and value that you are responsible for communicating and bringing to market through products and services. Wrapped up in those needs are expectations about the following. Take time to assess and document your expectations regarding each category below.:

- Implementation plans
- Product quality

- Project performance
- Due dates
- Teamwork
- Integrity
- Reliability

Management experts have recommended a bevy of solutions for addressing expectations in support of high-level business performance. I have seen program after program: managing by objectives, managing by outcomes, and managing by values, among them. The running thread is the need to set common expectations and align the business team around a shared vision.

A shared vision provides direction and fosters buy-in. When people know what is expected of them, they can map a route for getting there and figure out what's needed to stay on task.

So, how does work get done inside an organization? Leaders chart the course. They choose strategies that will position the brand, develop revenue potential, and deliver profitability. Managers orchestrate the solution. They translate the leadership vision to their teams by means of meetings, personal discussions, and internal communications. The manager's job is to ensure productive workflow. To ensure that everybody works toward the common goals, managers are responsible for communicating expectations. Their job is to lead productive meetings and make sure their teams stay on course.

Business success depends on accurate information and ongoing dialogue. As a manager, you cannot afford to leave outcomes to chance or assume that team members know what's on your mind and what you need from them. Specific communications will prevent and/or minimize the likelihood of disconnects and misinterpretations. Clear communication not only reduces risk but also lays a foundation for increased motivation. When people know where they are going, and understand the rationale, they are more likely to buy in and willingly move the process forward.

Managing by Leadership Expectations

Some say, "Walk the walk, talk the talk." Others say, "Walk the talk." No matter how you say it, you've got to actually *do* it. That means setting expectations high, but reasonably, and conducting yourself accordingly. While you may be a manager, rather than the top corporate kahuna, the people on your team look to you as leader of their department or division. How you conduct yourself and produce results communicates in itself. As a manager, it is your job to create the mirror in which your team members can see their own better selves. Reflect the behavior you want to engender.

CLARIFYING OBJECTIVES

To make sure your team knows what you expect, you must be specific about content, context, time frame, and anticipated impact. Use the following guidelines for clarifying objectives:

- Create an internal communication plan to inform team members and other internal stakeholders about the project and what you need from them.

- Communicate the project purpose with clarity and in appropriate detail for the individuals involved. Tell team members how this project serves the company in terms of brand management, customer service, financial advantage, or other relevant measure. Explain the anticipated project outcome and deadline as well as who needs what parts of the project by when, and why.

- Communicate honest urgency. Respect team members' time and the many projects on their plates. Be sure to let colleagues (i.e., your internal customers) know when a project is high priority within the context of your overall business plan, department plan, or marketing initiative.

- Spell out the process for communicating if a project gets off track. Ensure that people will carry the ball to completion. To do so, discuss in advance what to do if a project gets off track for some reason or has fallen through the proverbial crack.

- Make a plan for identifying needed resources in advance of project inception; also, identify and procure any special skills or knowledge required to successfully execute expected tasks and activities.

- Prepare a standard checklist that your team can use to track projects about issues of priority, purpose, deadlines, special information required, and communications vehicles.

- Assign a project liaison to you or your department whenever cross-functional responsibility is required.

- Share the consequences for missed deadlines and low-quality work. Do so in a way that does not generate fear but communicates its impact on the mission and the overall bottom line.

- Distribute a printed project spreadsheet or a collaborative spreadsheet that can be shared online and during meetings. All team members can then remain informed of project status, changing requirements, deadlines, and issues.

Quick Tips for Tactical Planning

Documentation is crucial to success. So, you need a reliable way to track deliverables, progress, and accountabilities in one place. Keeping information ready at a glance will show you exactly where you stand with each outcome. Tracking is done easily with Excel or any reliable spreadsheet software. Be sure to list all key tasks and associated activities. Include the following information:

- Deliverable (be specific: Is it a report, presentation, revised computer program, or anything else?)
- Start date (i.e., the date when it was assigned to a responsible party)
- Due date (i.e., when the deliverable must be completed)
- Responsible party (i.e., who has overall responsibility for the deliverable, at the key task level; others may be responsible for certain parts, and that responsibility needs to be identified as well)
- Status (mention any obstacles and how they have been resolved or if they are pending and why)
- Red flags
- Budget impact

Tracking engenders transparent communication about expectations and the importance of an organized, coordinated effort for ultimate success.

Managing by Customer Expectations

Marketing managers are responsible to two customers: internal colleagues and external customers. While this section concentrates on external customers, the same principles apply to your work relationships. Setting customer expectations begins with your first conversation with a prospect or repeat customer about a specific project. Whether you are asked to help solve a particular problem, deliver a service within a specific time frame, or produce something that has a special feature, setting the right expectations begins with honesty. If your experience tells you that the timing, process, or other variables need to be different than what the customer has asked for, then immediately explain why this is so.

Let the prospect or customer know that you want him or her to achieve the best possible outcome. Your competitor may agree to a prospect's initial request and not point out how it will cut corners. It is up to you to educate customers about what it really takes to get a job done right. This is part of your value proposition.

Setting expectations creates a foundation for long-term relationships. When a customer considers awarding you business, your behavior in the early stages tells the prospect or client how your company will approach the work and demonstrates your level of respect. Setting reasonable expectations about time frames and solutions is an important way to demonstrate respect. Whether you are releasing a request for proposal to an outside vendor or submitting a proposed solution and implementation plan to a client on behalf of your

sales department, always identify the factors that will impact success (include realistic time frames) and state what you need from the customer, by when.

Once you are awarded a contract, or asked to do a job for your own company, open communication will ensure that everyone is on the same page about the project's progress and the final deliverable. You can do this by creating an account packet, which should consist of the following:

- A project overview
- An implementation schedule
- A list of what is needed from your customer
- A list of key company contacts by area or customer need, along with phone numbers and e-mail addresses
- A process flowchart, if your business provides a product or service that has a complex delivery process that needs to be understood

Keep in mind that customers don't necessarily expect perfection. Everyone knows that even the best contingency plans can't cover every possible scenario. Customers do expect speedy, high-quality products and problem resolution, excellent follow-up, and a concrete explanation of what you have done to ensure that an out-of-plan event will not recur. How your team steps up to a challenge says a lot about how you view your customers and how you operate your business. Make sure your responsiveness conveys the brand message you want your customers to receive.

Incorporating Feedback

The purpose of asking questions of employees and customers is to get information that will help your business better deliver on your brand promise. Asking open-ended questions will yield more information, won't prejudice the content, and will demonstrate your sincerity about learning from what they tell you. Open-ended questions allow you to gather more information than a yes-no alternative or a rating scale would tell you. They encourage respondents to share their own knowledge, impressions, and feelings about a product or service encounter. Here are some examples of open-ended questions:

- Tell me about . . .
- How do you feel about . . . ?
- What did you think of . . . ?
- What else would you like to know?
- Whom would you like to share this information with?
- What does this mean to you?

Sometimes, what people omit from answers can tell you just as much as what they say. Listen for what people are not saying, and follow up with a question about that. For example, if you ask a customer whether she has received a product you sent (which is a close-ended question), and she answers simply yes or no, you may conclude that either she didn't try it, hasn't opened it, or didn't like it. Short responses may indicate that there is discomfort with a subject. Your job as a marketer is to probe for additional information. To enhance communication, work to uncover expectations and meet them whenever possible; make it a priority to seek the information you need. Doing so will help you make your product offering and/or marketing communication the best it can be.

Whenever possible, use person-to-person communication (e.g., by phone or face to face). That interaction will provide you with valuable insights that cannot be obtained through written surveys.

SETTING EXPECTATIONS ABOUT FEEDBACK

You can set your expectations and tone for feedback, too. To do so in an effective way, do the following:

1. If you don't intend to act on the information you gather, don't solicit it. You will lose credibility.

2. Explain why you are asking for feedback. Describe what the information will help you do for the customer.

3. Be prepared to answer questions that arise from your initial questions.

4. Designate the appropriate person(s) to conduct the discussions or ask customer questions. Consider which customer questions are best asked by different individuals within your organization: salesperson, account manager, senior management team member, customer service representative, or an outside consultant. You will get a more complete and accurate picture from your customer when you ask questions that address different aspects of the same topic from various perspectives, and this approach also will help you to identify any inconsistency.

5. Document the discussion in your business files.

6. Thank the customer for his or her time in a follow-up communication (e.g., in an e-mail message).

7. Send the customer an update on how you've incorporated his or her feedback into an improved operation, a better product, a quicker response time, or a more cost-effective alternative.

8. Set a schedule for follow-up feedback sessions, as needed.

9. Communicate that you appreciate your respondent's time and forthrightness.

Empowerment and Problem Solving

Setting expectations early on is a best practice for problem solving. It shows that you are proactive and have a plan in place to address events that are unexpected. It also provides you with the basis for how you communicate in a crisis. Employee empowerment has long been recognized as a lynchpin of superior customer service and customer loyalty. To cultivate superior customer service and customer loyalty, your business must do more than pay lip service to the phrase. Ask yourself the following questions to determine whether your business has an outcomes-focused, solution-oriented process in place:

- Do our employees have the skills and knowledge to solve problems?

- Have we conducted an evaluation of our employees? How often do we provide performance feedback? Do we have a formal performance management program?

- What do team members need to learn so they can solve customer problems?

- When we orient new hires and train employees, do we include sections on customer (and internal) problem solving?

- Does our performance management program evaluate our employees on problem solving?

- Do I tend to resolve problems myself because I fear someone else won't it get done the way I want? If so, what can I do about that? (Note that this is an issue of your own expectations. You can either adjust your expectations or train your team to resolve problems as you would.)

- Do I view disappointing outcomes as opportunities for employees to learn from their mistakes or simply as failure? Do I ever intentionally let employees fail, on the small things, so they will learn how to do things better the next time? What are my views on failure?

- Do we have a clear escalation process? If so, do all employees know what it is? Can they explain it?

Keep in mind that even if you have a customer service department or dedicated staff within your team, every employee must learn problem-solving skills—even if the solution is how to refer the customer call to the right person in your organization.

Honoring the Brand

When you promise something to someone, it means that you have told the other person what he or she can expect from you. The underlying message is that you are truthful and honest.

When you do what you promise, you honor your brand. How do you honor your brand? You ought to do the following things:

- Resolve the problem(s) for which your customer hired you in the way that you stated.
- Reply to requests and questions (via phone, e-mail, letter, and/or meetings) within the time frames that you have agreed to, in line with what is reasonable.
- Train your employees and provide them with the appropriate tools so they can do their best for your customers and business. Tell them what they need to do and why it honors the brand.
- Make product and service claims that are truthful and honest in your marketing and advertising.
- Never knock the competition; instead, persuade prospects and customers with your experience and value.
- Set the standards for behavior, attitudes, and beliefs about your brand, the operations, and communications, and then consistently act according to those standards.

Noticing Influence

Take note of who influences opinion within your company. Company leaders and brand influencers are not necessarily all C-level executives, such as chief executive officers, chief financial officers, or chief marketing officers. Very often, influencers are the people in your organization who make a difference in day-to-day outcomes, earn the respect of other employees, and are listened to by managers and executives when they provide feedback. Identify who the change leaders and influencers are in your organization. Pay attention to what they say and do, and file or use that information to build on, meet, and exceed expectations inside and beyond your organization.

Quiz

1. The benefit of creating a shared vision is that it:
   (a) Becomes immutable in the organization
   (b) Challenges teams to perform at higher levels
   (c) Provides direction and fosters buy-in
   (d) None of the above

2. You can demonstrate respect for clients by:

   (a) Staying late to work on projects

   (b) Setting reasonable expectations about time and solutions

   (c) Submitting a proposed solution to problems

   (d) All of the above

3. You can honor your brand promise by:

   (a) Resolving problem(s) in the way you stated

   (b) Replying to requests and questions within agreed-upon time frames

   (c) Giving employees tools

   (d) All of the above

   (e) Only choices (a) and (b)

4. When setting expectations around feedback, you should:

   (a) Explain why you are asking for feedback

   (b) Gather a team

   (c) Meet in private

   (d) Always use a written protocol

5. If you don't intend to act on the information you gather:

   (a) You will lose credibility.

   (b) It won't matter. No one expects you to use it anyway.

   (c) Your results will be skewed.

   (d) All of the above

6. Company leaders and brand influencers are:

   (a) Examples of role models

   (b) Not always C-level executives

   (c) Never leave companies

   (d) None of the above

7. Asking questions that address different aspects of the same topic:

   (a) Helps you identify inconsistencies

   (b) Reveals a more complete and accurate picture

   (c) None of the above

   (d) Both choices (a) and (b)

8. "What did you think of . . . "? is an example of:

   (a) Uncovering marketing strategies

   (b) An open-ended question

   (c) A close-ended question

   (d) None of the above

9. Setting expectations early on is:

   (a) A best practice for problem solving

   (b) Shows that you are proactive

   (c) Provides a basis for how you communicate in a crisis

   (d) All of the above

   (e) Only choice (b)

10. The manager's job is to:

   (a) Ensure productive workflow

   (b) Lead the organization

   (c) Provide market analysis

   (d) None of the above

CHAPTER 18

Integrating Ethics, Morality, and Social Responsibility

Whether plainly stated or implicit, every brand marketing effort centers on a promise. The promise itself may be wrapped in fantastic imagery, communicate a glowing benefit, or come with a money-back guarantee. But whatever your promise, it doesn't end with your message. As you know, messaging is a two-way street. After you launch your message, consumers will filter it based on their needs, perceptions, and expectations. Then, your company must act with integrity to make good on that promise by consistently delivering expected value. A consistent message reinforced by consistent high-quality service engenders trust, which leads to repeat sales. That sounds simple enough. Right? To be trusted, you just have to do what you say you're going to do.

But what about the implicit part of that promise—the part that says that the company that customers choose to do business with is worthy of their business? We've all heard the adage "people want to do business with people they know and like." You may be nodding your head in agreement right now. Later, you might furrow your brow, thinking the adage seems out of touch when applied to shoppers pulling products off a shelf. After all, how many shoppers really know the people behind the can of beans, jar of jelly, or panoply of cosmetics they might pluck from a shelf? For that matter, how many customers know the people running the local car dealership, or even more remotely, the car manufacturers themselves? You might say that consumers buy stuff anyway, without any personal relationships, which renders the adage meaningless. But then again, you are a marketer. By now, you have unwrinkled your brow. Now you are thinking about brand reputation.

As a marketer, you know that perceived value goes beyond the physical transaction to incorporate a customer's feelings about the brand itself and the company behind it. Today's marketing dialogue extends well past product delivery. Ethics, morality, and social responsibility have joined the marketing conversation. And consumers are proving it with socially conscious buying.

Socially Responsible Brand Management

Today's consumers are more aware of the social implications of their day-to-day buying decisions. Many consumers make purchasing choices that reflect their concerns about an array of issues, from environmental sustainability to health and safety issues, social needs, and business ethics, as well as cost. So, watching social trends presents an opportunity for observant marketers. Trend watching can unlock success secrets and help marketers generate results in new ways. To identify trends, pay attention to topics covered in articles in newspapers and magazines, broadcast news, movies, television dialogue, editorials, talk shows, advertising, commercials, blogs, and social media queries. The more often you see a topic discussed, the more likely it is that consumers consider it relevant. Reflecting on topics of concern will provide insight to social consciousness. By rolling that information into your marketing plan, you can position your company with a relevant premise for market differentiation and stronger competitive edge. Trend analysts contend that cultural values play a strong role in influencing buying patterns. Marketers who are the first to spot trends and the most in tune with cultural variations will be poised to seize and maximize market share.

Marketing and Social Values

Marketers who recognize the relationship between trends and cultural values will leap an extra step ahead. By monitoring social values, you can identify the motivating forces that drive business, societies and economies. Then, by aligning your company values so they match (or exceed) expectations of your market, you can tap into a powerful psychological marketing dynamic: the social belief systems that influence buying decisions.

Belief systems are based on *social norms*, which are the standards of conduct that moderate society as well as business organizations. Norms and ethics (i.e., accepted moral principles) are derived from *social values*, which are the ideals that communities find desirable, important, and morally correct. When company values align with a market's social values, marketers are better able to match messages, products, services, and actions in ways that mirror and/or exceed customers' expectations.

As a marketer, you can incorporate values as a guiding principle for planning and evaluating your marketing activities. By integrating your knowledge of your target market's values and concerns with your marketing plan, and blending that with your own corporate values, such as service, excellence, and philanthropy, you can add the clout of social responsibility to your marketing arsenal. Cause-related marketing is one effective strategy.

Cause-Related Marketing

Cause-related marketing is a collaborative strategy through which a for-profit corporation supports the message and/or needs of a not-for-profit organization for mutual benefit. The business benefits through access to the not-for-profit's stakeholders, the "halo effect" gained by doing good works, as well as the advertising value of association with a reputable nonprofit or charitable organization. The not-for-profit group benefits from support provided by its business partner, as well as the cachet of associating with a pillar of the community or respected community servant.

Through cause-related marketing, businesses may provide their not-for-profit partners with these things:

- Financial support for specific nonprofit programs
- Sponsorship of special events
- Personnel and resources for events and/or program delivery
- In-kind donations of equipment, intellectual resources, and consulting services
- Advertising services (as is often the case with media sponsors)
- Promotional products

In turn, nonprofit organizations may advertise the names of supporting companies on their Web sites and in newsletters, advertising, and viral marketing campaigns. In this way, a company can build its image as a socially responsible enterprise.

Supporting a cause is a win-win marketing opportunity that can advance your standing in the hearts and minds of consumers. Studies show that companies participating in cause-related marketing are valued by consumers as more trustworthy and innovative than those that do not. And, these attributes that help drive brand equity. The goodwill such companies generate often garners media attention and consumer loyalty. Leading companies have learned and have embraced social responsibility as a marketing strategy. For example, in early 2010, Pepsi television commercials communicated an *I Care about Community* theme.

Shortly after the 2010 earthquake devastated Haiti, Winn-Dixie supermarkets aired a television campaign promoting the relief effort. Why? Because socially responsible, cause-related marketing bridges relationships with people in target markets, especially when they have an affinity for the particular charity, nonprofit organization, or cause. With more than half of charities presently experiencing a downturn in contributions, cause-related marketing now presents an opportunity for companies to stand out by helping their communities.

BENEFITS AND IMPACT OF CAUSE-RELATED MARKETING

Good works increase brand loyalty within and beyond your organization. Socially responsible, cause-related programs return dividends to business in several ways:

- **Brand differentiation.** Ethical branding, developed as you walk your social responsibility talk, provides traditional and online public relations opportunities. Hosting events, press releases about your cause-related endeavors, and posting fan pages on which the community can comment can help build the buzz about your company. You may want to moderate your own self-promotion of cause-related marketing endeavors to avoid appearing to be self-serving. Allow savvy nonprofit partners, strategic partners, and consumers to share your brand story for you.

- **Employee morale.** Cause-related marketing and branding promotes organizational pride, contributes to status as an employer of choice, and helps attract and retain top talent. People, particularly younger workers, want to work for socially responsible companies.

- **Citizenship.** By educating legislators and participating in forums where you can share relevant information, insight, and concern about issues influencing society, you can codify your citizenship and strengthen your brand reputation.

- **Risk reduction.** Building an organizational culture tied to socially responsible activities makes a statement about your corporate values. Create policies that commit your company to socially responsible decision making, product development, and community action. Then, set expectations for walking the talk at all levels of your organization: from truth in advertising to recycling paper and cans, purchasing "green" cleaning products, developing green products, managing energy consumption in your office, and promoting philanthropy. As you do the right things right, you also will reduce risk caused by error and poor judgment.

- **Profitability.** By acting with integrity to bring value and substance to products, customers, communities, and society at large, companies build the foundation for sustainable client relationships. Leading by values also leads to customer loyalty.

DIFFERENTIATING YOUR COMPANY WITH CAUSE-RELATED MARKETING

Cause-related marketing works. For example, in 1983, American Express pledged to donate a penny to the restoration of the Statue of Liberty for every transaction made by its cardholders. As a result, use of American Express cards increased by 28 percent and new users increased by 17 percent.[1] Since American Express set sail on that social marketing regatta, cause-related marketing endeavors have consistently delivered strong return on investment.

EVIDENCE OF CAUSE-RELATED MARKETING SUCCESS

Cause-related marketing also impacts productivity and morale. Assuming equal location, pay, benefit, and responsibilities, 72 percent of Americans reported they would choose to work for a firm that supports charitable causes over one that does not.[2] Cause-related marketing is a proven differentiation strategy. Consider the evidence. Studies conducted in the United States and abroad consistently demonstrate the power of this approach. According to one study[3]:

- Seventy-seven percent of respondents state they were positively influenced by cause-related marketing programs during product decision making and at the point of purchase.

- Eighty percent of consumers say they will continue to feel positive about the companies that engage in cause-related marketing.

- Sixty-seven percent of consumers reported that they want to see more companies supporting causes.

- When price and quality are equal, more than 80 percent agree that they are more likely to buy a product that is associated with a cause they care about.

- Eighty-six percent have a more positive image of a company they see doing something to make the world a better place.

Managing by Values and for Value

It's clear that consumers want to do business with companies that do good works and operate with integrity, accountability, and transparency. But it is more difficult to know which values most strongly influence buyers. Spurred by greed, generations of profiteers have traded moral values for money. When greed overtakes integrity, quick, short-term

---

[1]www.causemarketingforurm.com.
[2]Deloitte & Touche USA LLP study conducted by Harris Interactive, as reported on www.causemarketingforum.com.
[3]Business in the Community study, Britain, 2009.

profits may result. But, profit mongering is not in the best long-term interest of shareholders, employees, consumers, or communities. For sustainable business viability, organizational leaders must stand strong on ethics and balance the dichotomy between managing for shareholder value and managing by values.

Over the last decade, we watched as greed ran the gauntlet. We witnessed the fall of Tyco and Enron executives. We saw the Dame of Home Entertaining imprisoned for insider trading. We were shocked by the gall and enormity of Bernie Madoff's far-reaching Ponzi scheme. As a nation, we still reel from losses resulting from recently uncovered financial industry mismanagement. When a business disregards morality, it compromises society at large. Over time, that enterprise and its constituents—employers, employees, investors, supply chain partners, and other stakeholders—will suffer from the erosion of consumer support. As perceptions about corporate-sector moral fiber shift downward, consumers will become more jaded.

Companies are not alone in their greed. Consumer lust for products, homes, and services they cannot afford has led to a society that buys and lives on credit. But, credit can be a safe bet when consumers have necessary income and a plan for paying that debt back in a reasonable time frame. So, why are we discussing credit issues in a marketing book? The current social circumstance of conspicuous consumption has been driven in a large way by advertising. Creative advertising has the power to lure consumers into buying beyond their ability to pay. As a result of expectations set by advertisements and society, many consumers believe that they will not be satisfied enough, good enough, or worth enough without the ability to procure more stuff. Banking and financial practices also have made it easy for consumers to accumulate extensive debt. Together, these factors created a recipe for unprincipled buying, in line with unprincipled selling and the strong shareholders' push for ever higher-level profits.

The good news is that marketers and business leaders can push back and positively influence perceptions by driving conversations, expectations, organizational behavior, and social behavior toward higher-level integrity and social responsibility. They can encourage consumers to buy responsibly. They can communicate consistent messages, inside and outside the company. They can help transmit a healthy vision and healthy values across their organizations. And, they can become powerful drivers of business integrity, processes, and profitability by promoting values-based, win-win customer-company marketing strategies and/or win-win-win customer-company-cause strategies. They also can promote socially responsible buying strategies.

For example, HumongousSavings.com is a relatively new socially responsible buying club run by individuals who guarantee a low price of 10 percent over cost. This guarantee benefits consumers with low-cost pricing (a win), while the company believes it will earn enough profit to stay viable based on sales volume (a win-win situation). Set up as a cause-related marketing firm, HumongousSavings.com further creates win-win-win outcomes by committing to contribute 50 percent of its profits to charities. This commitment is spelled out in its agreement with customers who buy through the Web site. Through alliances with RADD (Recording Artists Against Drunk Driving, the entertainment industry's voice for road safety), celebrities, and music producers, the company leaders also offer concerts and art events to support nonprofit causes.

Enlightened marketing leaders recognize the value of contributing to society through ethical business action and offerings. Leadership and marketing behavior speak volumes about company values. When both leaders and rank-and-file employees walk the values talk, companies do the following:

- Foster trust
- Strengthen internal and external relationships
- Enhance product quality and organizational productivity
- Communicate realistic and reasonable profit requirements
- Support the needs of individual consumers and society at large

Trends and Marketing

Marketers are uniquely positioned to help their organizations identify motivating forces in their markets and inside their companies. As a marketer, you can cultivate a values-based marketing mission, which acknowledges that profit flows from doing the right things right. You can advocate with company leaders to develop product value in line with societal needs, concerns, and expectations.

Business leaders and managers can identify the values driving them and their businesses, and use them as a marketing guidepost. According to Ken Blanchard and Michael O'Connor in their book *Managing by Values* (Berrett-Koehler Publishers, 1996), values-based management is a three-stage, people-focused process by which a company first clarifies its mission, purpose, and values, then communicates that information, and finally aligns its daily practices with mission and values.

To assess company values, business leaders must be courageous. They need to address business and discussions at all levels of the organization to get a handle on what is actually happening and to learn whether and how well people are walking the company talk. They must identify the link between company values and the company's place in the world. Today's consumers are instantly aware of needs, issues, problems, and concerns across the globe. They expect governments and industry leaders to be accountable for global problem solving. They expect to be satisfied with individual transactions, and they expect those transactions to occur in the context of their own beliefs and social mores. Marketers must gauge which values most strongly influence buyer behavior and how strongly they impact buying decisions.

VALUES-BASED MARKET POSITIONING MODEL

Modern management literature is preoccupied with success. Bestsellers, motivational theorists, and training consultants address the dynamics of change, frameworks for leadership, the relationships between customer expectations and service delivery, and quality management practices. Blanchard and O'Connor demonstrate in their book that businesses guided by strong moral principles can and do succeed despite bottom-line cost imperatives.

But how can a business leader know the true value of its offering? How can one evaluate the merits of an investment in a productivity enhancer, technical innovation, or a new product feature? Marketing research is one answer. Research into consumer values is another. Today's consumers seek value that feeds emotional and social needs, as well as physical. So, today's leaders need new ways of predicting and measuring the strength of value in changing markets, and adapting business tactics accordingly. For example:

- If you notice consumer concerns about the environment, you can respond with environment-sensitive promotions. You can run fund-raisers to help preserve rain forests or carry environmentally sensitive products.

- If you are in building and construction or pharmaceutical industries, you might refrain from using products harvested from rain forests, and work to develop suitable, environmentally safe products.

- When consumers complain about an imbalance in foreign trade, or when editorial pages of popular papers criticize low-paid foreign labor or sweatshops that exploit children, you can promote use of American-made products.

- When your target market is sensitive to issues of drunk driving, you can help support organizations such as RADD, or the SAFE KIDS USA campaign, which advocates unintentional injury prevention (through use of seat belts, bicycle helmets, flotation devices, and injury prevention education).

Understanding the interaction between cost-driven value (i.e., price) and consumer values can guide your market positioning. Figure 18.1 is a tool for rating consumers' own values and their perception of a company's values-based offering, then calculating the differential between personally held values and consumers' perception of company values. Figure 18.2 locates values compatibility and price tolerance. It provides a method by which companies can assess their own values-based positioning using a simple matrix. Together, these tools allow you to see whether your business is on trend with consumer values and can flourish as is or whether you should reexamine the principles influencing your value offering.

VALUE DIMENSIONS	RATING 0 to 10* Consumer values	RATING 0 to 10* Organizational values	ABSOLUTE DIFFERENCE Distance between consumer and organizational values
	*0 (not important at all) to 10 (highly important)		
PERSONAL			
Achievement	—	—	—
Belonging	—	—	—
Courage	—	—	—
Creativity	—	—	—
Education	—	—	—
Enjoyment/Fun/Entertainment	—	—	—
Family	—	—	—
Friendship	—	—	—
Fulfillment	—	—	—
Health and wellness	—	—	—
Honesty	—	—	—
Integrity	—	—	—
Leisure	—	—	—
Spirituality	—	—	—
Sports affinity	—	—	—
Trust	—	—	—
SOCIAL			
Connectedness	—	—	—
Communication	—	—	—
Community service	—	—	—
Compassion	—	—	—
Economic stability	—	—	—
Environmental sustainability	—	—	—
Freedom	—	—	—
Justice	—	—	—
Relationships	—	—	—
Peace	—	—	—
Philanthropy	—	—	—
Security	—	—	—
Sharing	—	—	—
Stewardship	—	—	—
Tolerance	—	—	—
Wisdom	—	—	—
BUSINESS			
Diversity	—	—	—
Efficiency	—	—	—
Excellence	—	—	—
Fairness	—	—	—
Initiative	—	—	—
Innovation	—	—	—
Knowledge	—	—	—
Loyalty	—	—	—
Recognition	—	—	—
Respect	—	—	—
Responsiveness	—	—	—
Risk taking	—	—	—
Safety	—	—	—
Success	—	—	—
Teamwork	—	—	—
Training	—	—	—

HOW TO USE THIS TOOL

PHASE ONE
Determine compatibility between consumer and organizational values in your target market.

1. Choose a random sample of consumers, and ask them to rate their own values. Also have them rate your organization's values, using their own perception of the organization's brand, products, customer service, business ethics, and social responsibility.

2. Calculate the absolute difference (the distance between the consumer's rating of values for him or herself, and that person's rating of perceived organizational values for each value dimension.)

3. Tally the absolute difference and record the total to determine your values-compatibility score.

4. Add totals from your entire sample, then divide by the number of individuals in your sample to calculate your *average* values-compatibility score.

5. Use your *average* values-compatibility score to determine your values-based market compatibility.
   0 to 160 = Congruent
   161 to 320 = Compatible
   321 to 480 = Incongruent

PHASE TWO
Understanding your values-based market positioning opportunity
Determine values-based compatibility with your market by applying your *average* values-based compatibility score, as indicated in Fig. 18.2.

VALUES-BASED MARKET COMPATIBILITY SCORE (TOTAL) _____

Figure 18.1   Values compatibility assessment.

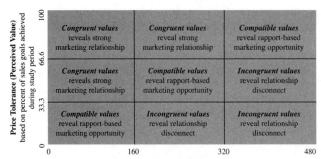

HOW TO USE THIS CHART

This table will help you assess your brand potential in a target market, by correlating values-based compatibility with consumers' price tolerance.

Locate your values-compatibility score, (calculated using the tool represented in Fig. 18.1) along the horizontal axis of the values-based positioning matrix at left. Position that value relative to your assessment of consumers' price tolerance across the vertical axis to locate your position on the chart.

Measure price tolerance as a reflection of the percentage of actual sales achieved by comparison to established sales goals for period in which the survey is conducted. (Or, you may survey consumers response to pricing directly, then measure results on a scale of 0 to 100 (0 representing no price acceptance and 100 representing total price acceptance) then locate price tolerance position on the chart.)

Once you have located your position on the matrix based on price tolerance (perceived value) and values-compatibility scores, refer to the values-based position information guide at left to consider your own compatibility with your target market. Use the information you gain through your values study to help guide discussions when you explore options for strategic decision making.

Source:
Concept for Fig. 18.1 and 18.2 adapted from General Electric Multi-Factor Portfolio Model and Growth Share Matrix

CONGRUENT VALUES POSITION

Product/brand offers based on value assignments in these positions are highly on trend with consumer values, and demonstrate strong values-based market positioning.

STRATEGIC DIRECTION

Consider bolstering marketing and business investment in values-compatible markets for ongoing growth. Periodically survey and observe consumer and organizational values for assessment of ongoing fit. Act to stay in alignment with consumer pricing expectations. Act to hold position and gains.

COMPATIBLE VALUES POSITION

Product/brand offers based on value assignments in these positions are moderately on trend with consumer values. This indicates acceptable values-based market positioning.

STRATEGIC DIRECTION

Review vision and values orientations. Examine market conditions. Seek ways to strengthen any disconnects. Concentrate investments where profitability is acceptable and risk is low. Act to hold business gains. Consider withdrawing from markets where indication of market growth is lacking or where values check-ups indicate disconnects.

INCONGRUENT VALUES POSITION

Product/brand offers based on value assignments in these positions provide little connection based on consumer values, or the ability to differentiate based on relationship between consumers and organization.

STRATEGIC DIRECTION

Seriously rethink vision, values, people strategies, priorities, and processes. Look for ways to align with consumers' personal, social, and business values and price tolerance to protect and grow your market opportunities. Train leaders to manage by values. Match product and quality efforts to consumer expectations to strengthen values-based market positioning and/or divest.

Figure 18.2   Values-based market positioning matrix.

Shifting Performance

Values are like body language. They speak more strongly than words. They drive the vitality of an organization and act as the eyes of a workforce. With clarity of vision and values, marketers can spark pride and bolster organizational performance. As more employees engage in living the company vision and values, organizational behavior becomes more consistent and collective.

Even with strong ethical values and a sound vision, circumstances and needs will change. Demographics will shift, new technologies will emerge, processes will need to adapt, and employees and market demands will rise or fall. So, how can your company chart and stay the right course? Try this pathway:

- Make an effort to understand and experience your corporate personality as it is now. Define what your company represents, and what it seeks to be in the future.

- Check your understanding. Ask your employees, investors, channel partners, and customers for information and feedback to help you see your company from the perspective of others. Test your assumptions.

- Gather the facts and use them to create a relational experience—using skills of emotional intelligence, social intelligence, strategic decision making, creative productivity, and impact on others—to strengthen your market connections. Make sure that your company is in sync with market values and demands. Decide if your assumptions hold true. Then act to close gaps or hold gains.

- When planning products and promotions, make a point of considering the anticipated impact of both products and campaign messages on target markets and the world at large. As a marketer you have responsibilities to both your company and society at large.

Marketing Integrity

A marketer's job is to stimulate demand, influence people, and develop competitive advantage. Marketers are charged with generating plans and advertisements that portray brands, products, and services in the most positive light. As a marketer, your job also comes with responsibility and accountability to a wide range of stakeholders: the company, community, channel partners, colleagues, and consumers. You are in a unique position to help balance the needs of company and community as you reach out to consumers.

Once a product need is defined, companies use advertising to promise benefits and solutions. Many use advertising to create fantasies of fulfillment for groups of human beings with specific needs and concerns. However, some target groups—the elderly, individuals with medical conditions, children, and underserved markets, among others— are more vulnerable to advertising messages than others. Marketers must take care to advertise with honesty and avoid unjust pressure.

When marketers subtly stage their products on television and talk shows, or when marketing messages are comingled with educational programming, edutainment, or new interviews, consumers can be hard pressed to discern opinion from reality. As marketers we have a responsibility to tell the truth. We also have an obligation to honor rules, such as guidelines from the FTC, Food and Drug Administration (FDA), and the CAN-SPAM Act (discussed in Chapter 15), which regulate commercial advertising.

As a marketer, you have a moral obligation to those whom you seek to influence. According to the American Marketing Association, marketers should adhere to the following ethical norms and values:

- Do no harm.
- Abide by laws.

- Foster trust in the marketing system.
- Create good faith.
- Provide fair value.
- Avoid deception in product design, pricing, communication, and delivery.
- Embrace ethical values, such as honesty, responsibility, fairness, respect, transparency, and citizenship.

As a marketer you can make a positive difference on behalf of your company. Here are a dozen ways:

1. Advocate for an ethics policy that addresses issues such as standards for professional behavior, gifts to and from outside vendors, media relations' protocols, confidentiality, and adherence to corporate values. Once you have a policy, you can help communicate it internally (and externally, as appropriate) to protect your company and community from risk and harm. If you are unsure how to create such a policy, speak with your human resources and/or legal team, or bring on a consultant to work with you.

2. Create marketing department standards, and follow marketing best practices. The American Marketing Association, International Association of Business Communicators, and the Public Relations Society of America all provide guidance and ongoing education for marketers. Attend local chapter meetings, as a visitor or a member, to stay on top of industry issues and concerns.

3. Create a customer bill of rights, and share it throughout your organization.

4. Familiarize yourself with fair market pricing, honesty in communications, industry and government regulations, product liability, and consumer protections.

5. Make sure your company has an employee handbook that clearly spells out expected ethical behavior and consequences for breaching it.

6. Define and honor product warranties, guarantees, and refund policies.

7. Develop purchasing guidelines and vendor guidelines. Know from whom you buy and why.

8. Establish your criteria for ethical business transactions, including assessment of values, decisions about tying or bundling agreements, special purchasing requirements, and societal impact created by your company or your vendors (e.g., impact on the environment, health, and safety or general societal well-being).

9. Provide honesty when describing product benefits and values.

10. Avoid exaggerated or unsubstantiated claims and comparisons that harm your competitors. Lead with integrity.

11. Do what you say you will do. Honor company commitments.

12. Treat clients' business and money as you would treat your own.

Money isn't the only currency in business. Reputation itself has value, as does every transaction inside and beyond your organization. Reputation is measured in consumer trust and brand loyalty. Relationship currency founded on truth, service, and integrity can generate short-term profit through individual sales and long-term profit through client loyalty, testimonials, and referrals.

Ethics in Advertising

While marketers and advertising agencies have the obligation to sell products, consumers have a different job. Based on their perception of advertising, they must make logical judgments and purchases based on sound reasoning. Some forms of advertising can make it difficult for consumers to discern fantasy from reality. In our digital age, videographers have mastered the art of special effects, and print designers can easily manipulate photographs and information; so, how can consumers trust that what they see is true?

In Chapter 6, onscreen product placement was mentioned as a marketing channel option. Now, consider that same strategy from another perspective—ethics. When consumers see evidence of brands and products—fancy cars, clothing, computers, stores, and music— on television and movie screens, they may not understand whether those items were chosen because they tell the story, or a company has paid to place their products on that show. When Bill O'Reilly wears a designer suit or tie on *The O'Reilly Factor*, producers clearly indicate the sponsor of those articles. But not all advertising is that up-front.

Recognizing that a marketer's job is to sell products, the marketer also must work within ethical guidelines discussed previously, with goals not to defraud and to do no harm. Deciding whether and how individual consumers or society may be helped or harmed is not always easy. So, whether selling your story in print or onscreen, do the following:

- Clearly identify paid advertising and product placements.

- Serve your community by providing seminars and articles on how to discern fantasy from reality.

- Communicate ethics inside your organization, and make sure that your advertising promotions meet socially responsible guidelines.

Assessing Organizational Integrity

Organizational ethics and overall business culture influence advertising and marketing behavior. What occurs on the outside is a reflection of what happens inside. To ensure that ethical practices transfer appropriately from internal behavior to external communications,

companies must assess and safeguard organizational integrity. Companies can evaluate organizational integrity by asking these questions of themselves:

- Does our leadership team clearly express expectations?

- Does our team understand those expectations and step up to the plate?

- Does our company allow certain people to misbehave when that misbehavior results in gains for the company?

- Are employees at all levels treated in a consistent manner?

- Does our company provide training and support services that ensure that employees learn how to do the right things right?

Assessing Marketing Integrity

To ensure that your marketing decisions reflect strong cultural ethics, marketing managers must evaluate all aspects of the marketing mix—planning, products, positioning, placement, price, people, and promotion—in terms of their influence on and responsibility to the company and consumers and community. Ask yourself the following questions to help you evaluate your own marketing mix:

- Do we translate our internal values appropriately through our products, advertising, and behavior with suppliers, sales channel partners, and customers?

- Does our product packaging reflect ethical and societal norms?

- Did we research the potential impact of our products and services on target markets, including anticipated and potentially unanticipated impact on vulnerable market groups?

- Is our marketing plan based on accurate research?

- Did our research and development team include features that matter to our customers and strive to offer them at the best possible price?

- Do our advertising claims match our product capabilities?

- Can we prove our claims?

- Has our advertising been approved by our investors, our company ethics board, and our attorneys?

- Does our advertising conform to regulations of the FDA, the FTC, and other government agencies?

- Is our sales team educated and skilled at communicating honestly and ethically with our customers?

- Does our sales team know what our company expects from them?

- Do we communicate the concerns of our marketing team back to organizational leaders honestly?
- Do we stay in touch with consumers' beliefs and expectations?
- Do we integrate customer feedback and marketing research into our marketing plan?
- Is our pricing fair and profit reasonable relative to our overhead costs and consumer value?
- Do we make our products affordable and accessible to markets in need to the best of our ability?

Quiz

1. To build stronger relations with internal and external stakeholders, you should:

    (a) Encourage leaders and rank-and-file employees to walk the talk

    (b) Choose internal or external stakeholders and pander to that group

    (c) Publicize employee announcements in newspapers

    (d) None of the above

2. Marketers can identify motivating forces in their markets by:

    (a) Monitoring trends and values

    (b) Monitoring the media

    (c) Monitoring what is happening inside the company

    (d) None of the above

    (e) All of the above

3. Values are defined as:

    (a) The jewels of an organization

    (b) The price of products

    (c) The ideals that communities find desirable, important, and morally correct

    (d) Quality divided by cost

    (e) All of the above

4. Social norms are defined as:

    (a) The standards of conduct that moderate society

    (b) The standards of conduct that moderate business

    (c) Neither choices (a) nor (b)

    (d) Both choices (a) and (b)

5. Social values are described as:

   (a) Having influence on buying behavior

   (b) The ideals that communities find desirable, important, and morally correct

   (c) Guidelines and criteria for planning and evaluating marketing activities

   (d) Only choice (b)

   (e) Only choices (a), (b), and (c)

6. One strategy for differentiating your company in a down economy is:

   (a) Cause-related marketing

   (b) Holding back on advertising and spending the money as the economy begins to turn

   (c) Following the rules of ethics

   (d) Giving discounts on slow-moving products

7. The three stages of values-based management are:

   (a) Evaluate your values; measure them; implement values in your marketing projects

   (b) Clarify mission, purpose, and values; communicate them; align daily practices with mission and values

   (c) Interview customers; integrate feedback; walk the talk;

   (d) Communicate values; train managers to deliver programs; evaluate results

8. According to the American Marketing Association, marketers should adhere to the following ethical norms and values:

   (a) Do no harm.

   (b) Foster trust in the marketing system.

   (c) Embrace ethical values, such as honesty, responsibility, fairness, respect, transparency, and citizenship.

   (d) All of the above

   (e) Only choices (a) and (b)

9. Consumer trust and brand loyalty are measures of:

   (a) Social values

   (b) Brand ethics

   (c) Brand reputation

   (d) Customer norms

10. Consumers may have difficulty separating fact from fantasy when:

   (a) Marketers place products on television and talk shows

   (b) Marketing messages are comingled with educational programming, edutainment, or new interviews

   (c) Advertisers provide product disclaimers

   (d) Only choices (a) and (b)

   (e) Only choices (a), (b), and (c)

CHAPTER 19

Developing a Marketing Budget

Budget development and analysis are exercises in best-practice planning and management control. Taking time to construct a practical budget will help you gain support for marketing programs, procure the means for executing them, and evaluate your team's ability to deliver on its marketing goals. Simply put, a *budget* is a financial planning document that enables you to allocate resources needed and manage costs associated with reaching your business goals. While many budgets focus on overall business and operating needs, this chapter focuses on budget considerations that will help you execute your marketing plan.

As you work through your budget needs, analyze costs and benefits, and chart your progress through the year, you will develop the insight and discipline needed for sound fiscal management. Unlike government officials, who often spend in excess of their funding streams, marketing managers are required to work within their annual resource allocations. As a marketing manager, you will be expected to present a balanced budget in which costs are equal to revenues. On occasion, you may be called to find money in your budget to serve an unexpected need. The budget you develop will demonstrate how you plan to execute on behalf of your company's goals and what you are capable of doing, given your departmental resources.

Make no mistake. Your budget has major consequences. It can mean the difference between success and failure of your marketing effort and organization. So, your budget development must address organizational needs and projects as well as desired success outcomes. It also must include a review process through which you can identify gaps, restructure priorities as needed, and assess what you may need to do differently in the future.

Whether you are managing a multimillion-dollar marketing enterprise or a do-it-yourself marketing campaign, you will get the best results by following a structured path. This chapter outlines a step-by-step approach that will help you simplify and master the budget process.

Budget Process

Your budgets must result in value for the organization while meeting the needs of your various internal and external consumers. To develop and manage your budget, you need a spreadsheet. (See Table 19.1.) Although it is possible to prepare your budget on paper in a ledger book, today's marketing managers and finance executives prefer to use electronic spreadsheets, since these are more efficiently shared across an organization and the documents are easier to revise. An Excel spreadsheet will address most budget needs, enabling you to list expenditures and resources, line by line. It also will allow you to prepare your budget in sections, with functional areas on separate worksheets, as needed. Most budgets are expenditure driven and constructed line by line, with each line representing one expenditure category. But ideally, a budget should include two sides: income and expenditures. In a perfect business scenario, the revenue side of your budget should exceed the expenditure side and reveal a profit.

However, in most companies, marketing is treated as a cost center. The organization allocates resources, and the marketing manager decides how to spend them. In some cases, the marketing manager builds a budget from the ground up and requests resources to get the job done. Drawing on your understanding of marketing opportunities and the resources of a creative team, the marketing team helps drive profitability for other strategic business units. But, with ingenuity, it also may be possible to transform your marketing department into a profit center of its own. The Orange County Public Schools in Orlando, Florida, is billed as the first school district to have its own advertising department. Through a unique promotion focused on selling advertising space in school district newsletters, on football fields, and even on student faces (logos can be painted on faces using ink black that lasts for one week), this school system's advertising executive generated more than $70,000 in revenues in the first season alone, helping to cover operating costs. With additional effort, the department could actually turn a profit.

Marketing budgets must cover day-to-day operating expenses as well as costs associated with market planning and promotion. Start by acknowledging that every

Table 19.1 Sample Budget Spreadsheet

Marketing Expenditures	Jan.	Feb.	Mar.	Apr.	May	Jun.	Jul.	Aug.	Sep.	Oct.	Nov.	Dec.
Research												
Advertising												
Television												
Newspaper												
Magazines												
Radio												
Internet/digital media												
Promotionals												
Agency fees												
Consulting fees												
Graphic design												
Copywriting												
Printing												
Mailing and distribution												
Networking												
Storage												
Product packaging												
Professional memberships												
Subscriptions												
Public relations												
Newswires												
Tracking and evaluation												
Internal communications												

(continued)

Table 19.1 Sample Budget Spreadsheet (continued)

Marketing Expenditures	Jan.	Feb.	Mar.	Apr.	May	Jun.	Jul.	Aug.	Sep.	Oct.	Nov.	Dec.
Signage												
Corporate identity												
Trade shows												
Web site												
Hosting services												
Search engine optimization												
Sales proposals												
Reward programs												
Special events												
Conference attendance												
Lunch and learns												
Seminars												
Blog maintenance												
Gaming programs, coupon programs, and reward programs												
Sponsorships and contributions												
Internal communications												
Speakers bureau												
Travel and entertainment												
Training and development												
Reserve												

company—for profit and not-for-profit alike—manages with limited resources. Money is finite, and managers must build budget programs that map to the company's most pressing needs and align priorities with available resources. When needs outpace resources, you may need to fine-tune your marketing plan so that it will help drive income needed for future business endeavors.

Budget Forecasting

Budget forecasting is a process for predicting business outcomes (in this case, marketing outcomes) by looking at past performance as well as current business indicators and trends. Businesses use forecasting techniques to predict sales revenues, expense patterns, seasonal requirements, and other business outcomes critical to success. Marketers can use forecasting to predict marketing needs and expenses. When you know what to expect, you can plan more effectively. Performance indicators may include actual money spent, markets served, customers reached, meetings generated, sales closed, and dollars earned as a result of a particular marketing intervention.

To forecast your budgetary needs, schedule a budget meeting with organizational leaders and department heads to review company strategies and departmental priorities. Since budgeting doesn't occur in a vacuum, your forecast also should take into account how the economy, industry, and competitive landscape will affect your ability to meet marketing goals and manage budget performance. In effect, you are conducting ongoing SWOT Analysis to keep your business on track.

Also meet with members of your marketing team (assuming you are not a one-person department) to gain additional feedback and determine what is actionable given the wish list you receive. When allocating money to budget areas, you must decide which projects are absolutely essential, which are nice to have, and which you can or must hold off for the future.

Don't be fooled by appearances. While budgeting may seem like a task that is all about numbers, budgeting may prove most effective when it is developed in collaboration with a team. While budgets themselves are driven by numbers, they are approved by, lobbied for, and executed by people. The early stages of your budget process will include gathering cost estimates and running preliminary budget projections. But winning budget approval may prove to be a political endeavor, since most organizations have competing needs. When you understand the needs, desires, goals, and challenges of the departments you serve, you will be in a better position to develop a budget that truly meets organizational needs. A best practice, from both marketing discipline and teamwork perspectives, is to address how your marketing efforts (in terms of dollars spent) will result in a specific positive impact (in quantitative terms, whenever possible) for other departments of your organization. Collaborative planning and teamwork increase the likelihood of gaining support for your budget proposal throughout the organization and budget approval process.

It also demonstrates how critically important marketing is to the ultimate success of the business.

As a marketer, your job is to advocate for and convince executives that there is a tangible return on investment for marketing dollars spent. So, you will need not only to predict costs but also to forecast results. In previous chapters, we talked about the need for conducting marketing research, polling and surveying prospects, assessing the best placement options, executing campaigns, and strengthening public relations, among other marketing tasks. The results of some tasks are easier to predict and measure than others.

Public relations and advertising, for example, create brand awareness and can impact brand preference, but customer attitudes (an intangible outcome) develop over time. Eventually, they may result in sales (a tangible outcome). Until those results occur, it may be difficult to draw a direct line between cause and effect. In such cases, you will need to present your rationale and justification—your own value proposition—when requesting money for projects with long-term benefits and/or intangible benefits. You can develop your budget justification in much the much the same way as you would construct a value proposition for customers.

By incorporating evaluation measures into every phase of your planning, and demonstrating that your marketing plan is strategic and maps to business drivers and/or revenues, you will increase the buy-in for your proposed expenditures.

Budget Cycles

Most budgets are developed on cycles that relate to the business operation at hand. Many companies require departments to submit their proposed budgets at the beginning of September, conduct their budget reviews in October and/or November, and then release budget funds in line with the new calendar year in early December. Because some of your marketing goals and objectives may affect more than one area of your company, be cognizant of the relative timing and implementation of business activities throughout the organization. Some companies determine an annual budget and release funds month to month, yet you may incur specific costs and payables according to a different schedule. When budgeting, take time to identify projected costs on month-to-month cycles and year-to-year cycles. Doing so will help you project cash flow and/or return on investment for projects whose benefits cross departments or span budget years.

Depending on project goals, you also may need to evaluate the best times to implement specific projects and tailor your time frame to generate the best returns in a budget year, as needed. For example, if your business demands adjust for peak seasons, you may also have peak cost periods that will influence your department's cash flow. When planning your budget, factor in timing and deadlines. This strategy can help you avoid budget conflicts and more effectively predict cash flow. Table 19.2 provides you with a guideline for working through potential budget planning issues.

Table 19.2   Sample Budget Issues Worksheet

Budget Process Task	Stakeholders Affected	Key Stakeholder Issues	Responsible Parties	Relevant Deliverable	Approval
Forecast need					
Identify funding source and decision makers					
Develop your annual (or time-based) marketing plan					
Establish project goals and tactics					
Identify budget categories					
Investigate costs for implementation and/or execution					
Determine best use of funds					
Set budget-based priorities					
Create line-item budget					
Document systems and results for transparency					

Step-by-Step Budget Planning

Budgeting is an essential component of your marketing plan process; it cannot be viewed apart from needs of the entire organization. Here's how to effectively plan the budget:

1. **Start with your organization's strategic plan.** This step provides an opportunity for you to uncover areas of need and map your marketing budget appropriately.

2. **Determine what type of budget is expected.** You may need to roll in all costs associated with your department, including staffing, office equipment, and a percentage of the overall infrastructure burden (see Table 7.1 in Chapter 7).

You may need only to present costs for specific marketing expenditures, such as marketing research, marketing campaigns, and special promotions.

3. **Identify where your budget funds will come from.** Determine who will control and decide on your resource allocation. Schedule a planning meeting with the decision maker to discuss your responsibilities and obtain information on strategic organizational goals.

4. **Review your marketing plan.** Your budget should flow directly out of your plan. Set your marketing priorities and goals (as discussed in Chapter 3). Break each goal down into specific objectives. Map each budget category to specific tactics. Calculate the costs associated with each outcome needed.

5. **Identify metrics.** Decide how you will measure your budget outcomes. Doing so will help you capture the evidence and data needed to assess return on investment and make future budget decisions. Your financial advisors will be looking for metrics. Decide what matters to your own department, what matters across the organization, and how your marketing budget will ensure that the business mission is accomplished.

6. **Decide how much money is needed to ensure product delivery and access to your target market.** This step requires you to assess various elements of your marketing mix, with particular focus being spent on your commitments to price, placement, and promotion.

7. **Choose the marketing strategies and tactics you intend to employ.** Consider how you will execute them. Who will do what? How many team members are needed? How much time will each team member need to dedicate to his or her assigned projects?

8. **Create a working budget document.** Use a spreadsheet or ledger to list categories of marketing deliverables (i.e., outcomes) and their associated costs, in line-by-line format. Provide as much transparency of detail and cost as is practical. Transparency will make it easier to discuss budget needs in an objective way and ascertain that allocations can support marketing goals.

9. **Review your budget, and solicit feedback.** Consult with team members and other department heads to review needs and solicit feedback. Repeat the process as needed to reassess priorities, and adjust expectations in line with available resources.

10. **Analyze your budget.** Assess the match between costs and your department's accountability for reaching specific target markets.

11. **Prepare for your budget presentation.** Unless you are the president of your company, you will need to present your budget proposal to a decision maker or

group of decision makers. To gain buy-in, you will need to know the value of every segment of your marketing budget and be able to justify it. For example, if you are budgeting for professional memberships, you must be able to explain in concrete terms how participating in those organizations will benefit your company. Will your attendance generate referrals? Do your clients and prospects also attend those meetings? Will it help you attract business? Prepare yourself by uncovering the implications of your budget decisions, and be ready to defend them.

12. **Present your budget recommendations.** Provide printouts of your budget, along with supporting assumptions and evidence on which you based your decisions. Be clear on your expected results and how you will measure them. You may be asked to go back to the drawing board and revise your budget. To do that, use the feedback gained during your presentation meeting. Also, draw peak performance skills and inner resilience needed to develop a consensus. Then prepare a budget that will win approval and support in the next round.

Budget Control

Once your budget is approved, you will need to monitor expenses and budget performance, and assess whether your objectives were met with the budget allocation. The information you gain will help you control expectations and budget performance going forward.

Planning Your Marketing Spend

There is no one-size-fits-all magic formula for determining how much money to allocate for marketing in a given year. Estimates may range from 2 to 20 percent of your overall operating budget, depending on your industry and business longevity. Start-ups need to allocate a larger percentage of their budget for marketing, while larger companies may allocate a smaller percentage but a bigger number. To determine how much you should spend, you must consider your company's overall sales goals and strategies as well as resources. Answers to strategy-related questions will help you estimate your marketing expenses. You also must decide how much to allocate among your varied marketing vehicles, particularly online marketing, which is gaining in popularity and effectiveness. Experts recommend allocating at least 10 to 15 percent of your marketing budget for online efforts. Of course, if your main business platform is e-commerce, your online marketing percentage must be significantly more.

Zero-Based Budgeting

As the marketing manager, you need to know why every number is on your page. When you build a budget with deep understanding of your budget decisions, you will be better able to justify it, and you will be passionate in the process. When you've been handling a budget from year to year, projecting expenses is relatively easy, but sometimes it is necessary to build a budget from the ground up. You start with an empty slate, with zero dollars allocated, and build your budget based on the results you need. This style of budgeting forces line-by-line accountability. You must determine your objectives, rationale, tactics, projected costs, and measurable impacts. This approach to budgeting is time consuming, but it creates more transparency than a budget that projects an arbitrary percentage increase or decrease year after year.

BUDGET ANALYSIS

A cost-benefit analysis will help you predict the consequences of your marketing and budget decisions. You can use a cost-benefit analysis to evaluate a singular event or to compare the anticipated impact of various marketing opportunities. As you analyze your budget you will probably have to make hard choices and trade-offs to justify costs as they relate to benefits. First, identify and rank priorities so you will be able to decide, for example, whether your budget will produce a better return on investment if it concentrates on marketing research and product development, internal communications, or marketing promotions. Decision factors may include the maturity of your business or product cycle, your entrenchment in your market, and your company's overall needs and earnings. By knowing your priorities, you can review (as needed) your budget when searching for dollars that may be reallocated to pay for implementation of more mission-critical projects.

When assessing which marketing actions will yield the greatest benefit, it is helpful to consider specific needs, time requirements, implementation costs, and returns in the short and long term. Table 19.3 provides a helpful approach for evaluating cost and benefit of multiple marketing options.

There are some marketing projects that, by virtue of their relation to the broader business, will have ripple effects in other areas. In Table 19.3, sales of software programs could translate into consulting work as customers connect with the company as a resource. As you evaluate anticipated results and actual outcomes, choose the tactics that will generate the most return in the shortest term at the best price. If you are unsure, go back to the evaluation criteria you set when starting your marketing plan and budget process. Choose the marketing projects that map directly to those criteria.

Table 19.3   Sample Marketing Tactic Cost-Benefit Comparison

Marketing Objective	Tactic	Specific Projected Outcome	Projected ROI	Projected Expense	Projected +/–
Raise awareness of additional accounting service and increase client comfort with changing providers.	Enhance sales presentations and develop an FAQ that addresses common sales objections while emphasizing value proposition.	Add 50 new clients.	$1,200,000	$257,000	First-year gain: +$943,000; second year: +$1,075,000
Expand branding of software package to new geographic market.	Invest in new trade show booth, attendance, promotion, and travel.	Generate 250 software sales	$74,250	$12,750	+$61,500

Quiz

1. A balanced budget refers to a:
   - (a) Budget in which costs are balanced with benefits
   - (b) Budget in which costs are equal to revenues
   - (c) Budget that balances costs with the needs of the strategic plan
   - (d) None of the above

2. Budget forecasting is a process for:
   - (a) Predicting business outcomes as well as current business indicators and trends
   - (b) Predicting marketing outcomes
   - (c) Using historical information to help support marketing decisions
   - (d) All of the above
   - (e) None of the above

3. Using transparency in your budgeting process:

   (a) Enables marketers to track expenses

   (b) Enables managers to question a budget allocation

   (c) Helps budget reviewers see how money will be spent

   (d) Only choices (a) and (c)

   (e) Only choices (b) and (c)

   (f) Choices (a), (b), and (c)

4. Marketing is typically treated as:

   (a) A cost center

   (b) A profit center

   (c) A strategic business unit

   (d) All of the above

5. Marketing budgets must:

   (a) Cover costs associated with market planning and promotion

   (b) Cover day-to-day operating expenses

   (c) Meet needs of internal and external shareholders

   (d) All of the above

   (e) Only choices (b) and (c)

6. Organizations have competing needs; therefore:

   (a) Marketers must balance them

   (b) Budgeting may become a political process

   (c) Team-built budgets have a better chance of being approved

   (d) All of the above

   (e) Only choices (a) and (b)

7. The best way to start a budget is:

   (a) With a collaborative team

   (b) By reviewing the overall strategic plan

   (c) By looking at the previous year's expenses

   (d) All of the above

   (e) None of the above

8. There is a simple formula for calculating budget based on overall revenues. True or false?

    (a) True

    (b) False

9. A zero-base budget refers to a budget that:

    (a) Is built from the bottom up

    (b) Forces line-by-line accountability

    (c) Begins with zero dollars allocated

    (d) All of the above

    (e) None of the above

10. Budget decisions following a cost-benefit analysis may depend on:

    (a) Product life cycle

    (b) Market entrenchment

    (c) Overall needs and earnings

    (d) All of the above

    (e) Only choice (b)

CHAPTER 20

Evaluating Marketing Performance

Throughout *Marketing DeMystified*, I have stressed the importance of tracking and evaluating results. Information gained through assessments and analysis provides direction for decision makers and enables marketers to judge the success of advertising and marketing strategies and tactics in the context of organizational success. Evaluation is more than a process. It is a discipline capable of supporting a company's bid for long-term sustainability. For ongoing success (or to achieve success at all), leaders and managers must identify and understand the impact of critical factors influencing performance:

- Organizational vision and planning
- Intellectual competencies, such as emotional intelligence, social intelligence, strategic decision making, creative productivity, and impact on others
- People strategies
- Process analysis
- Financial targets and decision making
- Individual responsibility in the context of a team

By measuring program performance, marketers are able to understand their own impact on their organizations. They can determine what changes are required for consistently

high-level performance as well as what is required to transform the organization and shift it to stronger leadership for products, markets, and brands.

As you learn what works and what doesn't, you will be better able to choose the best course of action for moving forward. You also will gather the information you need to establish your department's own value proposition. To get there, you must answer and explain exactly what you are doing for the organization and how it is working for you. By viewing evaluation as a learning tool, you can let go of any fear surrounding performance issues. Instead, you can focus on collecting information that helps you understand the significance of your actions and uncover sources of variation (i.e., what works and what doesn't under which conditions). Doing so will contribute to your development as a stronger, wiser, and more objective marketing leader.

Getting Started with Evaluation

The evaluation process will provide an eagle's perspective, enabling you to look down and identify the patterns, relative relationships, and interaction between marketing activities. It also can help you assess the influence of people on the process. Think of it this way: synchronized swimming looks very different from up in the stands than it does at water level. At the base level, it may look like just a lot of activity. From inside the pool, it may look like people flapping about. But from above, you can see the intensive coordination. Like the coach responsible for the training and orchestration of swimmers, the marketing leader needs to know how every aspect of a marketing program works, both alone and in context of the overall marketing plan. Evaluation can help you understand why you get the results you get. Table 20.1 demonstrates the link between specific strategic objectives and potential marketing results areas.

Once you have identified the results areas you want to measure and you collect relevant data, you can decide whether and what to change. By choosing performance metrics that allow you to evaluate strategic and tactical plans, you can determine how well each element of the marketing mix—plan, product, people, positioning, price, placement, and promotion—is working for you. Gathering market intelligence is just a first step. It's what you do with that information that really counts. To help your program achieve transformative success—the kind of success that shifts companies to their next level of business growth and cultural development—you must align your marketing endeavors with organizational strategies, goals, decisions, and actions. Then, you must track and measure outcomes and continually alter your marketing (and the organization must alter its training, sales, and operations approaches) in response to identified business priorities. Without measurement, you will not be able to enhance control or offer reliable predictions.

As a marketing manager, you must monitor your marketing plan and continually determine whether you are on plan (e.g., achieving goals, following specified tactics, or adjusting as needed) or off plan (e.g., foundering and unclear about what to do next). By identifying strategic and tactical initiatives, uncovering best practices, and measuring and balancing key objectives and results, you can develop transformative success.

Table 20.1 Key Marketing Results Areas

Key Marketing Results Areas	
Strategic Objectives	**Potential Marketing Results Area**
Strategic decision making and direction	Brand positioning, market planning, product development, placement strategies, and media planning
Overall brand performance	Awareness and interest
Mind share	Market preferences, market reach
Market share	Sales and sales reach
Tactical performance	Advertising layouts, advertising impressions, content, conversion rates, return on advertising investment, budget
Team competencies	Leadership, forecasting, planning, creativity, communication, implementation, teamwork
Integrated marketing disciplines	Research, development and evaluation, planning, branding, advertising, pricing, placement, public relations, community relations, publications, evaluation

Figure 20.1 demonstrates the actions required for transformational success. The process is mastered by tracking results and implementing improvements. When linked with mission-aligned goal setting and best-practice management, the cycle leads to improvements that help grow companies to higher levels of success.

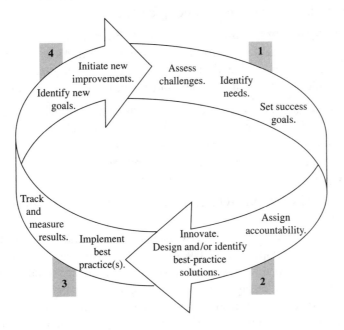

Figure 20.1 Transformative success cycle.

Marketing Audits

A *marketing audit* is an inquisitive review approach that helps reveal the strengths and weaknesses of marketing programs, processes, and practices. By identifying and reviewing key performance indicators, you can choose the marketing interventions required to ensure peak marketing performance. Before starting a marketing audit, you must decide what you hope to gain from the assessment and how you will measure effectiveness of various marketing elements in quantitative and/or qualitative terms. Table 20.2 provides insight to plan assessment by matching key assessment opportunities to related performance indicators. It provides questions and potential indicators for evaluating marketing plan performance. You can take a similar approach to evaluating every aspect of your marketing mix.

Measuring Your Progress

You can approach evaluation as you would any other planning exercise. Here's how you do so:

1. **Start by defining your objective.** For example, you may want to evaluate your marketing plan for strategic capabilities and/or deficiencies. Perhaps you need to know the impact of a specific market intervention or campaign. You may need to assess audience feedback, market potential, or cross-market results. Or you may want to assess online strategies, social marketing outcomes, budget effectiveness, call center results, or a customer-service program.

2. **Explain what you want to measure and why.** Be as specific as possible. First list the criteria that would make for an effective program. As an example, refer to the performance indicators listed in Table 20.2. Also list the type of information you plan to collect and why it is important to your overall marketing plan.

3. **Describe how you will collect your data.** Choose when and where you will collect data as well as which instruments you will use. You may choose surveys or focus groups, count calls, measure conversion rates, invite customer feedback, or hire a research team to do it for you, among other research activities. You also must decide how you will catalog and review results.

4. **Determine who is best suited to evaluate your data.** There will be some results that you can easily assess on your own. But it is not always easy to be objective when determining and evaluating performance measures. A cross-discipline team can provide a fresh perspective, as can an outside consultant. Depending on the scope of your study, you may want to consult with an external marketing research team. Experienced marketing researchers can recommend the right quantitative and qualitative data collection strategies for meeting your objectives. They also can employ the statistical tools needed to help you generalize results (or not).

Table 20.2   Matching Assessment Inquiry with Performance Indicators

Assessment Inquiry	Sample Performance Indicators
Did it help us align purpose, goals, and activities across our organization?	• Employees can describe work in terms of the mission. • Work has been completed on time. • There is little conflict between people and departments.
Did it help our company respond to competitive threats?	• Market hold has been maintained. • Market share has grown. • Sales have increased. • There's enhanced customer growth and acquisition.
Was it on target in identifying strengths, weaknesses, opportunities, and threats?	• We experienced no surprises. • The plan was executable. • Forecasts were on target. • Creative solutions were developed.
Did it account for industry shifts and/or predict regulatory changes?	• We experienced no surprises. • The budget served our plan projections.
Did it enable us to move forward as planned with new product development?	• Projects were completed on time. • Issues were overcome easily. • There were no cost overruns and/or there was money available to shift between lines, when needed, and still reach all plan goals.
Did it increase brand value and/or product value?	• Customers tolerated the price increase. • More units were sold during the plan period in which additional funds were invested. • Potential partners queried us for information. • Our plan garnered the targeted number of media hits.
Were pricing recommendations on target?	• We met sales goals and/or exceeded projections.
Did it move us toward effective placements and relationships with the right channel partners?	• Partnership implementations ran smoothly. • The rate in affiliation held steady. • Potential partners queried us.
Did it help us generate new revenues and/or higher profitability?	• New stores are profitable. • New target market was served. • Marketing costs were reduced through online services and viral strategies.
Did it effectively forecast success? Did it meet expected results?	• It met or exceeded targeted metrics for calls generated and sales closed.
Did it help enhance customer satisfaction?	• Customer satisfaction exceeded 90 percent. • There has been increased repeat-customer business.

(continued)

Table 20.2 Matching Assessment Inquiry with Performance Indicators (*Continued*)

Assessment Inquiry	Sample Performance Indicators
Did it strengthen our company's financial position?	• There has been top-line revenue growth. • The bottom line has held strong. • The bank credit line was increased. • Cash reserve has grown.
Did it achieve targeted or forecasted return on investment?	• Finance department analysis indicated a profitable period.
Did it facilitate decision making?	• Projects were implemented according to plan.
Did it properly assess the need for intellectual capital and human resource support?	• Collaborative decision making was evident.
Did it provide for superior implementation?	• Projects ran on time. • Satisfaction rates were very high. • There was increased brand visibility.
Did it identify critical performance measures and an approach to evaluation?	• The plan included measurement criteria. • Evaluations were conducted at required intervals. • Indicators were mapped to leadership goals.
How did brand or product awareness, share growth, advertising impressions, and/or sales revenues change as a result of the plan?	• There has been an increased number of ad impressions. • We've held market share or gained it. • Sales revenue has increased (or been lost). • Revenue has correlated with the volume of target market advertising.
Did the planning process involve the key knowledge holders and influencers from all levels of the organization?	• Interdepartmental planning meetings were held monthly. • Team meetings were conducted weekly. • Information was channeled through newsletters and meetings to employees.
Did the plan result in higher levels of product penetration?	• We entered a new market. • We increased penetration into our preferred niche.
Did the plan result in higher levels of customer satisfaction?	• Customer survey results have been favorable and increased two percentage points.
Did the plan result in higher levels of employee satisfaction?	• There has been a drop in terminations. • Survey results show increased satisfaction. • There was higher attendance during peak internal marketing periods.
Did the plan result in high levels or higher levels of channel partner and/or vendor satisfaction?	• Survey results are favorable. • There has been no turnover in vendor relations. • There has been no loss of partners. • Partner business referrals have increased by 10 percent.

(*continued*)

Assessment Inquiry	Sample Performance Indicators
Did the plan foster teamwork and communication among organizational units?	• No departmental conflicts are evident. • There is good employee humor. • Schedules are regularly met.
Was the plan understood, embraced, and facilitated across the company?	• Employees can describe work in terms of the mission. • Work was completed on time. • There has been little conflict between people and departments.
Was there consistency between the plan's internal and external messages?	• Questions and conflicts have dropped. • Employees act as brand ambassadors. • Product returns are fewer. • The number of complaints has dropped.
Where were the greatest sources of variation between expected and actual results?	• To be determined.
What areas failed to meet expectations?	• To be determined.
What factors influenced that difference between expectation and actual results?	• To be determined.
How will my answers to the above questions influence what I do going forward?	• To be determined.

5. **Conduct the evaluation.**

6. **Assess results and prepare a report of findings.**

7. **Use the report as a guide for developing recommendations for improvement initiatives, as needed.**

8. **Present your report and recommendations to key leadership and marketing team members.** Fold in to your plan their feedback, as needed.

9. **Implement targeted improvements.** Use the plan, do, check, act cycle (FOCUS-PDCA Model) described in Chapter 3.

10. **Track your improvement efforts.**

11. **Revive the evaluation process periodically.**

Marketing Report Cards

Using key results indicators, you can develop a report card that will help you track critical measures. A marketing report card can be as simple as a task list accompanied by goals measures. Or it can be a multidimensional report with various levels of feedback from customers, department heads, key staff, and decision makers, and it can include ratings along multiple dimensions. The complexity of your report card will depend on what you set out to accomplish and the needs and culture of your organization. Developing a report card, whether simple or complex, will help keep you on track and tell you how well you are performing in a specific area.

Dashboard programs—which provide at-a-glance performance indicators—can provide multiple measures, with sophisticated analytics and graphics that allow you to monitor strategic initiatives and specific performance areas that connect to bottom-line results. They can show you what must be fine-tuned so you can accelerate results. Marketers can use dashboards to track budgets, ad performance, sales conversions, customer satisfaction, employee involvement, and more. As a marketer, you are vested in enhancing organizational performance through integrated strategies and high-performing marketing campaigns.

If you are part of an organization, you probably have a performance management plan that measures your ability to meet the job requirements outlined in your job description. Your plan would provide recommendations for stretch goals (breakthrough outcomes) and periodic feedback to help you measure your progress. As a marketing professional, you can create a similar report card for your marketing initiatives. Look back over Chapter 3 and Chapter 14 for charts that can help you track your marketing performance and initiatives. Change the metrics as needed so they will be relevant to your needs.

In Chapter 3, we also talked about balanced scorecards (BSCs), a methodology for analyzing organizational performance. You can adapt the BSC framework to your marketing enterprise as well. Most important, by understanding the philosophy of a balanced scorecard, you will be better prepared to help support key organizational initiatives. With the end in mind—the transformative breakthrough outcome that will let you know you have made a real difference in your organization—you will be able to develop strategies, tactics, and daily actions to keep you on track. If you get off track, you can look at where you need to be and adjust your path accordingly. With a scorecard that measures key results areas that are tied to strategic organizational initiatives, you can monitor performance on multiple dimensions at once and keep responsible parties accountable to the plan. Customer-centric scorecards that incorporate the customers' needs, perspectives, and feedback can help you drive quality, increase efficiency, reduce cycle times, and meet customer expectations—each of which is critical to long-term success. As you strengthen your marketing capabilities and correlate them with customer concerns, you will pave the way to sustainable success.

Keeping the Momentum

Evaluation is not a one-time event. To ensure a long-term, high-quality enterprise, you must continually, consistently evaluate critical measures. Establish your planning and evaluation checkpoints in advance, and you will be better prepared to stay on track with your tracking. Also remember to test your marketing plan early, so you can identify what works in which markets and then adjust your plan, if needed. Responding along the way will help you identify and correct marketing mistakes before they become a serious problem.

By integrating evaluation into your marketing activities, here's what you can do:

- Learn which audiences are most responsive to your promotions.
- Understand the impact of campaign messages.
- Assess the effectiveness of language, tone, and content of print and online publications.
- Sample and assess the strengths of niche markets and target markets.
- Track budget effectiveness.
- Uncover areas needing improvement.
- Demonstrate effectiveness of marketing campaigns.
- Track changes in brand awareness.
- Assess the impact of internal marketing campaigns.
- Assess the feasibility of larger initiatives, based on results of test drives.
- Monitor the links between ad insertions, queries, and sales.
- Compare period-over-period results.
- Track sales conversions.
- Assess the strength of digital marketing platforms.
- Compare and evaluate the performance of marketing tests, both on- and offline.

As a result of your evaluation efforts, you will be able to do these things:

- Determine how to improve service.
- Justify budget allocations and expenditures.
- Identify need for training and/or additional staff.
- Complement organizational initiatives.
- Improve sales results.
- Enhance internal communication.
- Foster collaborative planning.

Quiz

1. The information gained through marketing program evaluations:

   (a) Provides direction for decision makers

   (b) Is used by marketers to judge the success of advertising and marketing strategies

   (c) Supports long-term success

   (d) All of the above

   (e) Only choices (a) and (b)

2. Vision and planning, financial targets and decision making, and individual responsibility are:

   (a) Critical factors in the organizational planning process

   (b) Examples of factors influencing organizational performance

   (c) Indicators of long-term success

   (d) None of the above

3. Understanding the marketer's impact on the organization and determining what changes are required for high-level performance are:

   (a) Topics for annual planning

   (b) Key results areas for the marketing department

   (c) Reasons for measuring program performance

   (d) All of the above

4. Marketing process evaluations can help justify the value of the marketing enterprise. True or false?

   (a) True

   (b) False

5. This chapter advises approaching evaluation:

   (a) As a practical experience

   (b) As part of an ongoing learning experience

   (c) Seriously and comprehensively

   (d) More than once a year

6. Defining your objective, explaining what you want to measure and why, and determining how you will collect data, are:

   (a) Early steps in the evaluation process

   (b) Guaranteed to get you the results you want

(c) Best practices for evaluation planning

(d) All of the above

(e) Only choices (a) and (c)

7. For a fresh perspective when conducting evaluations:

   (a) Consult recent marketing literature

   (b) Involve a cross-discipline team

   (c) Consult with an external marketing research team

   (d) All of the above

   (e) Only choices (b) and (c)

8. Multiple measures and sophisticated analytics and graphics are elements of:

   (a) Dashboard monitoring programs

   (b) Reports of findings

   (c) Evaluation criteria

   (d) None of the above

9. Monitoring strategic initiatives and helping to connect specific performance areas to bottom-line results are uses of:

   (a) Dashboard monitoring programs

   (b) Basic scorecard reports

   (c) Evaluation programs

   (d) None of the above

   (e) All of the above

10. To ensure a long-term, high-quality marketing enterprise:

   (a) Establish your planning and evaluation checkpoints in advance

   (b) Test your marketing plan

   (c) Respond along the way

   (d) All of the above

   (e) Only choices (a) and (c)

Final Exam

1. The integrated marketing platform:
    (a) Fosters communication between business functions and segments
    (b) Reduces red tape and lowers risk
    (c) Identifies marketing channels
    (d) None of the above
    (e) All of the above
2. Building a cross-functional team is important because:
    (a) Team members help pollinate ideas
    (b) They facilitate communication
    (c) Involved team members are more likely to support marketing initiatives
    (d) All of the above
3. If you use words such as *see, look*, and *imagine*, you are most likely:
    (a) To connect with your customers
    (b) Creative and inspirational

    (c) A visual learner

    (d) Able to create a good logo

4. To build a sustainable brand:

    (a) Develop a big budget

    (b) Call in a marketing consultant

    (c) Deliver on your brand promise

    (d) Capture attention in multiple markets

5. The executive summary:

    (a) Is the first section of your strategic plan

    (b) Not part of the plan

    (c) Belongs at the end of the plan

    (d) None of the above

6. The first rule of planning is:

    (a) Don't overplan

    (b) Use it

    (c) Make it as complicated as it needs to be

    (d) Start at the beginning of the calendar year

7. A strategic marketing plan:

    (a) Is scheduled during implementation planning

    (b) Maps marketing activities to specific organizational goals

    (c) Helps bring stakeholders on board and gains their confidence and support for moving it forward

    (d) Both choices (b) and (c)

8. _____ can help you determine which attributes of brands, products, and services are most valuable to prospective customers.

    (a) Competitor analysis

    (b) Market analysis

    (c) Marketing research

    (d) Online marketing strategies

9. The FOCUS Approach is designed for:

    (a) Statistical analysis

    (b) Quality management

    (c) Positioning strategy

    (d) None of the above

10. Positioning is a strategic component of the marketing mix that helps you determine:

    (a) How you will differentiate your company and/or products in the marketplace

    (b) Where you stand when compared to your competitors

    (c) Where you stand in the minds of consumers

    (d) All of the above

    (e) None of the above

11. A value proposition refers to:

    (a) Your company's pricing strategy

    (b) Employee benefits programs

    (c) Why a prospective buyer should choose you over your competition

    (d) All of the above

12. Three types of benefits described by Jack Trout and Al Reis are:

    (a) Functional, psychographic, and experiential

    (b) Profit, time, and productivity

    (c) Functional, experiential, and symbolic

    (d) None of the above

13. The downside of skimming strategies is:

    (a) They have a low profit margin

    (b) That skimmable markets attract competitors

    (c) They take a long time to return value

    (d) None of the above

14. Penetration pricing strategy is characterized by:

    (a) Competitive analysis

    (b) Low pricing

    (c) Strong customer relationships

    (d) Wide profit margins

15. People are considered part of the marketing mix because:

    (a) They contribute to a company's bottom line

    (b) They use training and development resources

    (c) They work for the marketing department

    (d) They are a source of differentiation and competitive advantage

    (e) All of the above

16. It is important to assess cultural fit with another business because:

   (a) It will help you qualify your prospect

   (b) It will provide information on what your prospect values

   (c) It will save money in the long run.

   (d) Only choices (a) and (b)

   (e) All of the above

17. Premiums are:

   (a) Discounts on closeout merchandise

   (b) Small gifts given as an incentive or reward

   (c) Undeveloped business ideas

   (d) Expensive services offered during holiday seasons

   (e) None of the above

   (f) Only choices (a) and (b)

18. Social aggregation tools make it possible to:

   (a) Create a thorough view of your target market

   (b) Integrate a blog and a Web site

   (c) Manage multiple social media updates from one place

   (d) All of the above

19. The purpose of business networking is to:

   (a) Close sales

   (b) Enjoy cocktail party conversation

   (c) Build relationships that lead to referrals

   (d) Qualify prospects

20. The $2 \times 2 \times 2$ and $4 \times 4 \times 4$ formulas are:

   (a) Product dimensions that help buyers double or quadruple their investments

   (b) Integral to every automated response program

   (c) Time-based contact points for ongoing customer service

   (d) Only choices (a) and (c)

21. A campaign management spreadsheet:

   (a) Enables you to track campaign progress

   (b) Helps communicate and reinforce accountabilities

   (c) Provides a guide for meeting agendas

(d) Should group items by categories such as advertising, public relations, and Internet marketing

(e) All of the above

22. Your ability to stay on message in a series of ads is known as:

(a) Call to action

(b) Consistency

(c) Context

(d) None of the above

23. The term "media hook" refers to:

(a) A way of pitching your story

(b) The positioning twist that makes your story appear to be novel and compelling

(c) The process of fishing for journalists online

(d) None of the above

24. When applying a series of small tasks to marketing and/or personal goals, peak performers:

(a) Ignore limiting beliefs and negative feelings

(b) Trust their own ability to learn what they need to succeed

(c) Cover cost overruns by zero-based budgets

(d) All of the above

25. The most important competency quadrant for peak performance is:

(a) Creative problem solving, because it leads to problem resolution

(b) Strategic thinking and decision making, because it creates a foundation for planning

(c) Emotional maturity and intelligence, because it forms the basis for the other competencies

(d) Impact on others, because it affects team building

26. A brand promise is:

(a) An element of the marketing mix

(b) The expectations set through marketing and service

(c) An example of a margarine marketing promotion

(d) Part of a mission statement

27. The right reasons for doing a trade show are:

(a) To foster brand image, make sales on site, and collect leads

(b) To reduce stress inside the company

(c) To give away premiums

(d) All of the above

(e) Both choices (a) and (b)

28. The four elements of the BOLD branding formula are:

    (a) Boldness, organizational development, loyalty, and differentiation

    (b) Branding, organizational development, loyalty marketing, and diversification

    (c) Branding, organizational development, loyalty marketing, and diagnostics

    (d) Boldness, operations, loyal customers, and differentiation

29. Segmenting, or separating, a potential market into groups helps businesses _____ and _____ target buyers.

    (a) Budget/promote to

    (b) Identify/cost-effectively

    (c) Scope/research

    (d) Understand/analyze

30. PDCA is:

    (a) An acronym for plan, do, check, act

    (b) A process improvement model

    (c) Part of quality management

    (d) All of the above

    (e) Only choices (a) and (c)

31. Background is information:

    (a) That you tell a reporter to create noise and deflect from negative news

    (b) Shared with the stipulation that it may not be attributed to you and must be verified by another person who will agree to attribution, before it can be published

    (c) Biographical information contained in a PR kit

    (d) None of the above

32. Two common research approaches are:

    (a) Formal/informal

    (b) Complex/statistical

    (c) Active/latent

    (d) Primary/secondary

    (e) Cause/effect

33. The goal of every positioning process is to:

    (a) Provide market analysis

    (b) Segment the audience

    (c) Find the right niche

    (d) Capture top-of-mind status in the mind space

34. Channel partners are a necessity for:

    (a) Penetrating markets that are difficult to enter

    (b) Reaching geographically dispersed markets' geographic spread

    (c) Maximizing physical and/or financial resources

    (d) All of the above

    (e) Only choices (a) and (b)

35. _____ is a supply chain system that covers the full product placement cycle, from online requisitioning, bidding and payment systems, to vendor management, sales help, online shopping carts, electronic order fulfillment, and inventory management.

    (a) A joint venture

    (b) A fulfillment service

    (c) An inventory system

    (d) E-procurement

36. Choosing a representative target market, estimating the cost of product runs, and establishing a test budget are methods for:

    (a) Testing the pricing strategies

    (b) Marketing principles

    (c) Cost-factor analysis

    (d) None of the above

37. You can make employees a core marketing resource by:

    (a) Educating them on your brand, your marketing strategy, and overall business objectives

    (b) Sending them outside with sandwich boards

    (c) Adding them into the marketing budget

    (d) Embracing telemarketing

    (e) All of the above

38. Companies that set a course, assign accountability, communicate, focus on quality, and build morale are:

    (a) Marketing geniuses

    (b) Organized

    (c) Mission centered

    (d) Employee-centric

    (e) Preparing to merge

39. The benefit of creating a shared vision is that it:

    (a) Becomes immutable in the organization

    (b) Challenges teams to perform at higher levels

    (c) Provides direction and fosters buy-in

    (d) None of the above

40. Target marketing helps companies:

    (a) Build rapport with customers

    (b) Concentrate budgets

    (c) Control market variables

    (d) None of the above

    (e) Choices (a), (b), and (c)

41. _____ will help you reflect on the potential of each market segment, assess market segments, and target segments that will work best for you.

    (a) Developing a market profile

    (b) Building an e-mail campaign

    (c) Creating a joint venture

    (d) None of the above

42. _____ are proven draws for joint venture marketing prospects.

    (a) Networking events

    (b) Free Web events

    (c) E-mail lists

    (d) None of the above

43. You can honor your brand promise by:

    (a) Resolving problem(s) in the way you stated

    (b) Replying to requests and questions within agreed-upon time frames

    (c) Giving employees tools

(d) All of the above

(e) Only choices (a) and (b)

44. Consumers may have difficulty separating fact from fantasy when:

    (a) Marketers place products on television and talk shows

    (b) Marketing messages are co-mingled with educational programming, edutainment, or new interviews

    (c) Advertisers provide product disclaimers

    (d) Only choices (a) and (b)

    (e) Choices (a), (b), and (c)

45. The information gained through marketing program evaluations:

    (a) Provides direction for decision makers

    (b) Is used by marketers to judge the success of advertising and marketing strategies

    (c) Supports long-term success

    (d) All of the above

    (e) Only choices (a) and (b)

46. Marketing budgets must:

    (a) Cover costs associated with market planning and promotion

    (b) Cover day-to-day operating expenses

    (c) Meet needs of internal and external shareholders

    (d) All of the above

    (e) Only choices (b) and (c)

47. Chunking projects down into long-term goals and short-term goals:

    (a) Is part of planning for next steps action

    (b) A strategy for reaching goals

    (c) Not a good way to get started on a project

    (d) Only choices (a) and (b)

    (e) Only choices (a) and (c)

48. Understanding the marketer's impact on the organization and determining what changes are required for high-level performance are:

    (a) Topics for discussion when making recommendations for annual planning

    (b) Key results areas for the marketing department

    (c) Reasons for measuring program performance

    (d) All of the above

49. The seven Ps of marketing are:

    (a) The marketing premise

    (b) Only as good as the CEO says they are

    (c) Known as the "marketing mix"

    (d) The most costly way to market

50. Culture is demonstrated through:

    (a) Leadership and employee actions

    (b) Mission, vision, and values statements

    (c) Communication methods

    (d) Business protocol

    (e) All of the above

51. Two elements that impact the productivity of peak performers are:

    (a) Setting a gold standard of performance

    (b) Strategic thinking and decision making

    (c) Emotional intelligence

    (d) Only choices (b) and (c)

52. Industry maturity, product cycle, and longevity represent:

    (a) Market analysis

    (b) Cost indicators

    (c) Branding factors

    (d) Factors that influence pricing strategy

53. A SWOT Analysis will not provide guidance for structuring a loyalty marketing campaign. True or false?

    (a) True

    (b) False

54. Market analysis requires:

    (a) Market research

    (b) Knowledge of competitors

    (c) Understanding of organizational goals

    (d) All of the above

55. You can demonstrate respect for clients by:

    (a) Staying late to work on projects

    (b) Setting reasonable expectations for time and solutions

(c) Submitting a proposed solution to problems

(d) All of the above

56. Asking questions that address different aspects of the same topic:

    (a) Helps you to identify inconsistencies

    (b) Reveals a more complete and accurate picture

    (c) None of the above

    (d) Both choices (a) and (b)

57. Setting expectations early is:

    (a) A best practice for problem solving

    (b) Shows that you are proactive

    (c) Provides a basis for how you communicate in a crisis

    (d) All of the above

    (e) Only choice (b)

58. Organizations have competing needs, therefore:

    (a) Marketers must balance them

    (b) Budgeting may become a political process

    (c) Team-built budgets have a better chance of being approved

    (d) All of the above

    (e) Only choices (a) and (b)

59. Integrated marketing principles:

    (a) Ensure that company teams speak the same brand language and understand their role in the marketing process

    (b) Make sense only for companies with large budgets

    (c) Focus entirely on branding

    (d) None of the above

60. Peak-performing marketing behavior includes:

    (a) Making decisions based on big-picture organizational goals

    (b) Incorporating marketing research into marketing plans

    (c) Assimilating customer input

    (d) Evaluating outcomes

    (e) All of the above

61. To ensure a long-term, high-quality marketing enterprise:

    (a) Establish your planning and evaluation checkpoints in advance

    (b) Test your marketing plan

    (c) Respond along the way

    (d) All of the above

62. Vision and planning, financial targets and decision making, and individual responsibility are:

    (a) Critical factors in the organizational planning process

    (b) Examples of factors that influence organizational performance

    (c) Indicators of long-term success

    (d) None of the above

63. Which one of the following is *not* part of pricing strategy?

    (a) Calculating costs

    (b) Analyzing business strategy

    (c) Advertising promotions

    (d) Demographic research

64. Brand value builds when:

    (a) People are willing to pay more for products

    (b) Marketers communicate in multiple ways

    (c) Customers ask a lot of questions

    (d) Customers experience positive outcomes

65. The marketing team should be called in after products are developed. True or false?

    (a) True

    (b) False

66. "What did you think of . . . ?" is an example of:

    (a) A way to uncover marketing strategies

    (b) An open-ended question

    (c) A close-ended question

    (d) None of the above

67. Effective networking happens when people:

    (a) Plan for referrals, not leads

    (b) Know your purpose

(c) Prepare in advance

    (d) Listen well

    (e) All of the above

    (f) Only choices (b) and (c)

68. Common networking mistakes include:

    (a) Not paying attention to the person you are speaking with

    (b) Asking for referrals before you build a relationship

    (c) Passing out business cards

    (d) Not shaking hands

    (e) Offering help too soon

    (f) Only choices (a) and (b)

    (g) Only choices (a), (b), and (d)

69. Logo and advertising art must:

    (a) Be colorful

    (b) Be short

    (c) Be designed by a professional

    (d) Capture interest quickly through distinct, recognizable design

    (e) Match a reader's language skills

70. Multiple measures and sophisticated analytics and graphics are elements of:

    (a) Dashboard monitoring programs

    (b) Reports of findings

    (c) Evaluation criteria

    (d) None of the above

71. Company leaders and brand influencers:

    (a) Are examples of role models

    (b) Are not always C-level executives

    (c) Never leave companies

    (d) None of the above

72. The manager's job is to:

    (a) Ensure productive workflow

    (b) Lead the organization

    (c) Provide market analysis

    (d) None of the above

73. Marketing is typically treated as:

    (a) A cost center

    (b) A profit center

    (c) A strategic business unit

    (d) All of the above

74. Creating a customer profile:

    (a) Is a strategy for segmenting your market

    (b) Improves your customer service attitude

    (c) Clarifies the characteristics of your target market

    (d) Gives you a basis for tracking

75. An elevator speech:

    (a) Is a short introduction that communicates business value

    (b) Is Web language for "small talk"

    (c) Should be limited to traveling

    (d) Is never more than 30 seconds

76. Article marketing has become a popular strategy for:

    (a) Communicating information to a target audience

    (b) Promoting the presence of a content expert

    (c) Both (a) and (b)

    (d) Only (a)

77. The Technorati.com Web site:

    (a) Tracks and ranks blogs

    (b) Tracks and ranks search engines

    (c) Ranks other Web sites

    (d) Provides technical information for Web analytics

78. A lead is as valuable as a referral. True or false?

    (a) True

    (b) False

79. Effective campaign management encompasses:

    (a) Tracking timelines, a contact database, copy and creative, placement venues, and calls to action

    (b) Management of third-party contractors

(c) Specific measurements of return on investment

(d) Communication with internal and external audiences

(e) All of the above

80. The purpose of using a metaphor is to:

(a) Create a perceptual shift

(b) Demonstrate literary skill

(c) Emphasize a point

(d) Enhance branding

(e) None of the above

81. To reduce risk with business blogs and Web sites:

(a) Issue a policy that explains your company's blogging rules to employees

(b) Limit your postings

(c) Add a disclaimer and/or limitation of liability to Web sites and blogs

(d) All of the above

82. Brand messages that target the senses are perceived faster. True or false?

(a) True

(b) False

83. Qualitative research is not measurable. True or false?

(a) True

(b) False

84. Studies in Neuro-Linguistic Programming demonstrate that information absorbed through the five senses is processed first through internal filters and influence:

(a) Positioning

(b) Beliefs

(c) Perceptions

(d) Results

(e) Only choices (b) and (c)

85. Useful information for marketing research can come from:

(a) Focus groups

(b) Telephone surveys

    (c) Anecdotal information

    (d) E-mail requests

    (e) All of the above

86. Alignment with goals, environmental assessment, and evaluative planning are predictors of:

    (a) Strategic marketing plan success

    (b) Vision-based planning results

    (c) Data-driven planning

    (d) None of the above

87. A graphic style manual is used to:

    (a) Reduce errors and increase compliance

    (b) Communicate expectations

    (c) Protect logo integrity

    (d) Illustrate best practices

    (e) Increase brand recognition and perception

    (f) All of the above

    (g) Only choices (c), (d), and (e)

88. Which of the following is more action oriented?

    (a) Strategic plan

    (b) Tactical plan

    (c) Hybrid plan

    (d) Organizational plan

89. Primary research is:

    (a) The first step in every research initiative

    (b) Data in an official database, such as the U.S. Census Bureau or the Bureau of Vital Statistics

    (c) Mostly qualitative

    (d) Data collected for the study at hand

90. Use your corporate blog to:

    (a) Inform and educate customers

    (b) Address client concerns and issues

    (c) Share important information and feedback

    (d) All of the above

    (e) Only choices (a) and (c)

91. HUT is a term used to describe:

    (a) The location of heavy coverage utility towers that broadcast commercially

    (b) The number of houses using television

    (c) Homes Under emergency Television broadcast reach

    (d) None of the above

92. When you are restricted from releasing information by legal or regulatory requirements:

    (a) Let reporters know that you are open to providing as much information as possible but that you are presently constrained from answering their specific question

    (b) State that you have no comment

    (c) Ignore reporter queries

    (d) All of the above

93. By creating a list of criteria, you can:

    (a) Identify your perfect customer

    (b) Build a better customer profile

    (c) Learn how to analyze your Web site

    (d) Get closer to your conversion target

    (e) Only choices (a) and (b)

94. Information gathering can help you learn about buyer preferences, buying culture, and what processes are most likely to influence buyers' behavior. True or false?

    (a) True

    (b) False

95. A logotype is a company emblem without text. True or false?

    (a) True

    (b) False

96. Marketing process evaluations can help justify the value of the marketing enterprise. True or false?

    (a) True

    (b) False

97. _____ research provides a picture of what is happening in a particular market.

    (a) Causal

    (b) Qualitative

(c) Exploratory

(d) Descriptive

(e) Primary

98. A statement that will help people remember you is called a:

(a) Reminder

(b) Personal statement

(c) Tagline

(d) Brand position

(e) Tip

99. A great way to network is to surround yourself with _____.

(a) People who can give you leads

(b) A diverse group of committed individuals

(c) People with money to buy services

(d) Social marketers

(e) Business service providers

100. Monitoring strategic initiatives and helping to connect specific performance areas to bottom-line results are uses of:

(a) Dashboard monitoring programs

(b) Basic scorecard reports

(c) Evaluation programs

(d) None of the above

(e) All of the above

Answer Key

Chapter 1

1. a	2. b	3. b	4. c	5. d
6. d	7. e	8. e	9. d	10. a

Chapter 2

1. c	2. a	3. c	4. a	5. b
6. a	7. b	8. c	9. d	10. c

Chapter 3

1. d	2. b	3. b	4. a	5. a
6. b	7. d	8. b	9. d	10. a

Chapter 4

1. e	2. d	3. b	4. d	5. b
6. e	7. b	8. c	9. a	10. e

Chapter 5

1. d	2. a	3. b	4. d	5. a
6. b	7. c	8. c	9. e	10. c

Chapter 6

1. a	2. b	3. d	4. c	5. d
6. d	7. a	8. b	9. d	10. a

Chapter 7

1. e	2. d	3. e	4. a	5. b
6. d	7. d	8. a	9. b	10. c

Chapter 8

1. b	2. e	3. c	4. b	5. a
6. e	7. a	8. b	9. e	10. d

Chapter 9

1. a	2. c	3. c	4. d	5. f
6. d	7. e	8. c	9. a	10. f

Chapter 10

1. b	2. c	3. a	4. b	5. e
6. d	7. a	8. c	9. d	10. d

Chapter 11

1. b	2. a	3. e	4. a	5. c
6. f	7. b	8. e	9. c	10. f

Chapter 12

1. a	2. d	3. c	4. b	5. f
6. c	7. e	8. f	9. a	10. c

Chapter 13

1. a	2. b	3. d	4. d	5. b
6. b	7. e	8. b	9. c	10. b

Chapter 14

1. b	2. a	3. d	4. e	5. c
6. d	7. b	8. a	9. a	10. b

Chapter 15

1. c	2. d	3. b	4. e	5. e
6. b	7. e	8. b	9. d	10. e

Chapter 16

1. d	2. c	3. b	4. a	5. b
6. c	7. a	8. d	9. a	10. e

Chapter 17

1. c	2. b	3. d	4. a	5. a
6. b	7. d	8. b	9. d	10. a

Chapter 18

1. a	2. e	3. c	4. d	5. e
6. a	7. b	8. d	9. c	10. d

Chapter 19

1. b	2. d	3. f	4. a	5. d
6. b	7. c	8. b	9. d	10. d

Chapter 20

1. d	2. b	3. f	4. a	5. d
6. e	7. e	8. b	9. d	10. d

Final Exam

1. a	2. d	3. c	4. c	5. a
6. b	7. d	8. c	9. b	10. d
11. c	12. c	13. b	14. b	15. d
16. e	17. b	18. c	19. c	20. c
21. e	22. b	23. b	24. b	25. c
26. b	27. a	28. c	29. b	30. d
31. b	32. a	33. d	34. d	35. d
36. a	37. a	38. c	39. c	40. e
41. a	42. b	43. d	44. d	45. d
46. d	47. d	48. c	49. c	50. e
51. d	52. d	53. b	54. d	55. b
56. d	57. d	58. b	59. a	60. e
61. d	62. b	63. c	64. d	65. b
66. b	67. e	68. f	69. d	70. a
71. b	72. a	73. a	74. a	75. a
76. c	77. a	78. b	79. a	80. a
81. d	82. a	83. b	84. e	85. e
86. a	87. f	88. b	89. d	90. d
91. b	92. a	93. e	94. a	95. b
96. a	97. d	98. c	99. b	100. c

INDEX

ABOUT THE AUTHOR

Donna Anselmo, M.S., is a strategic marketing expert and certified professional development coach. Founder and president of BOLD Marketing Solutions, Inc., an integrated marketing firm, Anselmo has helped small, midsize, and multinational companies enhance branding and business performance through targeted marketing programs, joint ventures, and/or professional development training. Formerly, she directed internal communications and publications for the $4.1 billion Olsten Staffing Services enterprise, where she was responsible for communications to 3,500 full-time employees and select external audiences. She also served on the firm's merger transition team, which facilitated an $11.8 billion merger resulting in the world's largest staffing agency, Adecco, S.A. Shortly after, she was named marketing vice president of Elite Technical Services, Inc., a national provider of information technology and engineering contractors.

Previously an award-winning journalist and managing editor for a group of community newspapers, Anselmo had been recruited to Stony Brook University's public affairs team, where she served as director of publications for the Health Sciences Center, and earned a master's of science (MS) degree in health-care policy and management. Anselmo has authored news and feature articles for various media, including *The New York Times*. She coauthored research articles published in *The American Journal of Maternal Child Nursing*, a peer-reviewed publication, and developed sales, marketing and entrepreneurship curricula for continuing education programs offered by Adelphi University, Hofstra University, and Stony Brook University.

Over the years, Anselmo has been tapped as an expert source for commentary by the news media. She has been quoted on topics as diverse as the economy, leadership, and change management, as well as marketing, employment, and public health issues. She has served as a speaker on best practices in leadership, marketing, and sales communications, business-to-business proposal development, as well as transformational strategies, for numerous organizations. Anselmo also hosts BOLD*TALK* Business Radio, a weekly broadcast on AM1300 WMEL (Cocoa, Florida) that also streams live over the Internet, and educates thousands of business leaders, managers, entrepreneurs, and individuals on marketing and business strategy. The BOLD Marketing Solutions, Inc. Web site is www.boldmarketingsolutions.com.